£2.sde.

The Fight for the Ashes

Also by Jonathan Rice
available from Methuen

One Hundred Lord's Tests: a celebration of the home of cricket

The Fight for the Ashes

THE STORY OF THE 2001 ENGLAND–AUSTRALIA TEST SERIES

Jonathan Rice

Methuen

1 3 5 7 9 10 8 6 4 2

First published in 2001 by
Methuen Publishing Ltd
215 Vauxhall Bridge Rd, London SW1V 1EJ
www.methuen.co.uk

Methuen Publishing Ltd Reg. No. 3543167

A CIP catalogue record for this book is available from the British Library

ISBN 0 413 77171 7

Designed by Geoff Green @ Geoff Green Book Design
Typeset in Utopia
Printed in Great Britain
at the Bath Press, Bath

Contents

Acknowledgements

There are many people who have contributed, deliberately or accidentally, to this book. At the top of the list I need to thank Peter Tummons, Eleanor Rees and Vicki Traino at Methuen, without whom this book would not have been put together at all. Without Peter's Yorkshire take on cricket, Vicki's amazing dexterity with an Apple and Eleanor's knowledge of Proust, the

book would have been very different. Thanks also to David Gower. This is the second time he has written a foreword to one of my cricket books. We must stop meeting like this. A cricket book needs Patrick Eagar's photographs to be a proper cricket book, and he remains on top form: we had a surfeit of riches to choose from. I would also like to thank Gary Franses and Mark Nicholas at Channel 4 television for giving me a fascinating tour of their facilities at the Oval, Michael Wolton at MCC for his cooperation and hospitality at Lord's and Arundel, and many former Test players, notably Alan Davidson, Mike Gatting and Neil Harvey, for their memories of Ashes series gone by. Others who deserve a mention are Anthea France, Ian Stephenson, Jonny

Chuter and my wife Jan, all of whom had something to say about the Tests which made its way into the text. The book was written on the hoof, so I would also like to thank the occupants of Brunswick House in Herefordshire, for allowing me to take over the dining-room table to write up the First Test, of Orchard House in Cornwall for granting me access to the Blair Suite to write up the Second and Third Tests, and of Dundonnell House in Scotland for showing me an attic where I wrote up the Fourth and Fifth Tests.

Finally I want to thank Steve Waugh for his captaincy and his batting, Shane Warne and Glenn McGrath for their bowling all summer, and Mark Waugh for that cross-batted hoick for six off Darren Gough which proved that my batting technique has been correct all along. It has been a summer of little comebacks, for Damien Martyn, Justin Langer and Mark Ramprakash and above all for Mark Butcher, who gave us all our moment of the year. They have all been a joy to watch.

Jonathan Rice
September 2001

Foreword

Without a shadow of a doubt one of the proudest moments of my life, and certainly of my cricketing career, was to be standing on the balcony at the Oval in 1985 as captain of England holding aloft the Ashes. For one of the most historic trophies in world sport it is a mighty small urn but it has quite simply inspired some of the most keenly fought cricket in the history of our game.

What a summer that had been with England and Australia one all after the first two matches (yes – we lost at Lord's again), still level after the next two games and then England able to beat both the opposition and the weather at Edgbaston to set up the finale at the Oval – a draw would do, a win would seal it in style.

As a captain one always wants to play one's part as either batsman or bowler. To lead by example is, to say the least, highly satisfying and the runs I made at the Oval on the first day of that test, all 157 of them, rank as some of the most enjoyable of my career. This was, in essence, as good as it gets.

It is wonderful to be able to look back on all that with great personal and collective pride. It was a job well done by a side including some who had long known the excitement of an Ashes series, and some for whom it was a first glorious taste. There

was the man who made a habit of bringing his best to the Ashes, Botham, and the likes of Richard Ellison and Tim Robinson for whom the glory might have been shorter lived but no less precious.

It is all the more galling to think that that 1985 series is still the last one to be have been won by England at home, Mike Gatting's team of course winning in Australia in 1986–7.

I, like many others, had high hopes of the 2001 series. I confess that my prediction was for the Aussies to win 3–1 but there were any number of good reasons to think that it would be a proper contest, a close and hard fought encounter. My prediction merely respected the outstanding and record breaking performances of the Australians and the fact that they were always going to be the side with the extra depth and dimension.

Against that we had the promise of resilience born of England's comebacks against West Indies, Pakistan and Sri Lanka. The key men would have to be Graham Thorpe as the most accomplished batsman of the team, Darren Gough and Andy Caddick, who, if they were able to bowl as they had done against the West Indies, would surely trouble even the most vaunted of Australian batsmen, and, of course, the captain, Nasser Hussain.

For Nasser it was the most agonising of summers.

Which hurt most I cannot be sure, the physical pain of his broken hands that kept him pacing helplessly in the dressing room or the anguish of seeing his team reduced to its own helplessness by the awesome efficiency of Steve Waugh's men. For England to compete on anything like level terms it was proven by events that they would have needed a full strength team to play out of its skin. The injuries to Hussain and Thorpe and even Craig White, who was to own up to having played while struggling for fitness, tilted the balance impossibly towards the Aussies.

Ironically they gave us Mark Butcher, England's most consistent batsman through he series, and he and all of us who watched him will treasure that magnificent innings at Headingley for ever – McGrath, Gillespie and Warne for once helpless themselves.

The Aussies have a point when they say that Headingley would have been different had the weather not prevented them batting England completely out of the game. It was the one blot on Adam Gilchrist's series.

In a way it was he who epitomised the strength of this Australian side. From the moment he smashed it all around the park in the Edgbaston test England were made brutally aware of the threat lurking at number seven. With Mark Waugh as elegant as ever, Steve as ruthless and Damien Martyn revealing his own silky skills superbly it seemed the visitors were never short of runs and at a pace that transcended the rules of test cricket.

In the end it is to Steve Waugh that one must pay the highest of compliments. I can think of no other man who would have made it back from that double tear of the calf as he did and his innings at the Oval was the ultimate demonstration of his and his team's determination to prove their ascendancy. He has always respected the history of the Ashes and that innings and the margin of victory in the series would have meant an awful lot to him.

To one of the finest sides ever to contest an Ashes series we must bow in due deference. They were magnificent.

David Gower
Hampshire, September 2001

Bring On The Aussies

Bring On The Aussies!

The summer of 2001 was going to be different. It was to be a season that would break with the past and establish cricket once again as a sport in which the English could be proud to proclaim their interest. There were new sponsors for most of the major competitions: the county championship became the Cricinfo County Championship, the NatWest Trophy became the Cheltenham and Gloucester Trophy, and the Test matches, which had for so many years been sponsored by Cornhill Insurance, were now under the corporate banner of npower, a name new to cricket.

There were to be seven npower Test matches, two against Pakistan and then five against the thirty-fourth touring team from Australia. This format had been tried, with great success, for the first time in 2000, but Australia traditionally had never shared the summer with another touring team, the only exception being in 1980 when they came to play just one Centenary Test after England had played a five-Test series against the West Indies. 2001 would also see a three-way One Day International tournament, following the success of the first such series in 2000. Then England had won the trophy against the West Indies and Zimbabwe, but this year the Limited Overs International series, sponsored for the first time by NatWest, was scheduled between England, Pakistan and Australia. This much tougher opposition would give us all an idea of how the English and Pakistani teams stood up to the world champions.

The last reason why 2001 was to be a different summer of cricket, and by no means the least important in the minds of all English cricket followers, was that England were on a roll: they had chalked up four consecutive series victories before the season began, against Zimbabwe and West Indies at home in 2000, and against Pakistan and Sri Lanka in the winter season of 2000–01. Their Australian opponents, on the other hand, had just lost a series for the first time in what seemed like many generations. Defeat had come at the hands of India, thanks mainly to the bowling of Harbhajan Singh and the astonishing batting of VVS Laxman. Since last failing to win a Test, Australia had beaten India four times, New Zealand three times, Pakistan three times, the West Indies five times and Zimbabwe once in a sequence which began in October 1999. Now at last the Indians had shown the rest of the cricketing world that this Australian side was mortal after all. The Test world champions, proud holders of the new trophy awarded by the ICC during the winter, were in for a tough summer.

So the 2001 season began with great optimism and excitement. English cricket was suddenly getting a good press. The leadership combination of manager Duncan Fletcher and captain Nasser Hussain could do no wrong, and the selectors, led by David Graveney, were being commended for their consistency and for the brilliance of some of their choices – Craig White and Marcus Trescothick in particular. However, for all their improvement over the past two years, England were still only third in the unofficial world rankings, and Australia were way out ahead at the top. So most level-headed commentators felt it was England who were in for a very hard summer, even if all the key players remained fit. Given that Nasser Hussain, Ashley Giles, Craig White and Graham Thorpe had returned from the sub-continent in varying states of disrepair, it seemed quite possible that England would find it hard to field a full-strength team all summer, making their task even more difficult. Australia too had injury worries, with Brett Lee and Jason Gillespie in particular needing to prove their fitness after long layoffs, but there was general agreement that they would be one of their country's strongest ever touring sides, even if they had to leave one or two men behind on the treatment table.

It had been a sad winter for Anglo-Australian cricket. Two of the greatest figures in Ashes history, one English and one Australian, had died either side of Christmas. Lord Cowdrey of Tonbridge – Colin Cowdrey of Oxford University, Kent and England – had died just before Christmas at the age of only 67. He had suffered a stroke in August 2000, the evening after hosting a day's cricket as President of Kent County Cricket Club during Canterbury Week, and although he had appeared to be making good progress back to fitness, he suffered a sudden heart attack and died on 4 December. Cowdrey had toured Australia six times – in 1954/55 when he celebrated his twenty-second birthday with a Test century, 1958/59, 1962/63 (when he scored his highest score, 307 against South Australia at Adelaide), 1965/66, 1970/71, and 1974/75 when at the age of 42 he was brought out to face Lillee and Thomson at their fastest, after Dennis Amiss and John Edrich had suffered broken hands in the onslaught. The moment when he went out to bat against Australia at the WACA ground in Perth, just four days after arriving in Australia, is enshrined in cricket folklore and was typical of the man. Cowdrey walked out to the wicket after his Kent team-mate Brian Luckhurst had been dismissed, and realised that he had not met all of his opponents before. He walked up to Jeff Thomson, held out his hand in greeting, and said, 'How do you do, Mr Thomson. My name's Cowdrey.' The fact that several thousand people were baying for his – and any Englishman's – blood at the time did not seem to matter. Courtesy to his opponents, indeed to everybody he met, came first. Most of the tributes after his death pointed out that Cowdrey was not ruthless enough to have been a great Test captain, but despite his lifelong devotion and service to cricket, it is as a great human being that he will be longest remembered.

Less than three months later, on 25 February 2001, the greatest batsman of all time died peacefully at home in Adelaide at the age of 92. Sir Donald Bradman AC, to give him his full title, dominated his sport in a way that few other sports personalities of this or any other generation have ever done. As a batsman, his test average stands at almost twice that of any other player, past or present. His superiority was so great that England resorted to tactics designed to hit the batsman rather than the stumps in an attempt to slow the flow of his runs. No other sportsman has ever been as far ahead of his contemporaries as Bradman was in the 1930s and 1940s. No other Australian was as famous or as revered around the world. No other Australian so defined the aspirations of the young country during the difficult years of the Depression, the Second World War and the austere post-war period. Bradman consistently lived up to the expectations of his countrymen, creating a national sense that success was Australia's due. The English reticence in the face of success, the desire to play the game for the inherent pleasure of playing rather than solely to win, is something Australians find hard to understand. It was Bradman as much as anybody who inspired a country that expected to come out on top. His legacy, still as powerful as ever, is embodied in the attitude of successive Australian cricket teams over the past two decades, led first by Allan Border, then by Mark Taylor and now into the new millennium by Steve Waugh.

The Australians of 2001, the thirty-fourth touring team since the first Test-playing Aussies of 1880, came to England via Gallipoli. They wanted to see the graves of the Australian forces who had died there in the ill-fated landings during the First World War, and to gain a strengthened sense of national pride from the visit. It was typical of the way that Steve Waugh leads his team. He thinks of the whole man, not just the cricketer, when he builds the bonds that have made his team possibly the best cricket side that the world has ever seen.

There were two Australian squads in England, one for the Limited Overs Internationals and one for the Tests. Of the seventeen players in the Test touring party, twelve were also in the one-day squad of fifteen. The men who were only here for the pyjama parties were Michael Bevan, Ian

Harvey and Andrew Symonds. Harvey and Symonds stayed on in county cricket after the one-day games, Harvey with Gloucestershire and Symonds with Kent, and were therefore theoretically available for a quick call-up to the main squad if injuries occurred. Other Australians playing county cricket in 2001 included Andy Bichel, Greg Blewett, Jamie Cox, Michael Di Venuto, Michael Hussey, Stuart Law, Darren Lehmann, Martin Love, Jimmy Maher and Daniel Marsh, so the Australian Cricket Board would not have had to pay much in the way of air fares if replacements were ever needed. After the tour of India which resulted in Australia's first series loss after sixteen consecutive Test match victories, the Australian selectors left behind their number two leg-spinner Stuart MacGill, as well as fast bowler Andy Bichel who had covered while reputedly the fastest bowler on the planet, Brett Lee, came back from prolonged injury.

The full Australian touring party was:

Steve Waugh (captain). Born 2 June 1965 in Sydney, the elder of the Waugh twins had played 135 Tests by the time he arrived in England, and had scored all but 9000 runs at an average just above 50. Since his first tour of England in 1989, when he scored 506 runs in the series at an average of 126.50, Waugh has feasted himself on English bowling. Though no stylist, he has nevertheless proved himself a great batsman, and a great competitor. His medium-pace bowling, which classified him as an all-rounder when he first appeared on the international scene, is now a thing of the past.

Adam Gilchrist (vice captain). Born 14 November 1971 in Bellingen, New South Wales, Gilchrist was making his first tour of England. As wicketkeeper and a very attacking left-handed batsman, he had stepped into the shoes of Ian Healy and by the start of the 2001 season, was already considered Healy's equal in the Australian team. In only 17 Tests, he had already scored almost 1000 runs at an average just a touch below 50, and had had a hand in 75 dismissals. His explosive batting style was eagerly anticipated by the English crowds.

Nathan Bracken, born in Penrith, New South Wales on 12 September 1977, was the surprise inclusion to the party. A left arm seamer in the tradition of Michael Whitney and Brendon Julian, Bracken had played only fourteen first class games before he was picked for the tour, taking 45 wickets at 25 each. He had played no Test matches, but appeared in eleven One Day Internationals for Australia, with mixed success. A graduate of the Australian Cricket Academy, he was known to be injury-prone and needed a solid tour to prove his long term fitness.

Damien Fleming, born in Perth, Western Australia on 24 April 1970, is one of three men in the Australian touring party to have taken a Test hat-trick, a feat he achieved against Pakistan in Rawalpindi on his Test debut in the winter of 1994/95. After twenty Tests, his right arm quick bowling had earned him 75 wickets at around 25 apiece. He also boasted a Test batting average of 19, with a highest score of 71* against England on their most recent tour, in 1998/99. He is, statistically, almost an all-rounder, but was expected to be used in Tests only if injury ruled out one of the three front-line fast bowlers.

Jason Gillespie, who was born in Sydney on 19 April 1975, now plays for South Australia. His career was put on hold for a season after a collision with Steve Waugh when both were going for a catch in the First Test against Sri Lanka at Kandy in September 1999. Gillespie broke his right leg and had to have a pin inserted in his right shin bone. By the beginning of the 2001 tour, he was back to full fitness and to the Australian Test side. As he arrived in England, he had played 21 Tests, and had taken 83 wickets at 22.53. At his fastest, he outpaces Glenn McGrath, but is perhaps not quite as quick as Brett Lee.

Matthew Hayden, born on 29 October 1971 in Kingaroy, Queensland, was one of only two recognised openers in the touring party. Well known to English cricket lovers after a season with Hampshire and two with Northamptonshire, his left-handed batting provided the stability in the opening partnership with Michael Slater, although with the speed at which the Australians score, stability is only a relative term. On the recent tour of India he hit 549 Test runs in the three games, resulting in a batting average of 109.80. This brought his career Test average over the 40 mark, and established him solidly at the top of the Australian batting order.

Simon Katich, born on 21 August 1975 in Middle Swan, Western Australia, is a left-handed batsman and occasional slow left arm bowler who played county cricket for Durham in 2000. He topped their batting averages with an average of 43, almost half as much again as any other Durham player, and he scored three of their five Championship centuries. An exciting player with immense power and a wide range of strokes, it was only a matter of time before Katich made his Test debut.

Justin Langer, born on 21 November 1970 in Perth, Western Australia, was coming to England having played 33 consecutive Test matches for Australia, most of them in the number three position. A disappointing tour of India meant that there was some threat to his place in the side, but his experience of English conditions after three seasons with Middlesex (culminating in being chosen as one of Wisden's Cricketers of the Year after another prolific season in 2000) made most commentators feel that his position in the Test team was secure. As captain of both Middlesex and Western Australia, he has also been mentioned as a possible successor to Steve Waugh.

Brett Lee, born on 8 November 1976 in Wollongong, New South Wales, came to England with the reputation of being the fastest bowler in the world, after a speed gun had timed him at 155 kph (96 mph). Unfortunately for him, like his only challenger for the title, Shoaib Akhtar of Pakistan, Lee is very injury-prone, and there was considerable doubt as to whether he would be available to tour England in 2001. He was, and English crowds awaited with eager trepidation the sight of this blond-haired whirlwind in action against the English team.

Damien Martyn, born on 21 October 1971, is the only Test cricketer to date to have been born in Darwin in the Northern Territory of Australia. He now plays for Western Australia. Martyn's Test career began in 1992/93, but at the age of almost 30, coming into the 2001 Ashes series, he had only played eleven Tests with a highest score of 89*. His attitude had been suspect in his early cricketing years, but he had shown a new maturity when given another chance in the Test side after Ricky Ponting suffered an ankle injury. He was not expected to be in the Test batting line-up from the start of the series, but he and Katich would keep the pressure on the men in possession throughout the summer.

Glenn McGrath, born in Dubbo, New South Wales on 9 February 1970, is one of the truly great fast bowlers in Australian history. In 70 Test matches to the start of the tour he had taken 326 wickets at a fraction over 21 apiece, placing him behind only Shane Warne and Dennis Lillee among Australia's most prolific Test bowlers of all time. His record includes the best analysis by a bowler in a Test at Lord's, 8 for 38 as England crumbled to 77 all out in 1997. However fast and dangerous Lee and Gillespie would prove to be, it was still McGrath for whom the England team had most respect.

Colin Miller, the oldest member of the oldest Australian touring party ever to tour England, was born on 6 February 1964 at Footscray, Victoria. His hair is often dyed violent yellow, or green, or whatever comes to mind, and his iconoclastic lifestyle has earned him the nickname of 'Funky'. His cricket career has taken him from Victoria to South Australia to Tasmania and back again to Victoria, and he is

also the only member of the Australian side also to have played for the Netherlands. His off-spin and medium pace seam-up bowling make him a useful bits and pieces bowler, but he would only be likely to play in the Tests if the wicket suited his spinning style, or if Shane Warne were injured.

Ricky Ponting, born on 19 December 1974 in Launceston, Tasmania, perhaps suffered from the weight of expectation since his time at the Australian Cricket Academy, where everyone who saw him bat concluded he was destined for greatness. He displaced Michael Bevan in the Test side after three matches of the 1997 Ashes series, and immediately hit a century in his debut Ashes innings at Headingley. England's bowlers know what to expect when Ponting is batting – a lot of hard effort, and a lot of watching the fielders chase the ball towards the boundary.

Wade Seccombe, born in Murgon, Queensland on 30 October 1971 (the day after Matthew Hayden was born just a few miles away in Kingaroy, and nine days after Damien Martyn was born in Darwin), was a late inclusion to the touring party as deputy wicketkeeper to Adam Gilchrist. Seccombe has yet to play Test cricket, but is used to the deputy role, having been Ian Healy's understudy in the State side for several seasons. Except in case of injury, Seccombe would not expect to do much more than play in some of the county fixtures when Gilchrist needed a rest.

Michael Slater is twelve days younger than his fellow New South Welshman Glenn McGrath, having been born on 21 February 1970 in Wagga Wagga. The other half of the well-established opening partnership of Hayden and Slater, he had now played 70 Tests and scored over 5000 Test runs at around 44 per innings. 'Dashing' is the word commonly used to describe his right-handed batting style, and those who saw him play during his two seasons with Derbyshire would certainly agree. The speed with which he compiles his runs means that the opposition are put onto the defensive from the very beginning of every Australian innings, a key feature of the positive Australian attitude to their cricket.

Shane Warne, the greatest leg-spinner the world has ever seen, was born at Ferntree Gully, Melbourne on 13 September 1969. Now Australia's all-time leading Test wicket taker, he has mesmerised batsmen the world over for a decade. His first ball in Ashes Tests, which bowled Mike Gatting at Old Trafford in 1993, changed the way the world's cricket tacticians thought of leg-spin, and at the end of the millennium he was the only current player to be voted one of Wisden's Five Cricketers of the Century. Despite shoulder problems that hampered his style a little, he was still a major threat in 2001.

Mark Waugh, the younger twin brother of his captain, Steve, is generally regarded as the more talented of the two as a batsman, and certainly as the more stylish. Though never quite matching his brother's achievements, still in 111 Tests he had scored over 7000 runs at over 41, and taken 152 catches, mainly at slip. It was expected that during the summer he would take the five catches necessary to overtake first Allan Border and then Mark Taylor to become the most prolific catcher in Test history. He might also prove a match winner, or at least a stand breaker, with his off-spin, the third string in this wonderful cricketer's bow.

The Australians' team manager was John Buchanan. A tall man with glasses and a moustache, Buchanan reminds many people at first glance of Ned Flanders, Homer Simpson's hapless neighbour in the hit television cartoon *The Simpsons*, to such an extent that one of his nicknames within the Australian squad is 'Ned'. However, even a cursory knowledge of the man will show that the resemblance ends there. For a start, he is not left-handed.

Buchanan's playing record at State level, for Queensland, was barely mediocre, but his career

as a schoolmaster obviously set him up well for cricket coaching. In 1994/95, his first season as Queensland's coach, the state won the Sheffield Shield, a feat that had eluded them since they first entered the tournament in 1926/27. His management style, aided by computer projections and statistics, discussions of each player's strengths and weaknesses and a determination to work on every aspect of their personalities as well as their cricket skills, has made him as likely to attract implacable enemies as devoted supporters. His one year as coach at Middlesex, in 1998, was a disaster despite his having an ally in vice-captain Justin Langer; Middlesex finished seventeenth out of eighteen, their worst result in their Championship history. However, in October 1999 Buchanan was appointed Australian national coach in succession to Geoff Marsh, and set about creating the team which won a record sixteen Tests in a row. Apart from cricket, he has been involved both as player and administrator in several other sports, and clearly enjoys his reputation for lateral thinking and creating surprises. In this he has been closely supported by his captain, Steve Waugh.

All in all, this was a very experienced touring party. Their average age was higher than that of any previous touring party, and with 665 Test caps between them, they presented a formidable array of experience and achievement for England to match up to. They also had three Test match hat-trick men, McGrath, Fleming and Warne, to England's two, Gough and Cork. If all five played in a Test match together, it would be the first time that five men with Test hat-tricks had appeared in the same Test.

Against these Australians, England were able to present a team that was growing in confidence, skill and determination with every match. During the previous summer and winter, England had moved up from the basement area of the Test cricket league table, into a very encouraging third place, although their record still did not begin to compare with Australia's. However, in the past twelve months England had fielded several players of genuine Test quality, and had enjoyed the bonus of success at the highest level for a couple of players some had considered past their sell-by dates, Michael Atherton and Alec Stewart. The emergence of Marcus Trescothick as a left-handed opening partner for Atherton, which had begun thanks to injury to Nick Knight before the One Day Internationals in the middle of the summer of 2000, was a major factor, while Caddick and Gough were establishing themselves as a new-ball attack which posed a genuine threat to even the best Test batsmen. Michael Vaughan's progress, despite injury, was noted when he scored his first Test century, against Pakistan at the start of the summer, and Craig White's abilities as an all-rounder capable of decent scores and very quick bowling added a new balance to the side. Nasser Hussain's batting form may have fallen away during 2000, but his captaincy had progressed to such an extent that he was now considered to be England's best captain since Mike Brearley. And in Duncan Fletcher, the quiet Zimbabwean, England had found a coach who brought out the very best in his charges.

The men most likely to face the Australians in 2001 were:

Nasser Hussain, the captain, was born in Madras on 28 March 1968. His family moved from Madras to England when he was five, and Nasser went on to become the youngest boy ever to represent Essex at Under-11 level; he was just eight. He began as a leg-spinner, but it was his batting that developed as he grew older and bigger. He played his first Test against West Indies on the 1989–90 tour, and soon earned a reputation as a very talented batsman but a difficult personality. Despite frequent injuries, he

has become a significant part of the England side, and since his appointment as captain in 1999 has led the side always with imagination and occasionally with brilliance.

Usman Afzaal, born in Rawalpindi, Pakistan on 9 June 1977, had never played Test cricket before 2001, and was not picked for either of the two Tests against Pakistan. However, the left-handed Afzaal had been the only Nottinghamshire player to score 1,000 runs in 2000 and was one of the successes of the England A tour to West Indies during the winter. His name was pencilled in to every armchair selector's list to move up to Test level as soon as a vacancy arose.

Michael Atherton, born in Manchester on 23 March 1968 (he is five days older than Hussain), has, like Alec Stewart, played over 100 Tests for England. He was captain in 52 of them and has established a reputation as a dour but often immovable opening batsman. He was known during his captaincy years as 'Captain Grumpy' for his unwillingness to suffer fools gladly, a tendency that was not helped by his apparent belief that most of the cricket press came into the category of fools from time to time. But nobody doubted his value to the England side, and his duels with Glenn McGrath promised to be a highlight of the Ashes summer.

Mark Butcher, born in Croydon on 23 August 1972, is the son of Alan Butcher, who played one Test for England, opening with Geoff Boycott against India at the Oval in 1979. Mark played 27 Tests between 1997 and the start of 2000, including one as captain when another injury sidelined Nasser Hussain, but his Test career seemed to have ended when he was dropped for the summer 2000 Tests. Having sorted out his personal life and his cricketing problems, he began 2001 well, but in a Surrey team with at least eleven internationals to call on at any time, he had to be at his best even to make the county side, let alone the Test eleven.

Andrew Caddick, born in Christchurch, New Zealand on 21 November 1968, enjoyed a wonderful year in 2000. He took 30 Test wickets during that summer in England, and became an essential part of a team which he had originally struggled to belong to. The ECB central contract system worked very well for him, keeping him fit and away from the daily grind of county cricket   to such an extent that he only took 25 first-class wickets for Somerset in 2000. All the same, his efforts earned him selection as one of Wisden's Five Cricketers of the Year. He is beginning to reach the veteran stage for a fast bowler, but as he has never relied purely on speed, he should have a place in the England set-up for as long as his 6'5" frame can stand it.

Dominic Cork, born in Newcastle-under-Lyme on 7 August 1971, is an enigma. Since his first Test cap against West Indies in 1995, when he took 7 for 43 at Lord's, the best analysis ever by an England debutant, he has been in and out of the side. Injuries as well as loss of form had limited his Test appearances to just 33 by the start of the 2001 Ashes series, but the responsibilities he took on when he became captain of Derbyshire in 1998 have made him a more mature and reliable team member. He missed the winter tours through injury, and there was some doubt, even after the home Pakistan series in which he played, whether he would ever come back to the form that brought him a Test hat-trick in 1995, and helped win the epic Lord's Test against West Indies in 2000.

Robert Croft, born in Morriston on 25 May 1970, is the first Glamorgan player to win twenty Test caps for England. A great future was predicted for him when he made his debut in 1989, but he has never quite fulfilled that early promise. England's reluctance to use off-spin has not helped his cause. Too often Graeme Hick or Michael Vaughan have been asked to plug the off-spin gap while Croft waited in the wings. However, 37 wickets at 34 apiece in 2000 was not the sort of return that would quickly bring a man back into selectorial favour, particularly as his high-est Test score is still only 37*, an under-achievement for a man of his batting skills.

Ashley Giles, born in Chertsey, Surrey, on 19 March 1973, played for Surrey in the early 1990s as a left arm fast medium swing bowler, but failed to make the grade until he switched to Warwickshire and to left arm spin. Like several of his predecessors as a left arm spinner in the England side, he is a tall man (6'3") and no mean batsman. His elevation ahead of Phil Tufnell into the England ranks has been consolidated with a very successful tour of Pakistan in the winter, where he took seventeen wickets in the three-Test series. If he could keep fit – the same old story – he had the potential to be a key player during the summer.

Darren Gough, born in Barnsley on 18 September 1970, was bound to be a key player, fit or not. He had taken 211 wickets in 51 Tests by the time the Australians arrived, including three in consecutive balls at Sydney on the 1998/99 tour, the first hat-trick by an Englishman against Australia since JT Hearne at Leeds in 1899. By far the most popular of English cricketers with the general public, Gough had taken over the mantle once worn by his fellow Yorkshireman Fred Trueman as England's leading strike bowler with attitude. His catch off his opening partner Caddick's bowling at the Lord's Test against West Indies in 2000 turned the Test match, and the summer, England's way. His presence in the side was vital if England were to have a chance against the Australians.

Matthew Hoggard, born in Leeds on 31 December 1976, is the latest in a line of Yorkshire quick bowlers of whom great things are expected. Yet, once again, his fitness is an issue. With Gough, Gavin Hamilton, Ryan Sidebottom, Chris Silverwood and Craig White, Test players all, he forms by far the most feared county attack in the country, and yet he had not yet translated his performances at county level into great things at Test level. 2001 was going to be a make or break summer for Hoggard, in terms of fitness as well as ability. Most watchers felt he had what it takes to succeed at Test level.

Ben Hollioake, born in Melbourne, Australia on 11 November 1977, was a youthful prodigy who failed to make the most of his enormous talent. Still only 23 in 2001, he had already gone three years since the second of his two Test appearances, and a poor summer in 2000 had left him languishing in Surrey's second eleven for several matches. However, a very encouraging winter and a solid start to the summer brought him back into the selectors' minds for the One Day Internationals, and although his bowling seemed to lack a little edge, his batting and his electric fielding did not let him down. If only he could marshal his undoubted talents, he would be a pillar of England's team for years to come.

Mark Ramprakash, born in Bushey, Hertfordshire on 5 September 1969, has been another Test match enigma. At county level he has always succeeded (averaging 64 for Middlesex in 2000), and boasted a career average of over 46 as the season began. However, at Test level he has been a disappointment, often getting in and then getting out before making the big score his supporters felt he was capable of. Being asked to open the England batting at the beginning of the previous season had not worked, but a switch of counties, across the river from Middlesex to Surrey, over the winter, would, it was hoped, bring him back into the selectors' calculations.

Owais Shah, born in Karachi on 22 October 1978, came to England as a child, and was soon picked out as a cricketer of exceptional promise. He made his county debut for Middlesex at the age of seventeen, and won his county cap at 21. All the same, 2000 had been a season of under-achievement for him, perhaps because Middlesex relied for most of their runs on Ramprakash and their Australian star Justin Langer. With both of them gone in 2001, it was time for the younger Middlesex batsmen, led by Shah, to take the responsibility on themselves. A promising start to the

season, and several injuries at the highest levels, gave Shah an opportunity in the One Day International series, which he took well. A Test debut might not be far away.

Chris Silverwood, born in Pontefract on 5 March 1975, played the first of his five Tests for England against Zimbabwe on the 1996/97 tour, but by the beginning of 2001 had not claimed a regular place in the side. He was one of six Yorkshire fast bowlers with Test caps, and had to wait in the queue for the Test place that became available whenever injury hit somebody higher than him in the pecking order (which it seemed to do with monotonous regularity). Most critics would place him very high on that particular list, as they knew that Silverwood would let nobody down. Whole-hearted effort, in the style of his county colleague Gough, was his trademark. His Test record, 11 wickets at 37 each, understated his worth to the team.

Alec Stewart, at 38 the oldest man in the England side, was born in Merton on 8 April 1963. As the son of England's manager (and former opening batsman) Micky Stewart, his entry into the England side in 1989/90 was greeted with some scepticism, but 110 Test matches later he has proved his critics wrong. This was definitely his last chance to wrest the Ashes from the Aussies' clutches, and there were strong rumours before the series began that Stewart would be retiring from Test cricket at the end of the summer. However, his fitness and dedication to English cricket has never been in doubt, and even at an age when many of his contemporaries have pulled on their carpet slippers in the place of cricket boots, he is still one of the best wicketkeeper/batsmen in the world.

Graham Thorpe, born in Farnham on 1 August 1969 had claimed his place as England's premier batsman at the start of the season. He scored 114* against Australia on debut in 1993, the only England cricketer playing today to have a that distinction, but then took some time to hold down a permanent place in the batting order. A brilliant tour of Pakistan and Sri Lanka in the winter, in which he hit 553

England Captain: Nasser Hussein

Australia Captain: Steve Waugh

runs at an average of 61.44 including two match-winning centuries, established him as the England batsman opposing bowlers want to see the back of, and only a perceived lack of ruthlessness in his play prevents him from being one of the greats of today's batting scene. Maybe 2001 would change all that.

Marcus Trescothick, born in Keynsham, Bristol on Christmas Day 1976, came to the England one-day side in 2000 thanks to injury to Nick Knight and the fact that he had impressed Duncan Fletcher with a big century, 167, for Somerset against Glamorgan in September 1999. Trescothick, a schoolboy wonder and an England Under-19 captain who had then seen his career falter for a couple of years, made an immediate impact, and by the winter was not only Atherton's permanent opening partner but also a member of the tour committee, a sign of a possible Future England Captain. He began 2001 in brilliant form and scored his second Test century in the Old Trafford Test against Pakistan. Remarkably, his three centuries for England colours (two in Tests, one in Limited Overs) have all been scored in a losing cause.

Alex Tudor, born in London on 23 October 1977, came to every cricket watcher's attention when he made his debut for Surrey aged only seventeen, and was chosen to tour Australia and New Zealand in 1998/99 at the age of barely 21. His bowling, very fast when he puts his back into it, his batting, which almost qualifies him as an all-rounder, and his brilliant fielding should give him a permanent place in the England side, but the same old problem arises when we talk of Alex Tudor as with many other members of the England squad: injuries. He has been unavailable for selection almost permanently since his brilliant 99* as nightwatchman which won the Edgbaston Test against New Zealand in 1999. But if he is fit, he is a strong contender for the third or fourth seamer's slot.

Michael Vaughan, born in Manchester on 29 October 1974, is another man beginning to earn the tag of Future

England Captain. Although, born a Lancastrian, Vaughan went to school in Sheffield and plays for Yorkshire. His career average at the start of the 2001 season was a comparatively unimpressive 34.59, but his correct style and cool temperament have singled him out for some time as an England batsman, a position he seemed to have made his own when he hit his first Test century, against Pakistan at Old Trafford in the Second Test of 2001. Despite being centrally contracted for 2001, Vaughan had missed out on the Pakistan leg of the winter tours, and had only forced out Graeme Hick in the Third and final Test against Sri Lanka in March 2001. His off-spin bowling is seen as an added bonus, but to be honest, it is no better than Hick or Ramprakash bowling their little offies – a stopgap while the frontline bowlers take a breather.

Ian Ward, born in Plymouth on 30 September 1972, has already enjoyed two careers at Surrey. He came into the side in 1992, after leaving Millfield School, but dropped out of Surrey's thoughts after a disappointing 1993 season in the Second XI. He then played league cricket until 1996, when he was given another chance by Surrey, and he grabbed it. Selection for the A tour of West Indies in the winter of 2000/01 gave him the chance to show his mettle in the spotlight: he scored 769 runs at an average of 64.08, and at the start of the 2001 season was next in line for a batting place in the England line-up. Although an opening bat for his county, he played at number seven in both Tests against Pakistan, doing enough with both the bat and his brilliant fielding to retain his place, but he knew he needed to play a big innings in one of the early Tests against Australia.

Craig White, born in Morley on 16 December 1969, emigrated with his family to Australia as a child. He played two games for Victoria in the 1990/91 season, but decided that his best opportunities lay with the country and county of his birth, and he has been a regular in the Yorkshire side since earning his cap in 1993. In 1994 he made his Test debut, but his appearances in the national side were sporadic until 2000, when he seemed to gain a yard of pace with his bowling and a greater confidence in his batting. Although he narrowly missed a first Test century during the winter, being dismissed for 93 in the First Test against Pakistan at Lahore, he had a good winter (274 runs at 34.25 and 13 wickets at 39.30) and looked to cement his place at number eight in the side for the summer.

Unless the season were to reveal a new star from an unheralded direction, England's stock of likely Test cricketers was limited to these men. Of course there were many other names bandied about in the press during the early part of the season, like that of Paul Collingwood of Durham who had a run-out in the NatWest Limited Overs series, and the season also pulled some unexpected rabbits out of hats: who would have guessed that David Fulton of Kent, a man who in nine years in and out of Kent's county side had never scored 1000 runs in a season, would in 2001 be the first man to reach that mark? Who also would have guessed that Devon Malcolm, 38 years old and playing for his third county, would be the leading wicket-taker in the first part of the summer? All the same, there were not many pundits prepared to nominate either of these players for elevation to the England team (or in Malcolm's case, a return to the England team). The older faces, a gang that also included Graeme Hick, Angus Fraser, Martin Bicknell and Phil Tufnell, were assumed to be not in the running for the Test side, however well they might perform at county level in 2001.

The Tests against Pakistan were to be a yardstick for the English audience of how the team had progressed through the winter. Of course, we had all watched and listened in amazement during the winter to the two astonishing series wins in Pakistan and Sri Lanka, both series culminating in quite outstanding matches to clinch victories for England. As Thorpe and first Hick, then Hussain, batted through the intense gloom at Karachi to inflict on Pakistan their first ever Test defeat at that stadium, we marvelled at the sheer unlikeliness of it all. When Thorpe, again, herded his less competent partners to the grand total of 74 for 6 to beat Sri Lanka in the scorching heat of Colombo in mid-March, we could hardly believe that victories like that could come twice to England in such a short space of time. Clearly Graham Thorpe's knighthood as English cricket's equivalent of Sir Steve Redgrave would not be long in coming.

However, for all the euphoria of the winter, and the cries of 'Bring on the Aussies' in the tabloid press, there was no doubt that the Aussies to be brought on were the most formidable side seen anywhere in the world for many seasons. There were some who went so far as to say they were the greatest side ever. In preparation for this onslaught, Pakistan, beaten by the narrowest of margins in the winter, were to be this brave new England's whipping boys. Unfortunately, the Pakistanis had not read the script.

Reality Bites

Pakistan and the One Day Internationals

Reality Bites

Pakistan and the One Day Internationals

England's mini-series against Pakistan got underway in mid-May.

The First Test, at Lord's, was won by England by an innings and nine runs, and it looked as though everything in the garden was lovely. Ian Ward and Ryan Sidebottom were given their first Test caps, and England hoped that in the batting line-up at least they were as strong as they could be. Injury worries to Thorpe, Hussain and Vaughan had been overcome, and all were in the top five of the order, along with Atherton and Trescothick opening. Ward, Cork, Caddick, Gough and Sidebottom made up the rest of the team, and only Sidebottom owed his place to injury (to Craig White and possibly several others).

Ryan Sidebottom is an interesting character. The son of Arnie Sidebottom, who played for many seasons for Yorkshire and also as a pillar of Manchester United's defence (and Huddersfield's and Halifax's), Ryan has hair cascading onto his shoulders in golden ringlets, making him look like Roger Daltrey, lead singer of the Who, in his prime. His left arm fast medium bowling brought him 24 wickets at 12.50, and his county cap, for Yorkshire in 2000, but by the start of 2001 he had only played 29 first-class

matches and taken 76 wickets in them at 23.93 each. His father played just one Test match, against Australia at Trent Bridge in 1985, taking the wicket of Bob Holland before breaking down and dropping out of the England reckoning for ever. After Ryan's one Test, in which he took no wickets for 64 runs without bowling either well or badly, there were many who were secretly hoping that he would also be a one-cap wonder, so that he and his father would forever be the only father and son who each played just one Test. Realists considered that Ryan had little chance of adding to his one cap, and that he would be another of the left arm seamers, like Simon Brown of Durham and Mike Smith of Gloucestershire, who have just one Test cap to their credit. Still, one cap is one more than most of us can ever hope to claim, so we should not be too dismissive.

However, it was hard to understand the selectors' motives in picking Sidebottom. If they needed a left arm over the wicket seamer, why not go for Alan Mullally? If they just needed someone to fill the gap while Craig White, Matthew Hoggard and Alex Tudor, to name but three, were nursing themselves back to fitness, why choose a raw

23-year-old? The only reason had to be that he had topped the bowling averages for England A in West Indies during the winter, and therefore had to be considered as the next choice when a gap in the England team arose, a logic that had already ensured Ian Ward his selection as well. But the England A party is made up not necessarily of the next best fifteen or sixteen players in England: it is meant to be a development project, made up of some hardened county pros and some youngsters who need to cut their teeth in competitive cricket overseas. And that is what Sidebottom began to do in the West Indies during the winter. Nobody begrudges Ryan Sidebottom his Test cap, but one wonders if he was ready. Will the selectors' decision to pick him and then discard him so soon really help his career? Let us hope he proves us all wrong and goes on to become a major force in Test cricket. The raw talent is there, at least.

That first Test was, in retrospect, a false dawn for the Ashes series to follow. The fact that the opening day's play was entirely washed out by rain was a reasonable augury of things to come, meteorologically speaking, but the England performance was, sadly, good enough to paper over the cracks in what is still a developing side. All the batsmen got a start, but only Thorpe (80) and Hussain (64) got past fifty. The total of 391 was very high for a side that had no individual century makers, and you could argue that it showed a solid team batting performance. But Ted Dexter always used to say that a good team score was built around one (or more) big individual scores and a number of lesser ones. The big individual score was missing. Then when England bowled, the top three bowlers, Gough, Caddick and Cork took the twenty wickets needed between them: Gough 8 for 101, Caddick 8 for 106 and Cork 4 for 83. The other bowlers, Sidebottom, Trescothick and Vaughan, were only given a few overs between them, but went for 78

runs without taking a wicket. The support bowling was not strong enough.

In the Second Test at Old Trafford, the old failings came back, even though the batting looked more solid in the first innings, and with Hoggard back in the side the bowling looked more likely to keep the pressure on the opposition all through the match. The difference between the two sides was Inzamam-ul-Haq, who scored 199 runs in the match. Inzamam is just one example of a continuing failing of English Test sides – the unorthodox player on top form. When a Test opponent goes about his cricket in an unorthodox way, and when he does it brilliantly, the England teams tend to struggle to find a response. Inzamam is by no means a classical batsman. His running between the wickets is truly lamentable for a top-class cricketer, and he has almost given up fielding altogether. But he has very quick and powerful hands, a wonderful eye, and a way of adapting his shot at the very last minute which keeps him out of trouble, and helps him to dominate any bowler. There is no set way of bowling to him: he has an answer to most forms of attack. When a player like Inzamam is in form, he can tear apart almost any bowling attack, but he seems to relish his successes against England more than most.

County cricket in England tends to breed orthodoxy. We play much more cricket than other countries of the world, and to survive at county level a cricketer needs to put in solid performances week in and week out. This tends to eliminate the flashy touches of genius and replace them with risk-free cricket – the accumulation of runs and the application of line and length. In other parts of the world, the unorthodox is given its chance. The training manual is ignored when it needs to be. Players like Inzamam or Saqlain Mushtaq, Shane Warne or Adam Gilchrist present any Test side with problems they do not encounter elsewhere, but it seems that the English struggle more to come to terms with them. We do not produce the unorthodox in England any more. Since the days of Denis Compton and, before him, Harold Larwood and Bodyline, it is hard to think of any player who has prospered in the English county set-up with a different way of going about his cricket. Derek Randall is the nearest example, and even he played much less Test cricket, with much less freedom to play in his own style, than he might have done if he had been West Indian or Australian or Pakistani. Is it a pure coincidence that the 'overseas' players who have represented England in the past fifteen years or so have, in almost every case, proved to be not quite as good as their home-grown counterparts? Why have we produced Devon Malcolm and Norman Cowans rather than Courtney Walsh and Curtly Ambrose (both of whom also played a great deal of county cricket, of course, but who joined the circuit from a position of established power)? Why do we have Graeme Hick and Jason Gallian rather than Andy Flower or Ricky Ponting? What is there about English cricket that takes the spark of greatness and crushes it to mere competence? Perhaps 2001 would show us some of the answers.

The Second Test against Pakistan, and especially the final day, Monday 4 June, marked the beginning of a rapid dip in England's confidence and form which seemed to be bringing the side back to the bad old days of two or three years earlier. For the first four days of the game, the sides had been evenly matched. Inzamam had scored a bruising and brilliant 114 in the first innings, around which other players like Rashid Latif and Younis Khan were able to build a Pakistan total of 403. This followed first innings totals of 401 and 405 by Pakistan in two of the three winter Tests, so their batsmen were nothing if not consistent. England replied with 357, built around Graham Thorpe's 138 – equalling his highest Test score –

and Michael Vaughan's first Test century, a beautifully crafted 120. When Pakistan batted again, Inzamam hit 85 and seemed all set for a second century of the match when he mishit a catch to Trescothick off Matthew Hoggard. Still, a total of 323 meant England needed 370 to win, a daunting task.

The side got off to a perfect start. Mike Atherton and Marcus Trescothick put on 146 for the first wicket, and had given England a good chance not only of saving the game, but even of winning it. At 174 for 1, they were all but half way, there was every expectation of an exciting finish and an England victory. What happened was quite different: another loss of nerve by England. Apart from Mike Atherton's 51 and Trescothick's solid 117, no other batsman made more than Darren Gough's 23 at the end. So 174 for 1 became 261 all out. Vaughan, Thorpe, Stewart and Ward all got to double figures without any of them going on to 20, and Nick Knight completed a match he will want to forget by adding a duck to his dropped catches. Saqlain Mushtaq, another player of unique style and genius, took 4 for 74 in 47 overs, twenty of which were maidens, as the England batsmen suddenly decided that he was unplayable. There were a few umpiring decisions that rankled – four wickets falling to what should have been called no-balls – but that still did not justify the attitude of the English batsmen. Suddenly it seemed as though the world was conspiring against them again, and Pakistan duly won by 108 runs.

The NatWest Triangular Series of One Day Internationals between England, Australia and Pakistan served only to accentuate the negative. Australia are world champions at the short game, and Pakistan were the team they beat in the final, so it was bound to be a tough series for England. However, it proved even tougher and even more humiliating than the most carping of English critics (of whom there were plenty) had expected. Nasser Hussain was injured and unavailable for the entire series, so Alec Stewart captained, and then a day or two before the series began, Graham Thorpe dropped out with a mysterious calf injury. Before the matches had all been played, Michael Vaughan had joined the hospital waiting list, and although there were occasional encouraging performances by Owais Shah and Ben Hollioake the end result for England was Played 6 Lost 6. A couple of those matches, against Australia at Bristol and against Pakistan at Lord's, looked harder to lose than to win, but there were also a couple of severe trouncings, by Pakistan at Edgbaston on the day of the General Election (one contest the English could win, at least) and by Australia at Old Trafford a week later, where England were all out for 86, their lowest ever One Day International total. Against Pakistan at Headingley, England conceded the match when Pakistan needed another 4 to win with ten overs to play: a pitch invasion by a significant section of the crowd bent on celebrating a Pakistan victory made the match unfinishable and the situation dangerous for the players.

The NatWest Series was about as bad a preparation for the Ashes series as England could have had. The key Test players involved – Trescothick, Stewart, Vaughan, Cork, Gough, and Caddick – did little to advance their reputations, apart from one Trescothick innings at Lord's, but even he was now going into the Test series with two consecutive international ducks to his name, not to mention the published opinion of Glenn McGrath that the Aussies had worked him out. Two players, Thorpe and Vaughan, were now unavailable for the First Test because of injury. The borderline players, Knight, Croft, Ealham and Mullally, had done nothing to strengthen their Test claims, while Paul Collingwood and Ally Brown had looked out of their depth. Things could hardly get worse.

The Australians, for their part, had three first-class games to play to get back into five-day form before the First Test. Everybody knew now that their one-day form was as brilliant as the Australians had hoped and the English had feared, but would all their players take to English county conditions as easily? Nathan Bracken, the surprise choice left arm fast bowler was forced by injury to return to Australia, and his replacement was not one of the Australians already playing county cricket in England, like Andy Bichel at Worcestershire, or even a man the English public had heard of, like Mike Kasprowicz. It was another wild card as far as the English public were concerned, 24-year-old right arm fast medium bowler Ashley Noffke from Queensland, who was asked to join the party.

The first game after the Australian NatWest triumph in the final at Lord's on 23 June began two days later against an MCC side at Arundel Castle, the home of the Duke of Norfolk in West Sussex. It was a friendly fixture, with MCC putting out a combination of Test players, old county pros and international prospects to give the Australians a stretch of their three-day legs before the serious business against the counties got under way. The Test players in the MCC team included Shahid Afridi, Asif Mujtaba and Azhar Mahmood from Pakistan, Mark Richardson from New Zealand and Aminul Islam from Bangladesh, as well as the captain Jimmy Adams of West Indies. The old county pros were David Ward of Surrey, who was now 40 years old and had retired from county cricket five years before, and Colin Metson, the former Glamorgan wicketkeeper. Among the international hopefuls were two South Africans, Gideon Kruis and Charl Willoughby, and a Queensland teammate of Ashley Noffke's, 30-year-old Joe Dawes. Australia rested Glenn McGrath and Mark Waugh of the definite starters for the First Test, but the rest of the main contenders for places were on parade.

The Monday morning was very hot, almost sultry, and despite the heat, it was no surprise when Steve Waugh chose to have a bat on winning the toss.

Before the innings began, there was a minute's silence, in honour of both Lord Cowdrey, whose widow was a daughter of the late Bernard, Duke of Norfolk, and Sir Donald Bradman. The large crowd, dressed for a day basking in the sun on the edge of the Sussex Downs, got up from their deck chairs and their rugs to stand for a minute in silent tribute. The flags, set at half mast on the pavilion, rustled only slightly in the faintest of breezes.

By the time the midday sun had reached its sweltering height in an azure blue sky, there were no mad dogs in sight and only two Englishmen, but the morning belonged to an Australian. The Australian was, unfortunately for the tourists, not playing for them. The burly figure of Joe Dawes, steaming in from the Castle End, was the success of the morning, claiming the wickets of Slater, Hayden, Langer and Martyn and leaving Australia at 64 for 4. Dawes, a part-time policeman, with a big chest and a pounding run-up which brought to mind Kent's Irish Australian Martin McCague, was, however, unable to inflict further damage on the Australians, and after lunch, Simon Katich and Shane Warne set about repairing the damage to both the scorecard and the Australians' self-esteem. They put on 190 together for the seventh Australian wicket, with Katich making a powerful and stylish 168 not out, and Shane Warne, who had vowed to hit a Championship century for Hampshire in 2000, equalled his best score of that year, 69, to continue his good batting form of 2001. By the time the pair were parted when Warne hit one of Jimmy Adams' little spinners to Shahid Afridi, the score was 365 for 7 and the match was safe. From then on it became an exhibition, which the Australians duly won on the third day by 280 runs.

Simon Katich, who would celebrate his twenty-sixth birthday the day after the scheduled finish of the Fourth Test at Leeds, came to England with good memories of a successful season with Durham the year before, and with high hopes of breaking into the Test side. This was Katich's second tour with the full Australian squad, but his first had ended early and disastrously when he contracted chicken-pox and had to fly home from Sri Lanka after playing only one match of the 1999/2000 tour (in which he scored 40 and 36 not out). His strength of purpose, however, was shown in his action of giving back his 'baggy green' cap on his return to Australia, saying he would have it back when he had earned his place in the Test team. He had been selected for that tour on the strength of five centuries in the 1998/99 season, but the illness took its toll on him even after he came back into the Western Australian side. In 1999/2000, his batting average dropped to a fraction below 30. So it was with mixed feelings that the Durham authorities welcomed Katich as their overseas player in 2000. They need not have worried. He scored 1089 runs at 43.56, 408 runs more than anybody else, and at an average 14.51 above his nearest rival. He scored three of Durham's five Championship centuries, and his was the one wicket that Durham's opponents valued above all others. Many people in the know about Australian Test politics have earmarked him as a future Test captain, but he has to break his way into the brilliant Australian batting line-up first.

From Arundel, the Australians moved to Chelmsford, a ground that only the most fervent Essex supporter would dare to compare with Arundel, to take on Essex, who were in the throes of one of their worst seasons for a long time. Nasser Hussain decided to play, but the Australians rested Steve Waugh and gave the captaincy to Adam Gilchrist. Waugh had very recently gone on the record to say that the Australians would be playing all their games against the counties to win, and that they would not use them merely for batting practice. Unfortunately, Adam Gilchrist was clearly not listening at the time.

After the Australians made 405 for five declared in their first innings (Gilchrist 150 not out, Damien Martyn 114 not out), they disposed of Essex for 231, with Jason Gillespie taking five for 37. Nasser Hussain, opening the batting, barely got into double figures, and it was only 21-year-old James Foster, with 74, who prevented a complete rout. (This was the first clear public sighting of Foster in the first-class game, and he laid out his credentials as a batsman/wicketkeeper so well that before long he had moved into pole position to take over from Alec Stewart in the increasingly unlikely event that he ever decides to retire. Stewart is, after all, only 38.) The Australians did not enforce the follow-on, a permissible tactic, but they then made no attempt to force a result. They declared their second innings only when there was no time for Essex to bat again, at 569 for 9, a lead of 743. Rather surprisingly, no Australian hit a century, but Hayden (98), Ponting (70), Lee (79), Miller (62) and Slater (58) all scored fifties. Langer failed again, twice, and his Test place was suddenly in jeopardy. Gilchrist was much criticised for not making any attempt at all to make the match competitive, but the Australians had the luxury of going into the first Test knowing that all their squad was fit and that most of the batsmen and bowlers had struck form. England were not nearly so lucky.

The England selectors had several problems to contend with. There were many players out through injury, the most notable being Graham Thorpe, whose mystery calf strain had kept him out of the NatWest one-day series and now sidelined him for the First Test against Australia, and Michael Vaughan, whose knee required surgery which would keep him out until the Fourth Test at

the earliest. In the end, the England selectors made no real leaps of faith from the squad that had worked pretty well together over the past twelve months, and picked Nasser Hussain (Essex, captain), Usman Afzaal (Nottinghamshire), Michael Atherton (Lancashire), Mark Butcher (Surrey), Andrew Caddick (Somerset), Dominic Cork (Derbyshire), Ashley Giles (Warwickshire), Darren Gough (Yorkshire), Alec Stewart (Surrey, wicketkeeper), Marcus Trescothick (Somerset), Ian Ward (Surrey) and Craig White (Yorkshire). The two surprises were the return of Mark Butcher, whose early season form had been so patchy that he had been in and out of Surrey's first eleven, and the inclusion for the first time of Usman Afzaal, the young Nottinghamshire batsman. In the one-day series the selectors had been watching Paul Collingwood of Durham, who had not, in truth, done anything to merit promotion to the Test team, and Owais Shah, who had. Nevertheless, it was Afzaal who got the nod, and on the morning of the Test, earned his first England cap. Dominic Cork was relegated to twelfth man duties.

Australia had no worries, mate. On the Monday before the Test, they had announced their team – just eleven, mind. No dropping one of twelve depending on what the pitch looked like. Just eleven men to beat England, the best eleven Australia could muster. The psychological warfare for the Ashes had begun, and Australia took the first round, even before England had heard the bell.

The Australian eleven were Steve Waugh (New South Wales, captain), Michael Slater (New South Wales), Matthew Hayden (Queensland), Ricky Ponting (Tasmania), Mark Waugh (New South Wales), Damien Martyn (Western Australia), Adam Gilchrist (Western Australia, wicketkeeper), Shane Warne (Victoria), Brett Lee (New South Wales), Jason Gillespie (South Australia) and Glenn McGrath (New South Wales). For the Western

Australian pair of Martyn and Gilchrist it was the first Ashes Test, but otherwise they were all used to playing against, and beating, England.

The dropping of Justin Langer after 33 consecutive Tests, to make way for Damien Martyn, was the only slightly surprising or controversial selection, but on the evidence of the tour so far, there was little doubt it was justified. Langer had not been among the runs, while Martyn seemed to get to three figures every time he went to the crease. Langer's disappointment was obvious, but it was probably his series against the West Indies at the end of 2000 that had signalled his possible exclusion. In five Tests, all of which Australia won handsomely, he scored only 203 runs at a fraction over 25, a lower batting average than every other Australian batsman and four of the defeated West Indian side. In the one Test which Martyn and Langer played together, Martyn made 46 and 34 without once being out, while Langer made 6 and 48, out both times. That series was followed by unexceptional form in the three-Test series against India, which Australia lost, so Langer was in need of heavy scoring in the first few games in England if he was to retain his Test place. In the event he was dismissed cheaply and often, so Martyn took over.

Australia would not have professed to any weakness at this stage, but their one concern must have been in the form of Brett Lee. Billed as the fastest bowler on earth, with the potential to become the first to break the 100 m.p.h. barrier, he had arrived in England as a hugely exciting prospect for English audiences if not for English batsmen. But in the first few matches of the tour, he did not live up to his reputation, bowling quickly but no faster than Jason Gillespie, and taking fewer wickets than everybody had expected, at a greater cost. His Test place was not in doubt, but one or two suspicions that he had not completely recovered from his recent back problems were beginning to be voiced. Lee needed this Ashes series as an opportunity to silence his critics.

No Great Hopes From Birmingham

The First Test, Edgbaston, Birmingham
5–8 July 2001

No Great Hopes From Birmingham

The First Test

The first day of a new Ashes series, the first day of the 297th Test match ever staged between England and Australia! The sense of anticipation and excitement was palpable, and had the spectators known what a feast they were in for there would have been no empty seats, even from the first over. The match was a sell-out, and before long all the seats were full, but those who missed the first few overs, or even who blinked during the day, failed to get full value for the price of their tickets. New Test match sponsors npower, who had laid out their startlingly bright logo in the outfield in the customary manner, could not have asked for a better first day's play.

As usual, England lost the toss. Nasser Hussain tossed and Steve Waugh called correctly. Without any hesitation and to the surprise of nobody, Waugh invited England to bat first. What followed was one of the most remarkable days of play in all those 297 matches, the equivalent of around a thousand days of Ashes cricket.

Atherton and Trescothick opened the batting, despite the presence of both Surrey's regular openers, Butcher and Ward, in the side. I am sure it would be possible to find out whether a Test team had ever before been picked including both opening batsmen from one county, neither of whom were asked to open for their country. In fact, there were three Surrey openers in the team, because Alec Stewart was also in the eleven. The Australians, who had said often enough that they had worked Trescothick out, dismissed him for a duck with the first ball bowled by Jason Gillespie in the series, the seventh ball of the morning. Warne took a good catch in the slips and the trend for the series was set. England were under the hammer from the very start.

It was left to Atherton and the first of Surrey's opening bats, Mark Butcher, to try to repair the damage. In this they proved quickly to be very successful. Neither batsman is known particularly as a dasher, but Butcher obviously reckoned he had nothing to lose, having been summoned in the first place to resurrect his career as the replacement for a replacement, so he went for his shots. The weather played its part as well – bright sunshine and a glorious summer's day made conditions very good for batting, helping even this suspect England batting order against the best bowling attack in the world. The Australians attacked from the start, with what fifty years ago was known as a Carmody field, after the New South Welshman Doug Carmody who was credited with the idea of employing an umbrella-field of slips and gullies, with perhaps one man on the leg side, and a forward off-side fielder as cover. That type of attack relies for success on great catchers, and the Australian side of 2001 has plenty of those.

Unfortunately for the Aussies on the first morning, one of them was not behind the stumps. For a man who would prove so brilliant both in front of and behind the stumps before the summer was out, Adam Gilchrist had a terrible first morning of Ashes cricket. He dropped Butcher before he was off the mark, and also put down Atherton off Brett Lee. England's second-wicket partnership yielded 104 runs, the first century partnership of the innings but not the last, before Shane Warne, England's nemesis for the best part of a decade, was given an over before lunch. His second ball caused Butcher to give a catch to Ricky Ponting at silly point, and England went into lunch at 106 for two. The runs had come in 24.2 overs, at a rate of more than four an over, reckless stuff for the first day of any Test series, let alone an Ashes series, but the crowds did not mind.

After lunch, England's middle order forgot all the good work of the winter and slipped back to its old ways. Nasser Hussain, in slightly better form than the previous year, but still not threatening to dominate any bowling attack, joined Michael Atherton as they regrouped. But seven overs later Atherton was out, for 57. At least it was not McGrath who had dismissed him, but Atherton no doubt saw it as a job half done rather than a job well done. It was his first fifty in sixteen innings in Ashes Tests, his last one coming in the second innings at Lord's in 1997, when his 77 in an opening partnership of 162 with Mark Butcher was the same score as the entire England team had man-

aged in their first innings. Since then, his scores in Ashes Tests had been 5, 21, 24, 19, 27, 8, 5, 13, 0, 28, 1, 35, 41, 5, 0 and 0, for an average of 14.5. Eight different Australian bowlers had claimed his wicket during that run, but it was Glenn McGrath who sent him most often back to the pavilion, eight times in those past sixteen innings. His average in those innings in which he had been dismissed by McGrath was just 8.25, so the lesson was clear. If even an out-of-touch Atherton can survive McGrath's opening spell, he will go on to make a useful contribution to the total. But enduring that spell is a feat that has tested all of the world's greatest batsmen of the past ten years. This time Atherton resisted McGrath, only to fall, with the score at 123, when he nudged a ball from Gillespie to Mark Waugh, who rarely drops catches, and duly caught this one.

Ian Ward, Surrey's other opener, now joined Hussain for what was undoubtedly the quietest period of batting during the day. Ward was prolific in the West Indies for England A during the winter, but all the commentators and journalists picked up his weakness very quickly – he does not play straight when he defends. He has a tendency to try to turn everything to the leg side, and although this has worked very well for him against county sides and West Indian island sides, it is not a technique that will ensure a long life against a world-class attack. Nevertheless, it was Hussain who was first to go, lbw to McGrath offering no stroke when he had reached 13 and the total was 136, in the 38th over. Ricky Ponting had dropped Ian Ward at third slip one ball earlier, so although Australia had only one wicket to show for their efforts, they had England very much on the defensive. Alec Stewart came in at number six, leaving the number seven position to debutant Usman Afzaal, and almost immediately he tried to increase the tempo.

Ian Ward built his score up to 23 before his

weakness was exposed: he played with his bat angled towards leg at a ball from McGrath, mistimed the shot and dragged the ball on to his stumps. The score was 159 for 5. 'I told you so,' was the cry from the know-it-alls in the stands. This is not what England's middle order are supposed to do.

Afzaal, on his debut, did not look at all nervous, but underneath the helmet and behind the ice cool expression he must have felt the occasion. He lasted just seventeen balls, of which he faced nine, before he left a Warne leg break alone and learned to his cost how far the great man can make the ball rip and turn on only a slightly helpful pitch. The Warne leg break is of course an off break to a left-hander like Azfaal, but the effect is the same. At least he had made four runs, four more than Len Hutton or Graham Gooch made on their Test debuts. But if 170 for six was not good, then 174 for seven was even worse. Craig White, also on four, tried to sweep Warne, did not pick the straight one and was lbw. Ashley Giles came in to join Stewart, and between them they took the score to 191 for 7 at tea.

The final session of the day, only 35.3 overs long, yielded 236 runs and five wickets at a rate of 6.65 runs per over. It would be heady stuff in one-day cricket; in a Test match it was almost unprecedented. A Test crowd who went home at the end of a complete day's play with the score at 236 for 5 would not really complain, but to enjoy it all in one session was a wonderful advertisement for Ashes cricket. The crowd at Edgbaston, including the usual complement of fancy dressers – nuns, convicts, Merv Hugheses and so on – roared the players on, but the session began on a down beat, at least for England. Giles was caught behind by Gilchrist, for seven, as he tried to play Warne through the covers immediately after tea, and Darren Gough played a very stupid shot just three

balls later, trying to whack Warne into the crowd but succeeding only in finding Gillespie, who had been placed at square leg with great ceremony only a couple of balls earlier. Gillespie accepted the catch with gratitude. Suddenly England were 191 for 9 at the end of 53 overs.

Alec Stewart had been watching much of the mayhem from the other end. When Andrew Caddick came in at number eleven, he realised that there was little to do but to play their shots, and Caddick – who has a lesser range of shots than Stewart but is a good six inches taller – realised it too. Within a few balls, the Australians and the entire Edgbaston crowd had got the message. In twelve overs and four balls, occupying a couple of minutes less than an hour, Caddick and Stewart added 103 for the last wicket. It was exhilarating stuff. Both men swung the bat at almost everything, but somehow it did not seem risky or reckless. When Caddick lofted Warne into the stands beyond square leg for six, it was a perfectly respectable hit, no wild swing with the eyes shut but a wonderfully timed pull-hook into the crowd, the kind of shot that Darren Gough had perished attempting. All the same, nobody recognised it at the time as the opening salvo in an onslaught that would change – albeit only temporarily – the whole face of the match.

Andrew Caddick is not picked for his batting, but there have been times during his Test career when he looks as though he is a respectable Test number nine, at least. But in 2000 and on the winter tour his batting had slipped to the extent that he was now below Darren Gough in the order, and although his bowling was plenty good enough to keep him in the Test side, his admirers wished that his batting could regain some of its former sparkle. None of his most recent fourteen Test innings had got beyond single figures, but he has five first-class fifties to his name and should be

The first wicket to fall: Trescothick is caught by
Warne off Gillespie for a duck. The series is just
seven balls old.

Debutant Afzaal is bowled by Shane Warne for 4. The ball has turned a long way from outside the left-hander's off stump.

nobody's pushover when he comes to the wicket. Today he was not. The sparkle was back.

Gillespie, whose second spell of six wonderful overs had yielded only eleven runs and included the wicket of Atherton, now found himself going for 26 in four overs. Lee was brought on in place of Warne, and went for fifteen in his first over, six more in his second. McGrath, replacing the severely mauled Gillespie, was hit for thirteen in his first over, thanks mainly to two wonderful cover drives by Caddick, who used his feet to give himself room to have a full swing of the bat, but still kept his head over the ball and his eyes on the task in hand.

There were some signs that the Australian fielding buckled a little under the pressure of the onslaught. The 200 came up when the ball went through Brett Lee's hands on the fine leg boundary, and Michael Slater and Matthew Hayden, too, were guilty of sloppy fielding as the stand gathered pace. The Englishmen in the crowd began to taunt the Aussies: 'You're not singing any more'. Stewart brought up his thirty-seventh Test fifty with a four off McGrath over mid-on, and by this time the record tenth-wicket stand for England against Australia at Edgbaston, an undefeated 81 between Lockwood and Rhodes in 1902, was under threat. Stewart and Caddick would have had no idea of this, of course, and even less that the 1902 side is often described as the strongest batting side ever to have represented England, all eleven players having scored centuries in first-class cricket. What's more, having made 376 for 9 declared, the 1902 side then bowled Australia out for 36, their lowest ever score in Tests, but could not force the victory because rain intervened. This England team 99 years later had similar bad luck with the weather – it didn't rain enough to cause the match to be drawn.

Stewart and Caddick bludgeoned their way past Edgbaston's record tenth-wicket stand, and had their sights on the record in all Ashes Tests, as they took the partnership into three figures in just 56 minutes off 74 balls. This was one of the fastest hundred partnerships in England's Ashes history, although the one longer tenth-wicket partnership for England, 130 by Tip Foster and Wilfred Rhodes at Sydney in 1903, took only 66 minutes in all. The crowd showed its appreciation with a standing ovation, and Caddick allowed himself a rare smile. He was by now on 48 not out, equalling his highest ever Test score, and three runs ahead of Derek Underwood's 45 not out at Headingley in 1968, until now the highest score ever made by an English number eleven in Ashes history. He was indeed only two runs short of the highest score ever made by a number eleven in Ashes history, FR Spofforth's 50 out of 64 for Australia at Melbourne in March 1885. The records beckoned.

But it was not to be. Stewart was lbw to McGrath a couple of minutes later, a decision that provoked no controversy whatsoever, and the fun ended at five past five. England were all out for 294, presenting Australia with a target far higher than either side could have envisaged at tea.

If the spectators thought they had had their feast of batting for the day, they were sorely mistaken. The Australian innings had a mere 22 overs to run, but in that time – about an hour and three-quarters – they scored 133 runs for the loss of two wickets. The prime mover in this hectic session was Michael Slater, though he had fine support from Matthew Hayden. Darren Gough, having had an hour's rest since his three-ball innings, took the first over, and began with a no-ball which Slater hit for four. The tone was set for the rest of the evening. Three more boundaries and one more no-ball followed in Gough's opening over, by the end of which Australia were 18 for no wicket. Hussain handed the ball to Caddick, and hoped that

Hayden had not had whatever Slater had eaten for tea. Caddick, incidentally, bowled with his fingers bandaged, the aftermath of a broken hand. During his innings, his main ambition had been to make sure he was not hit on the hand yet again.

Hayden played a far more circumspect role. Yes, he hit Caddick's first ball for four, though that was an uppish half-chance to Ward in the covers, but then he played the rest of the over serenely. The tally of 22 for 0 after two overs became 37 for 0 after five overs, and from there the assault on England's bowlers slipped into top gear. Slater, still a little upset at his continued absence from the one-day side, played Test match cricket as though it was a ten-over slog, but with perfect style and grace. It was classical and it was brutal at the same time, a heavily armed gladiator against a hapless tiger, cheered on by a full stadium of enthralled spectators in the sunshine. Hayden was scarcely less violent, indeed it was he who hit the only six of the partnership, but he had less of the strike and it was therefore his partner's batting which caught the eye. Slater gave one chance, to Usman Afzaal at square leg when he was on 43, but otherwise it was dispiriting stuff for the England players. After fifteen overs, the score was already 98, and at this point, the left-handed Hayden chose to hit Ashley Giles with all his might to the mid-wicket boundary. Craig White, who until this moment had been having a very quiet day, launched himself at short mid-wicket to catch the ball as it flashed into the top left-hand corner of his goal. It was already past him when he stuck out his left hand, and it stuck. It was a catch of such brilliance that we expected it to change the whole course of the match: it deserved to, but in the end it didn't. It sent Hayden back to the pavilion, though, and allowed Ricky Ponting to come to the crease.

Ponting had been in such good form during the One Day Internationals and in the county warm-up matches that the English team cannot have been too excited at the thought of seeing the back of Hayden. But Ponting was moving up from number six to the number three slot that Justin Langer had vacated, and perhaps he was not as assured as he liked his opponents to believe. In the next four overs and four balls, he and Slater added another 32 runs, of which Ponting's share was 11, including two boundaries. He then became the first Australian victim of the curse of the no-ball: Darren Gough bowled what umpire Steve Bucknor should have called a no-ball but didn't. The ball hit Ponting on the pad and Gough's appeal went through, despite the fact that television evidence suggested the ball may not have gone on to hit the wicket, even if it had been fairly delivered in the first place. It was 130 for 2. Ponting's Ashes series had not begun well.

The final fourteen balls of the day were an anti-climax. Mark Waugh faced nine of them and failed to score. Michael Slater took his score to 76 not out in 77 balls, bringing the total up to 133 for 2, and then the day's play was over. The players were applauded all the way back into the pavilion. Australia had the edge at the end of the first day's play, but if the whole series was to be played at this breakneck speed, then anything could, and quite possibly would, happen.

Close of play: England 294 (Atherton 57, Stewart 65, Warne 5 for 71); Australia 133 for 2 (Slater 76 not out)

Second Day, 6 July 2001

The Friday was far more overcast. The sun was not visible at all as the players came out to resume the Australian innings, but still the ground was full, as it should have been after that electrifying first day's cricket. But if the fans were hoping to see a

Stewart plays the West Indian pull off Brett Lee to add four more to his score during his bravura last-wicket century partnership with Caddick.

lot more of Michael Slater, they were to be disappointed. He faced just five more balls and made one more run before Darren Gough's first ball of the morning knocked back his off stump. It was a great start for England, and for Gough, but in case the English supporters got carried away, the big television screen reminded them of the background of the new batsman, Steve Waugh. This was his thirty-eighth Test match against England, and his 136th overall. Although his career Test average was a modest 50.93, (nine runs per innings higher than any current England batsman) against England it was 58, and against England in England it was almost 70. He already had 8965 Test runs under his belt, and if these days of helmets meant that he could not always wear his old baggy green on his head, he still had his lucky red handkerchief peeking out of his left trouser pocket. At 36, he was just about the best Test batsman in the world, and in no need of help from lucky charms.

The Waugh twins set about building an impregnable score to mock England with. It was not spectacular, but it was ruthless, it was clinical and it was effective. The Hawaiian Elvises in the crowd, and the men with the curly green wigs, and all the others in fancy dress or gaudy club ties cheered and drank and sang throughout the morning, but it did not seem to affect the Waughs. Andrew Caddick ran in as consistently as ever, his stiff-legged run bringing to mind a flamingo struggling to take off from the surface of a lake, and Gough buzzed around all morning like an eager puppy hoping somebody would throw him a stick. Craig White, who had bowled three overs for 24 runs the previous evening, enjoyed bowling against the Waugh twins much more: in a long spell both sides of lunch he bowled thirteen overs for 28 runs, but did not make the breakthrough. Steve and Mark Waugh moved serenely on, with Steve outpacing his brother as the morning progressed.

The session settled down to what the pundits had expected all along – the compilation of runs by a superior batting side against the best efforts of a fine opening pair who lacked support. The Waughs picked up runs off everybody, Mark the more elegant, Steve the more assured. We have been told over and over again how Steve, and indeed Mark, eliminated the pull and the hook shots from their repertoire in about 1992, and there was very little evidence to the contrary as the twins nudged the scoreboard along. But obviously nobody had told Andrew Caddick about the Waughs' nine years of abstinence from hooking: he was cautioned by umpire George Sharp for intimidation after bowling consecutive deliveries above shoulder

height to Steve Waugh. The Australian just watched them go by. There was not even an involuntary muscle twitch to invoke memories of a Waugh hook or pull.

The twins took the score to 238 for 3 at lunch, England's solitary success becoming an ever more distant memory as the morning wore on. There was an occasional flurry of excitement, as when Mark Waugh survived a stumping chance off Giles, who was getting a great deal of turn and bounce from this second-day wicket. The run rate had slowed, however, since Slater left. Where the Australians had been rattling along at six an over, the Waughs took things more steadily. The last ball before the interval was hit for four by Steve Waugh, off Giles, bringing him to 62 not out and his brother to 29. Their partnership of 104 had occupied 27 overs – a rate a little below four an over, much more like Test match cricket. Sanity was being restored by the Australians, but hope was dying in English hearts.

After lunch, Trescothick gave Mark Waugh another life, a hard chance in the slips put down, and Steve Waugh was almost run out by Ward when he had made 63 – a great effort by Ward, whose throw missed the stumps by a whisker. That seemed to be the only way the partnership might be broken. When the Waugh twins get together against England, they like to stay together. At Edgbaston eight years earlier, they had put on 153 together, and they looked like repeating or even exceeding the dose this time.

Ian Ward, playing his third Test match, was having a tough time of it to establish himself as a batsman in the side, but his fielding was almost always brilliant. Ward's early career had marked him out as no more than a journeyman county player, but in 2000 he had struck a rich vein of form for Surrey as their opening batsman with Mark Butcher, and was rewarded with selection for the England A tour of West Indies. Even so, by the time he left England for that tour, he was already 28 years old and had scored only four first-class hundreds. His career batting average was just under 34 and he had never made 1000 runs in a season. However, on the tour of West Indies, he was England's biggest batting success, and came back to Surrey with the confidence of knowing that he was next in line for selection when the season began. Despite a less than prolific start to the season, he was duly chosen for the Pakistan series, to bat at number seven and, despite not making a fifty, let nobody down. Everybody remarked how at home he looked in the England set-up, perhaps because the England team was stuffed to the rafters with his county colleagues. However, after a few Tests, Ward knew that looking at home in the side was not enough: his batting had to come into the equation quite soon against the Australians or he was in danger of being branded yet another county pro who was not quite up to the standard of Test cricket.

When the fourth wicket finally fell, it was not a run-out. Mark Waugh was tempted by a short ball from Andrew Caddick and nicked a catch to Stewart behind the wicket. He had made 49 and thus missed his forty-third Test fifty by one run. During his innings, he overtook Greg Chappell's aggregate of runs for Australia, moving up to fifth place on the all-time list, behind Allan Border, Mark Taylor, David Boon, and his brother Steve who was inexorably widening the gap between them. Steve also reached a major landmark in this innings, becoming only the third player in history to reach 9000 Test runs. The two who still lurk ahead of him, Allan Border (11 174) and Sunil Gavaskar (10 122) are still a few seasons away, but it would be a brave man who would bet against him getting there.

Mark Waugh's successor at the wicket was Damien Martyn. For Martyn, this was a crucial innings. Now 29, he has been on the fringes of the Australian Test eleven for years, but has never made a permanent place his. This was only his twelfth Test cap in eight years, and the first time he had faced England. Now with Langer out of form, he was given the chance to take over the sixth batting position on a permanent basis. He had never previously scored a Test hundred, but was averaging 42.53 all the same, so bringing him into the side was rather less of a risk than the England selectors had been forced to take with the range of injuries afflicting the English players.

Martyn clearly felt that the situation called for the brisk approach, and having come in at 267 for 4, 27 runs behind the England total, he set about knocking off the deficit in as short a time as was feasible. One over from Ashley Giles went for fourteen runs, and Australia had soon established their lead. There was no surprise in this. From the moment that Slater had set Australia on their way the previous evening, it had looked inevitable that any terrors in the wicket were in the England batsmen's minds, and Australia's progress towards a useful lead was largely untroubled. However, the job for England was to ensure that the lead remain merely useful, and not a match-winning one. Martyn and Steve Waugh had the task of thwarting even this minor ambition.

The weather became ever gloomier in a summer of gloomy weather, but despite the quality of the light Steve Waugh flicked a Craig White delivery off his legs to bring up his century shortly before tea. This was his twenty-sixth Test hundred in his 136th Test, and his eighth against England. It was the first century of the 2001 Ashes series, and it took him 164 balls spread over three and three-quarter hours. To their credit, the England players all applauded his hundred, a courtesy that has been all too lacking in recent years. Waugh acknowledged the applause by removing his helmet, holding up his bat and flashing his steely smile. Then he settled down for the next hundred.

At 3.35, Nasser Hussain turned to Mark Butcher. He bowled one over of his occasional gentle medium-paced swingers (Test career record, 3 wickets for 169 runs) and then the players went in for tea. The score was 332 for 4, with Steve Waugh on 101 not out, and Damien Martyn on 34, made from 51 balls in just over the hour.

After tea, umpires Steve Bucknor and George Sharp made their way out to the middle, but the players did not follow them. The umpires consulted, decided that the light was too bad to play, and they marched back into the pavilion again.

Forty-four minutes later, the players came back out onto the pitch. During the hiatus the crowd had cheered loudly on hearing that the Australian Patrick Rafter had beaten Andre Agassi in the semi-final of the Wimbledon Men's Singles, 8–6 in the fifth set, but otherwise the gloom of the afternoon had projected itself onto the mood of the crowd, who were patient enough, but restless.

Nasser Hussain took the new ball straight away, in the eighty-second over of the innings, and asked Darren Gough to make first use of it. The light was still not good. Gough bowled two balls with it, no runs were scored and the umpires offered the light to the batsmen. Steve Waugh immediately accepted their invitation to go back into the pavilion, and so after just two balls, the square was empty again. Within fifteen minutes, the bad light had developed into drizzle, and then into fully fledged rain. By just after five o'clock it was chucking it down. Play for the day was abandoned. The ground staff battened down the hatches and hoped for better things on Saturday.

Close of play: England 294; Australia 332 for 4 (Slater 77, SR Waugh 101 not out)

Third Day, 7 July 2001

The Saturday weather showed little sign of improvement. The players came out onto the playing area on time despite the very heavy overnight rain, but the conditions remained poor. The atmosphere was oppressive, it was muggy and grey and rain was threatening all the time. England needed quick wickets and Australia needed quick runs. The only thing the weather could guarantee was a foreshortened day and the possibility of a rain-affected draw, which was not on the Australian agenda at least.

For the third day in a row, the second over of the morning provided a wicket. This time it was Steve Waugh, whose innings had started almost exactly 24 hours earlier. As before, it was Gough who struck, this time by trapping the Australian captain lbw with a ball that kept low. Waugh's 105, made from 181 balls, had ensured that Australia had a chance of creating the mountain of runs that England would never be able to pass beyond.

Conditions should have favoured the England seamers, but after Gough's early strike you would have thought it was the most perfect batting track in the world, a shirt-front flat and grassless strip bathed in bright sunshine and with a gentle breeze to make batting not only easy, but also fun. Well, watching the batting was easy and, unless you are a diehard England supporter, a lot of fun too, and it was clear that the two Ashes debutants, Martyn and Adam Gilchrist, were enjoying it too.

Gilchrist came in with the score at 336 for 5, a lead of 42 over England, with a partner who was already going very well at the other end, and with virtually three days' play in hand. Hardly a crisis, but it still called for a special effort to turn the screw on England and make sure there was no chance that they could inch their way back into the game. Gilchrist and Martyn made that effort.

The left-hand right-hand combination forced England's bowlers to keep on adjusting their line, but the way that the pair added 160 runs in 34 overs and one ball owed nothing at all to the short-comings of England's bowling and everything to the skills of the batsmen.

Damien Martyn is a big man whose batting style is powerful but orthodox. His fifty, which came during the morning session, took him 76 balls and included six boundaries. There were some lucky runs in among the great shots, but he always played as though he was in total control. In the first hour of the day he took two fours off Darren Gough from consecutive balls, the second one lifted majestically over cover, and it was bursts of activity such as this that kept him on top of the English bowling, which, if truth be told, was not at its best. Caddick was doing his best to re-establish his reputation as a great second innings bowler, a reputation he had shrugged off over the past twelve months. There was a strong feeling that a good second innings bowler was surplus to requirements against a side that seemed unlikely ever to need a second innings.

Gilchrist is an astonishing player. His wicket-keeping is nothing more than average in interna-tional terms, but his batting is so good that he could drop three catches an innings if he wanted to, or let through twenty byes a session, and still show a positive contribution to the team from his batting alone. When his score reached 6, he passed 1000 runs in Test cricket in only his eighteenth Test, at an average of just a notch under 50. Such has been Australia's dominance since he came into the side that this was only his 26th Test innings. As the number seven batsman, he hasn't needed to bat twice in

Craig White holds his head in his hands. Where will the next wicket come from?

even half his Tests played to date.

At Edgbaston, where there have been many fine Test innings over the years, Gilchrist batted as well as anybody ever has done. The bowling may not have been as testing as that May and Cowdrey faced when they put on 411 against Ramadhin and Valentine at Edgbaston against the 1957 West Indians, but the runs still have to be made. The statistical extent of Gilchrist's innings is easily told: 152 runs in 143 balls, includ-ing twenty fours and five sixes. He went from his 100 to 150 in just 23 balls. This was the second highest score ever made by an Australian in an Edgbaston Test, beating all but Dean Jones' 157 in 1989. With Damien Martyn, he added 160 for the sixth wicket, a ground record for Australia, and with Glenn McGrath, who made just one run, he added 63 for the last wicket, another ground record for Australia. McGrath did not score his one run until over 50 had been added since his arrival at the crease. Gilchrist hit Mark Butcher for three

To bring up his hundred, Gilchrist plays a remarkable but completely controlled shot off a Caddick bouncer, off the face of the bat and to the boundary directly over Alec Stewart's head.

sixes in five balls after Butcher had taken 4 wickets for 20 runs, and to bring up his hundred he played a remarkable but completely controlled shot off a Caddick bouncer that came off the face of the bat and raced to the boundary directly over Alec Stewart's head.

To describe the aesthetic of the innings is less simple. Gilchrist is not a beautiful stroke player, nor is he merely a bludgeoning slogger. Yes, he hits the ball very hard and very accurately, and he uses his feet to give himself room to have a full swing of the bat. But he is also very correct in defence and blessed with an ability to concentrate for long periods which may well be the legacy of his wicket-keeping. He has complete confidence in his own skill, and the ability to improvise which allows him to keep one step ahead of the bowlers and fielders. He also has the great advantage of coming in at number seven behind six of the world's best batsmen, so that he usually has a very firm foundation for his innings. Despite the fact that he was batting with Martyn for most of the time, and despite the fact that Martyn also scored a maiden Ashes century in his maiden Ashes innings, Gilchrist scored 152 of the 240 runs added to the total while he was batting. It was a wonderful innings to watch, and it eventually won Gilchrist the Man Of The Match award. It put the game well beyond England's reach, and it established Gilchrist in their minds as a man of skill, power and, above all, danger to England's prospects in the series.

That the innings totalled only 576, and was all over less than an hour after tea was mainly due to the bowling efforts of Mark Butcher. The overcast conditions lasted throughout the day, and led to a stoppage and lunch interval which lasted from midday until half past two as a storm swept through even the posher parts of Birmingham. Despite the low cloud, Caddick and Gough were finding little swing, and White none at all. Butcher

began promoting his own cause to his captain well before lunch, as Martyn and Gilchrist were getting into their stride. Hussain had both Butcher and Trescothick available if he wanted a few overs of medium pace, but apart from giving Butcher one over at the end of the second day, Hussain maintained an orthodox attack and used the men chosen for their bowling skills rather than risk any of the part-timers. It was not until tea time that Hussain tossed the ball once again to Butcher to see what he could do with it.

What he did with it was to cut short the Australian innings. In just eight overs of his gentle swing, he got the ball to move significantly, and by dropping it on the right line and the right length, he worried all the batsmen, with the possible exception of Gilchrist. Butcher has a modest bowling record – just over 100 wickets at about 33 runs each – but he has often chipped in with vital wickets for Surrey when he has been feeling confident of his bowling. If he is to stay in the England side, then he could take on the role that Doug Walters had for the Australians of thirty years ago: he is the man who breaks up the stubborn partnerships, the man with the golden arm who bowls five overs, takes a wicket and then retires back into the field before the batsmen work him out. This time Butcher bowled eight overs, three of them maidens, and took 4 for 40 in the spell. Martyn nudged to Trescothick in the slips, Warne and Lee were both caught by Atherton at first slip – Lee first ball – and Gillespie was blatantly lbw. Butcher's figures would have been even more respectable if Gilchrist had not taken to him during the last wicket thrash (63 in eight overs), but that just proves the point. The skill of bowling a man like Butcher is not only in when to bring him on, but also when to take him off. He probably bowled two overs too many in this innings.

He was not the only one, though. Caddick's final

spell of four overs went for 26 runs, and even Craig White, who took Gilchrist's wicket with the fourth ball of his seventh spell of the innings, had been hit for ten runs from the first three balls. When the Australians were finally all out, it was with a total almost double England's, a lead of 282. Despite Slater's opening barrage of boundaries and the mayhem of the latter stages of Gilchrist's innings, their scoring rate, 4.44 runs an over, was marginally less than England's 4.48. The difference was that Australia batted for twice as long.

England were left with a short spell of batting at the end of the day – how long depended on the weather. Bad light extended the break between innings to 35 minutes, and in the end England had to face thirteen overs. Michael Atherton was caught by Mark Waugh in McGrath's second over, the fourteenth time McGrath has dismissed him in Tests, for four, but that was the only alarm. Trescothick and England's hero of the day, Mark Butcher, batted out the remaining overs until bad light ended play at just past seven o'clock.

Close of play: England 294 and 48 for 1; Australia 576 (Slater 77, SR Waugh 105, Martyn 105, Gilchrist 152, Butcher 4 for 42)

Fourth Day, 8 July 2001

Oh dear. Having competed in a spirited way against far stronger opponents, for three days England fell apart on the fourth, like a tennis player who gets to two sets all and then loses the decider 6–0, or a 1500 metre runner who blows up in the back straight on the final lap. England never really looked like winning, but they should not have been humiliated. But they were. This Australian team is really very good, and if England did not know it before, they knew it now.

The overnight total of 48 for 1 became 99 for 1 in the twenty-fourth over as Butcher and Trescothick worked their way steadily towards the 282 that would at least prevent the ignominy of an innings defeat. The plan was to lose no more than one wicket in the first session, and battle on from there. Butcher, who had scored 38 in the first innings, had reached 41 when a vicious lifter from Brett Lee gave him no room for manoeuvre and he edged it to Gilchrist. It was by far Lee's best ball of the match. Lee had come to England as the phenomenon of the age, the fastest bowler on Earth and the man whose strike rate in Test matches was bound to terrify even the best batsmen, let alone England's flimsy top six. In the event, he clearly had not recovered full fitness after the arm injury which had kept him out of much of the domestic season in Australia, and his performance at Edgbaston was probably the one real worry that the Australians took away with them. But in a side of this quality, you can afford to have one bowler not always operating in top gear. McGrath, Gillespie and Warne were more than enough to dispose of England, so Lee's match figures of 2 for 108 in 19 overs of merely average pace did not matter. But he needed to get himself a little fitter for Lord's.

Butcher's exit brought in Nasser Hussain, who scratched around for almost half an hour making nine runs before a sharp rising delivery from Jason Gillespie, who bowled quicker than anybody in the match, caught the little finger of his left hand and broke it. This was the moment when England's fate was decided. At least the ball did not carry for a catch to the slip cordon, which would have added insult to injury, but although Hussain faced one more ball after extensive treatment on the pitch, but then had to retire hurt when it became obvious he could not grip the bat, and he took no further part in the match.

Hussain's finger injuries are becoming a real

issue for England. His captaincy is always good and often brilliant, but his batting has suffered, and probably as much because of a subconscious and very natural fear of having his fingers broken again as because of the added responsibilities of captaincy. Hussain has an odd way of playing the quick bowlers, so that he seems to lead with his bat handle held far away from his body, and his hands seem to follow the ball so that collision becomes inevitable. But even if technically he were perfect against all types of bowling, he needs to take greater efforts to protect his fingers. His Essex team-mates apparently call him 'Poppadom' because his fingers break so easily, but anybody's fingers are likely to break if they are caught between a piece of wood and a leather ball travelling at ninety miles an hour, unless they are properly protected. And that's the key. Alec Stewart had similar troubles a few seasons back, but he kept free of injury by wearing specially made gloves with added protection to the fingers. Can he not tell Hussain where to buy these things? It would help England's cause no end.

With the captain heading off to the hospital for an X-ray, England crumbled. Ward came and went, bowled by Lee. A Test batsman should not be bowled out in both innings of a Test match, especially not for a match aggregate of just 26. Stewart got a leading edge as he tried to turn Gillespie to leg, and the ball was well caught by Warne at slip. Afzaal was lbw to Gillespie, who also clean bowled White for a duck with the last ball before lunch. Gillespie took 3 for 24 in this seven-over spell, and tore the heart out of England's middle order. By lunchtime, England were staggering along at 154 for 6. Trescothick was still there as planned, not out 76, but his partner was not Butcher

England captain Nasser Hussain is hit by a lifter from Jason Gillespie. This delivery broke the little finger of his left hand, and he missed the next two Tests.

or even Hussain, it was Ashley Giles, chosen in preference to Cork in the first place because the ball was not expected to swing. In the event, the ball did not swing for England, except when Butcher was bowling, but if Cork had played instead of Giles, maybe it would have done. This was a difficult call, even in retrospect. Giles was clearly not fully fit, but Cork was not having a good season, and the stresses of a benefit season (a stress he shared with Gough) did not help. Now Giles had to prove his batting skills were a clear advantage in this time of crisis.

They were not. He lasted for twenty minutes after lunch, but by the time he was out, the rest of his team-mates were back in the pavilion, so his wicket finished the match. The first to go after lunch was Marcus Trescothick, who the Australians clearly had not entirely worked out despite their pre-match propaganda. Warne's first ball after lunch popped a bit, and Trescothick touched to slip, where Mark Waugh does not miss them. Next ball, Darren Gough was completely unable to read Warne's top-spinner, and he was lbw. Caddick stopped the hat-trick and even managed a boundary off Gillespie before the end. Giles perished the way Trescothick had done, caught by Mark Waugh off Shane Warne, but for 76 fewer runs than the Somerset opener had made. At one minute past two on the fourth day, Australia completed their victory by an innings and 118 runs.

Depression immediately fell over the England camp, but in reality the situation was no worse than it had been at the beginning of the summer. It was just that some dreams had evaporated. Duncan Fletcher and Nasser Hussain tried to put some positive spin on the match by pointing out a couple of positives from the game, Mark Butcher's bowling and Andy Caddick's batting. Unfortunately, Butcher had been picked for his batting (which hadn't been at all bad) and Caddick for his bowling (ditto), and the one man who had been picked for both his batting and his bowling, Craig White, had clearly failed in both departments.

But as Michael Henderson wrote in the *Daily Telegraph*, 'Even if they lose all five Test matches, it is not the end of the world. ...These tourists have stretched the game beyond what was thought possible and they are such an extraordinary side, from number one to number eleven, that all cricket-lovers should rush to watch them, and cheer them on their way. We may never see their like again.' England are still probably the third best team in the world. It's just that the best in the world might as well be on another planet.

The Ashes 2001 First Test
England v Australia
Edgbaston, Birmingham
5, 6, 7, 8 July 2001
Australia won by an innings and 118 runs

England 1st innings

MA Atherton c ME Waugh b Gillespie	57
ME Trescothick c Warne b Gillespie	0
MA Butcher c Ponting b Warne	38
*N Hussain lbw b McGrath	13
IJ Ward b McGrath	23
†AJ Stewart lbw b McGrath	65
U Afzaal b Warne	4
C White lbw b Warne	4
AF Giles c Gilchrist b Warne	7
D Gough c Gillespie b Warne	0
AR Caddick not out	49
Extras (b 10, lb 8, nb 16)	34
Total (all out, 65.3 overs, 289 mins)	294

FoW: 1–2 (Trescothick, 1.1 ov), 2–106 (Butcher, 24.2 ov),
3–123 (Atherton, 31.3 ov), 4–136 (Hussain, 37.4 ov),
5–159 (Ward, 43.2 ov), 6–170 (Afzaal, 46.1 ov),
7–174 (White, 48.3 ov), 8–191 (Giles, 52.2 ov),
9–191 (Gough, 52.5 ov), 10–294 (Stewart, 65.3 ov).

Bowling	O	M	R	W
McGrath	17.3	2	67	3 (3nb)
Gillespie	17	0	67	2 (4nb)
Lee	12	2	71	0 (7nb)
Warne	19	4	71	5 (2nb)

England 2nd innings

MA Atherton c ME Waugh b McGrath	4
ME Trescothick c ME Waugh b Warne	76
MA Butcher c Gilchrist b Lee	41
*N Hussain retired hurt	9
IJ Ward b Lee	3
†AJ Stewart c Warne b Gillespie	5
U Afzaal lbw b Gillespie	2
C White b Gillespie	0
AF Giles c ME Waugh b Warne	0
D Gough lbw b Warne	0
AR Caddick not out	6
Extras (b 1, lb 5, nb 12)	18
Total (all out, 42.1 overs, 218 mins)	164

FoW: 1–4 (Atherton, 2.3 ov), 2–99 (Butcher, 24.2 ov),
3–142 (Ward, 32.1 ov), 4–148 (Stewart, 33.1 ov),
5–150 (Afzaal, 35.3 ov), 6–154 (White, 37.3 ov),
7–155 (Trescothick, 38.1 ov), 8–155 (Gough, 38.2 ov),
9–164 (Giles, 42.1 ov).

Bowling	O	M	R	W
McGrath	13	5	34	1 (5nb)
Gillespie	11	2	52	3 (4nb)
Warne	10.1	4	29	3 (1nb)
ME Waugh	1	0	6	0
Lee	7	0	37	2 (2nb)

Australia 1st innings

MJ Slater b Gough	77
ML Hayden c White b Giles	35
RT Ponting lbw b Gough	11
ME Waugh c Stewart b Caddick	49
*SR Waugh lbw b Gough	105
DR Martyn c Trescothick b Butcher	105
†AC Gilchrist c Caddick b White	152
SK Warne c Atherton b Butcher	8
B Lee c Atherton b Butcher	0
JN Gillespie lbw b Butcher	0
GD McGrath not out	1
Extras b 3, lb 7, nb 23)	33
Total (all out, 129.4 overs, 545 mins)	576

FoW: 1–98 (Hayden, 14.6 ov), 2–130 (Ponting, 19.4 ov),
3–134 (Slater, 23.1 ov), 4–267 (ME Waugh, 63.6 ov),
5–336 (SR Waugh, 83.2 ov), 6–496 (Martyn, 117.3 ov),
7–511 (Warne, 119.6 ov), 8–513 (Lee, 121.1 ov),
9–513 (Gillespie, 121.4 ov), 10–576 (Gilchrist, 129.4 ov).

Bowling	O	M	R	W
Gough	33	6	152	3 (10nb)
Caddick	36	0	163	1 (12nb)
White	26.4	5	101	1 (1nb)
Giles	25	0	108	1
Butcher	9	3	42	4

Umpires: S. A. Bucknor and G. Sharp   3rd Umpire: K. E. Palmer
* captain † wicket keeper

Back to Basics

The Second Test, Lord's Ground, London
19–22 July 2001

Back to Basics

The Second Test

England retreated from Birmingham assessing their wounds, the most notable of which was the broken little finger of Nasser Hussain's left hand. Word soon emerged from the English camp that the injury would keep him out of cricket for three weeks, which meant that for the second consecutive Lord's Test England would have to be led by a stand-in captain. Hussain's fingers have been broken time and again, sometimes when he has been hit while batting, and sometimes when he has been hit while fielding. When he made his first overseas tour, to the West Indies in 1989/90, the great West Indian batsman Everton Weekes saw him batting and remarked, 'That boy's fingers are going to get mashed.' He saw something in Hussain's technique, holding the bat low on the handle with the fingers pointing towards the bowler, and in his tendency to play the ball well away from his body, that made him fear for the young man's fingers. His technique may make his batting better – or it may not – but Weekes was very prescient about his vulnerability to injury.

The Australians, with no such worries, took advantage of the spare day their efforts at Edgbaston had earned them to watch the men's singles final at Wimbledon between Goran Ivanisevic and the Australian Pat Rafter. The match had been postponed from the Saturday because of rain at Wimbledon (which had stubbornly refused to spread a hundred miles further north and wash out the Edgbaston Test), and the Australians, many of them wearing their baggy green caps in support of Rafter, confidently expected a third major Australian victory of the weekend, following the Edgbaston Test match and the British Lions' defeat in the Second Rugby Test in Melbourne. It is now history that Ivanisevic won in five sets, and no doubt the English cricket team took heart from this piece of evidence that not all Australians are invincible. The fact that Ivanisevic had beaten both Greg Rusedski and Tim Henman in earlier rounds could now be forgiven.

The main issue that occupied the back pages between Wimbledon and the Second Test was the question of who should captain England at Lord's. Many names were put forward: Alec Stewart (who had covered for Hussain a year earlier); Graham Thorpe (who had led England in the One Day Internationals in Sri Lanka in the spring); Mike Atherton (a former England captain who by all accounts

Mark Waugh ducks a Craig White bouncer on his way to the Lord's Test century that had eluded him on previous tours.

wanted to remain a former England captain); Marcus Trescothick (currently the front runner to succeed Nasser Hussain in the long run); Mark Butcher (who had captained England once before when injury had robbed them of Hussain's services); and a host of other more speculative guesses ranging from Darren Gough – the people's champion – to Adam Hollioake, Mark Alleyne and even David Byas as captains of successful county sides. There was even mention of Dominic Cork, the captain of an unsuccessful county side, Derbyshire, who were languishing at the foot of the Second Division of the county table as the selectors discussed their choices. While the Australians continued on their gentle rampage through the counties between the Tests, the debate raged.

In the end, the appointment was the one that most commentators had hoped for – Michael Atherton. The selectors let it be known that they had considered a number of options, but Stewart and Butcher had also both let it be known that they did not want to be considered for the role. Trescothick was left to concentrate on his batting, and the more whimsical choices such as Gough, Cork and Alleyne were left for another day. There was some criticism of both Stewart and Butcher for not wanting to be considered as stand-in captain, on the basis that anybody should leap at the chance of leading his country, but both players felt they could be of more use to the English cause by concentrating on what they had been selected for, batting, and in Stewart's case wicketkeeping as well. Atherton thus added to his English record 52 Test matches as captain. It was his seventh Test as captain at Lord's, a ground where he had yet to score a Test century. He was also taking into the match a few memories of the last time he had captained in an Ashes Test at Lord's. In 1997 England were all out for 77, thanks to Glenn McGrath's best-ever Test bowling analysis at Lord's – 8 for 34 – and the match was only saved for England by the rain.

The squad that was chosen to try to lay the Lord's jinx in Tests against Australia (England's last victory was in 1934) was probably the best that was available, but there were still several gaps through injury.

It was: Michael Atherton (Lancashire, captain), Usman Afzaal (Nottinghamshire), Mark Butcher (Surrey), Andrew Caddick (Somerset), Dominic Cork (Derbyshire), Ashley Giles (Warwickshire), Darren Gough (Yorkshire), Mark Ramprakash (Surrey), Chris Silverwood (Yorkshire), Alec Stewart (Surrey, wicketkeeper), Graham Thorpe (Surrey), Marcus Trescothick (Somerset), Ian Ward (Surrey) and Craig White (Yorkshire).

The announcement, usually made at eleven o'clock in the morning on the Sunday before the Test, was delayed until noon while David Graveney and his fellow selectors checked on the fitness of Alex Tudor, who had just taken three wickets for Surrey in the Benson and Hedges Cup Final against Gloucestershire, thereby helping to condemn Gloucestershire to defeat in a Lord's final for the first time in five consecutive appearances. Nasser Hussain had not found it easy to check personally on Tudor's fitness because he was refused entry to Lord's no fewer than three times that day by the ever-efficient Lord's gatemen. He got in at the fourth time of asking, and was eventually able to report on the match as both journalist and selector. In the end, it was felt that Tudor was not fit enough to withstand the strains of a five-day Test match, and Chris Silverwood of Yorkshire was called up instead. The prospect of bowling for much of the five days at the broad and intimidating bats

of the Australian top seven is far more daunting than that of getting through ten overs on a Saturday afternoon against a Gloucestershire batting line-up with only one Test player, Jack Russell, in the top half.

Even so, the team was missing at least three first choices – Hussain, Vaughan and Hoggard – and the risk of playing Graham Thorpe, who had not played any competitive cricket since finishing the Second Test against Pakistan on 4 June, was still being considered right up to the moment the teams were announced. If we assume that Tudor would have been selected ahead of Silverwood, and that White had still not fully regained his bowling fitness, it still looked as though the England selectors were having to make the most of a bad hand rather than putting out the cream of their cricketers to face the Australians, who had no such injury worries. The prospect of an England batting line-up from numbers three to seven made up entirely of Surrey players would be an interesting statistical first for England, but it seemed very likely that Afzaal of Nottinghamshire would be given a second chance to show the skills and determination that had all the best judges raving about him. This meant that Ward or Ramprakash, Hussain's direct replacement, would be most likely to miss out if Thorpe was declared fit.

In the mean time, the Australians were getting themselves fully prepared for the Lord's encounter. It was surprising to note that since 1997 the Australians had made seven changes to their Test eleven, with only the Waugh twins, Shane Warne and Glenn McGrath surviving, while England, the weaker of the two sides then as now, retained six of the side that had performed so poorly four years earlier, and would have had a seventh if Hussain had been fit. What's more, given that Robert Croft, who played at Lord's in 1997, was in the squad for the First Test, out of 1997's players really only John

Crawley, Mark Ealham and Devon Malcolm were not in the frame for the Second Test. Of those three, John Crawley still had a few backers, Devon Malcolm was at that stage the county circuit's leading wicket-taker and Mark Ealham had played in the Limited Overs Internationals earlier in the summer. Australia had lost Mark Taylor, Paul Reiffel and Ian Healy through retirement, and Matt Elliott, Greg Blewett, Michael Bevan and Michael Kasprowicz had been replaced by Hayden, Martyn, Ponting and Gillespie. The new eleven was stronger than the old one.

Against the counties between Tests, the Australians tried out their second string players. McGrath, Gillespie and Lee, their front-line quick attack, sat out the ten days along with Steve Waugh and Adam Gilchrist, giving Katich, Noffke, Langer, Seccombe, Fleming and Miller a day or two in the sun. Brett Lee had a slight side strain, and Hayden and Slater were nursing minor knocks, but otherwise the touring party were fit and raring to get stuck into England once again. Justin Langer took the opportunity to score 104 not out against Somerset, but when Damien Martyn scored 176 not out in 231 balls in the second innings of the same game, his fourth first-class century of the tour, any thoughts of tinkering with the Test top six went by the board. Damien Fleming took 6 for 59 in the same match, but unless Lee's strain were to prove more troublesome than was at first thought, Fleming would do no more than carry the drinks at Lord's.

The county opposition was becoming a matter of some concern. Somerset's two centrally contracted players, Caddick and Trescothick, both missed the game against the Australians, and their replacements were two men not even on Somerset's books – Aamir Sohail and Shoaib Akhtar, the Pakistan Test players. The overall standard of county opposition put out against the touring sides had been of barely second eleven quality for some seasons, which meant that the tourists often found themselves able to have not much more than an extended net practice, while the England players and leading contenders for Test places sat out these matches, as though by keeping their powder dry the England selectors could frighten the tourists into submission. The impression this tactic actually gives is that the English players are frightened of showing their weaknesses to the tourists before the serious business begins, which can only serve to bolster the touring team's confidence. Not that the Australians in 2001 needed much confidence-boosting.

The team they chose was exactly the same as the team for the First Test: Steve Waugh (New South Wales, captain), Michael Slater (New South Wales), Matthew Hayden (Queensland), Ricky Ponting (Tasmania), Mark Waugh (New South Wales), Damien Martyn (Western Australia), Adam Gilchrist (Western Australia, wicketkeeper), Shane Warne (Victoria), Brett Lee (New South Wales), Jason Gillespie (South Australia) and Glenn McGrath (New South Wales). They were ready for their favourite hunting ground.

First Day, 19 July 2001

The first day of a Lord's Test is always special, although the weather conspired to put this particular one, the hundred and second opening day of a Lord's Test since the first ever on 21 July 1884, among the less distinguished. As the crowds arrived, there was no sign of play, and the outfield was full of players from both teams warming up for the match. Colin Miller, in pink hair at this stage in the tour, was practising with Glenn McGrath, Jason Gillespie, Brett Lee and Adam Gilchrist, and Duncan Fletcher was giving Dominic Cork and Andrew Caddick catching practice.

Michael Atherton and Steve Waugh did not even come out to toss until noon, Waugh in his faithful baggy green, Atherton in his England blazer. Play was scheduled to start at 12.30. Waugh called correctly yet again, and put England in. This was the ninth consecutive toss lost by England: the change of captain made no difference. England would have liked to have won this toss, that's for sure, but the importance of winning the toss can be overestimated. More often than not it makes little difference, and the better team wins anyway. The South Africans under Shaun Pollock have been as unlucky as England, losing nine consecutive tosses, but they still win their matches, and represent the only credible sustained challenge to Australia today.

The toss has become a major media opportunity these days. Where once two men strolled out to the middle, flipped a coin, and one of them mimed a forward defensive stroke to his teammates as they walked back into the pavilion, nowadays the captains are accompanied to the square by the groundsman, several cameramen, even more reporters, probably a selector or two and a few people standing solemnly under umbrellas. It soon emerges that some of these people are there to have a word or two with the captains as they toss. Dermot Reeve, given the task of getting some newsworthy comment out of the captains, came up with the brilliant question to Atherton, 'So it's going to be an interesting first hour then?' Atherton's reply was to the point: 'There's only half an hour until lunch.' In the event, there was no real need for newsworthy comment. At about the same time as the captains were tossing, at the Old Bailey Lord Archer was found guilty of perjury and sentenced to four years in jail. The papers would have no trouble filling their pages for the next day or two, with or without the thoughts of Captain Atherton.

Waugh took the modern route and put England in to bat. Giles and Afzaal were left out of the England thirteen, which meant that England had five men from the same county batting in positions three to seven, the first time this had happened in English Test history. It was the first time that five members of the same county side had played together in a Test since 1949 when five Middlesex players had played in the Lord's Test against New Zealand, a match that had ended in a draw.

As 12.30 came round, Glenn McGrath marked out his run from the Pavilion End and Atherton prepared to take strike. Waugh gave McGrath four slips and two gullies, a silly mid on, a fine leg and an extra cover. Two lights glowed from the scoreboard as Atherton faced his nemesis through the gloom. The hundred and second Lord's Test was under way.

McGrath's four slips and two gullies lasted only five balls. Then Waugh took two of them out into the off-side field, and immediately McGrath dug in a ball short, which Atherton hooked well for four. The trap was set, and the bait had been taken; this time, the batsman won. Atherton had also signalled England's intention to play positively, which was good for the crowd to know. All the same, batting in the gloom against McGrath, Gillespie and Lee was a tough situation in which to play positively.

Only ten minutes later a third light came on, and the umpires, John Holder and Steve Bucknor, conferred. This time they did not offer the light to the batsmen, and Trescothick celebrated with a fierce cut for four. Next ball, he was dropped at slip by Mark Waugh, of all people, but it had been called a no-ball. This prompted the umpires to confer again, no doubt on the basis that if Mark Waugh drops a catch the light must be really poor. And this time they offered it to the batsmen, who

Of the many odd engagements the Queen has fulfilled, giving a cake to five middle-aged gentlemen
in recognition of their abilities as cricket commentators must be among the most bizarre.

retreated eagerly
to the pavilion.
Lunch was taken
early, after only 3.2
overs, with England
11 for no wicket.

The lunch break was extended due to bad light
and rain. Play could not restart until 2.30, and then
it was more of the same: McGrath and Gillespie
bowling very quickly and with pinpoint accuracy
as the England openers attempted to play themselves back in. Trescothick's method seems to
involve a great deal of swishing at balls outside his
off stump without much use of his feet, but this is
his style and he got away with it. Gillespie was
timed at 88.8 m.p.h. for one delivery, which
Trescothick played a touch streakily between third
and fourth slip for four.

All the time, the light was deteriorating again,
but this did not prevent Atherton hitting two
delightful fours off McGrath, a cover drive followed
by a square drive. The positive attitude seemed to
be working. But then, with his score at 15 and the
total on 33, Trescothick had another waft at
Gillespie and edged it to Gilchrist. He made way

for another left-hander and the first of the five
Surrey batsmen, Mark Butcher. Butcher's arrival
was accompanied by the first light on the scoreboard coming on, but that did not stop Atherton
hooking McGrath for four again, nor Butcher himself square-cutting Gillespie to the Grandstand
boundary.

After ten minutes of this, Her Majesty the
Queen arrived. As monarch of both England and
Australia (and several other places besides) she
could of course choose which team to support,
and anyway need never back the loser. In 2001 it
was certainly more profitable to back Australia, but
probably a certain regal impartiality enters into
her thoughts, and it seems unlikely that she ever
cheers very loudly for either side, preferring to
maintain a dignified silence. As the Queen arrived,
Brett Lee was introduced into the attack, bowling
from the Nursery End. The two events were probably not connected in any way other than chronologically, but Lee failed to excite his monarch, or
anybody else. His first ball was a wide, one of those
which start wide down the off-side and move even
wider, aiming almost exactly at the Committee
Room window where the Queen was sitting. Atherton was unimpressed. Quite probably, the Queen
was also unimpressed.

A few minutes later, Shane Warne was brought
into the attack. His first ball was hooked for four by
Butcher, and then the 50 came up thanks to three
byes, the result of a poor ball backed up by poor
wicketkeeping. The score moved on to 55 for 1
when the rain came back again, and tea came
early. In one hour's play since lunch England had
made 44 runs for the loss of one wicket in 14.4
overs – a fair result given the conditions.

Tea, like lunch, lasted for over an hour, and the
crowds bore it all very patiently. During the tea
interval, the teams were presented to the Queen,
in the pavilion rather than out on the pitch as is

traditional, and she in turn presented the BBC Radio Test Match Special team with a Dundee cake baked in the royal kitchens. Among the many odd appointments she has been asked to fulfil in the 49 years of her reign, giving a cake to five middle-aged gentlemen in recognition of their abilities as cricket commentators must be among the most bizarre. The cake was officially to mark the fortieth anniversary of the first Test Match Special broadcast on an Ashes Test in 1961, but we can only assume that the whole thing was to appease irate listeners to TMS. There are senior figures in the BBC who can pull strings to ask the Queen to present a cake to Aggers, Blowers, Bearders, CM-J and the rest, but there is apparently nobody with the clout or the desire to ensure that TMS becomes once again what it always used to be, a ball-by-ball commentary with never a ball missed nor a shipping forecast halfway through an over. If I were a sailor in Dogger, Fisher or Finistere stuck in the middle of a hurricane, I'd almost rather hear the gentle banter of Jonathan Agnew and Henry Blofeld describing the field set by Shane Warne for Mark Butcher than a complacent continuity announcer in a nice warm studio in London confirming my suspicion that it was chucking it down in a hundred-mile radius around my ship.

After tea, play resumed at 4.50 pm, and by this time only 34 overs remained to be played. The Queen made her excuses and left and the Royal Standard came down from the top of the pavilion. The cricket was a curious mixture of the daring and the attritional, with Atherton the more attritional and Butcher the more daring. The Australians never let up for a minute, and Atherton found himself playing that characteristic shot of his time and again. You will not find it in any coaching manuals, but it is effective, for Atherton at least. He comes half forward and the bat swings like a pendulum in a lazy arc from off to leg. The

ball makes contact with the bat at the central point of the arc, and the ball, usually, is nudged across to the leg side for a run or two. Sometimes he misses altogether, and sometimes the ball takes a leading edge. Given the purity and orthodoxy of the rest of his shots, it is an odd stroke for Atherton to have invented, but he has used it throughout his career, and it has generally served him well.

Lee was beginning to work up a real pace (a no-ball was timed at 90.2 m.p.h.), but he was not taking wickets. Waugh brought on McGrath for Lee and almost immediately Butcher nicked one to second slip, where Mark Waugh took the hundred and fifty-seventh catch of his Test career, to equal the record set by his former captain Mark Taylor. Butcher had made 21 in just under an hour of batting, about two and a quarter hours altogether since Trescothick's dismissal. England were 75 for 2.

This brought Graham Thorpe to the crease for his first innings since the beginning of June, since his mystery calf injury which kept him out of the one-day matches and the First Test. Such is his importance to the England team that even with no match practice at all, and no guarantee of fitness, he is still the first name linked to the list when the selectors meet. There was really no doubt that he would play: the only surprise was that it was Afzaal who made way for him.

Thorpe proved his fitness and his value to the crowd by tucking his first ball away square for a single. The roar of approval was as much an expression of relief as applause for the shot. A little later, a magnificent extra cover drive off Gillespie brought cheers for the quality of the shot, although the wet outfield stopped it earning the full four it deserved. Atherton joined in the strokeplay with an on-driven four off Gillespie, followed by three more runs through the off side field. In the same over, Thorpe hit another three, so Gillespie had gone for ten in the over. Poor Brett Lee chased each ball to the boundary, proving his fitness and the strength of his throwing arm, but not having much chance to rest between his bowling spells.

If Gillespie was giving the batsmen a few problems, McGrath at the other end was a real handful. There was a feeling in the crowd that this could be the crucial partnership: if Atherton and Thorpe could last the day and build tomorrow a decent platform for a good total, then who knows? But, as my grandmother used to say, if ifs and ands were pots and pans, we'd have no need of tinkers. McGrath was determined to play the role of tinker, demolishing those ifs and ands. One over to Thorpe was majestic, but as it finished a third warning light came on and the umpires conferred.

Steve Waugh then did an odd thing: he brought Brett Lee on in place of Gillespie. With three lights blaring out through the gloom, Waugh could have tried Warne or his brother or even carried on with Gillespie, but to bring on the fastest of his bowling attack invited just one response from the umpires. They offered the light to the batsmen, who marched off at once. The crowd began to wonder whether there would be any more play. But before most of them could work their way to the front of the queue for a beer, the players were back on again, at just before 6.00 pm and now with a theoretical twenty overs remaining. Brett Lee carried on where he left off, with a no-ball.

Disaster struck at five past six. Atherton, who had been playing very well all day despite the interruptions, suddenly decided to leave a ball from McGrath that jagged back in to him from the off-stump line. The umpires had no hesitation in giving him out, and although the television replays seemed to show that it might have been too high to hit the stumps, at the time there could have been little doubt even in Atherton's mind that he was

going to have to pay for that misjudgement. Atherton out for 31, England 96 for 3.

This brought Mark Ramprakash to the wicket, in what was his first Test as a Surrey player, and also his first since the Lord's Test against the West Indies a year before, when he had been Atherton's opening partner. England had already lost one more wicket than they had hoped, so another before close of play would be a major blow. Ramprakash looked, amazing to relate, very relaxed and more at home in England's colours than at any time in his long, stuttering career. To match his mood, by 6.15 there was blue sky visible overhead and no lights shining from the scoreboard. Lee was trying his best to disconcert the two England batsmen, with a no-ball and then his slower ball (timed at 54.6 m.p.h.) followed by a full blooded 81.6 m.p.h. delivery. But for all his efforts, the ball was not doing much in the air or off the wicket, and Thorpe and Ramprakash coped quite easily. Their running between the wickets was excellent, and gave us hope that Thorpe's calf injury was truly a thing of the past.

These things cannot last. A quick ball from Lee did, for once, cut back in on him and Ramprakash was bowled through the gate for 14. Ramps always seems to score 14 in Tests: it is a great irritation to his supporters, and no doubt to the man himself, that he gets himself in so often and then does not go on to build any sort of a substantial score. England were 121 for 4, at 6.45 and with ten overs to go. Who would come in? A nightwatchman or the next man on the list, Alec Stewart?

No question: the true professional, Alec Stewart, marched through the pavilion gate and out to do battle. His arrival coincided with the third light coming on. The umpires conferred, but let play continue, at least until a fourth light came on for the first time. At that point the light was offered to the batsmen, and that, gentlemen, as Alec Skelding used to say, concludes the entertainment for today. Not much entertainment for the full house, it must be admitted, but in the end it was Australia's day. England lost at least one too many wickets.

Close of play: England 121 for 4

Second Day, 20 July 2001

The weather on the Friday was beautiful. The sun shone and the crowd basked in the best conditions for cricket imaginable. The best cricket imaginable did not, sadly, come from England, who were bundled out rather too quickly for all but their opponents' tastes, but from the Australians, especially the elegant and ruthless Mark Waugh. Glenn McGrath did not bowl too badly either.

In only the third over of the day, McGrath got rid of Alec Stewart, who snicked a ball into Gilchrist's gloves. Stewart had failed to score, and England were 126 for 5. Two overs later, McGrath and Gillespie did it again, this time removing the top scalp of the innings, Thorpe, for 20. Thorpe had added only 4 to his overnight score, and now the wheels were well and truly coming off the England bandwagon. Waugh was able to carry on attacking with four slips and a gully, and no England batsman was able to get off the hook.

Only two runs later, Craig White became McGrath's fifth victim of the innings, caught by Hayden for the same score that Stewart had made. McGrath had now taken 5 for 31 in 20 overs and was chasing his own Lord's record bowling analysis of 8 for 38 four years ago. But he had not counted on a counter-attack, led by Dominic Cork with some help from Ian Ward. In the space of ten overs the pair added 47, which might under some circumstances have been described as a useful eighth-wicket stand, but today just rescued England from complete disaster and pulled them into the merely dismal category. Cork relishes these situations, but in the past couple of seasons has become less able to exploit them. However, he no doubt remembered his brilliant cameo 33 not out here in 2000 to win the Test against the West Indies, and that inspired him to achieve a little more than some of his team-mates higher up the order. In the course of his 24 – not many, but still England's third best effort of the innings, after Atherton's 37 and Extras' 28 – he struck McGrath for an all-run four through mid-on and a hook for six into the Mound Stand. The 150 came up from four byes off a wild McGrath delivery, and at the end of that over the crowd in the Allen Stand, in front of which McGrath was fielding, gave him a far bigger cheer than when he was taking wickets. Irony lives in the Allen Stand (or at least, Australians don't).

But it could not last. Cork was caught quite brilliantly by Ricky Ponting at square cover off Gillespie and England had slipped to 178 for 8. Warne, who had replaced McGrath, then bowled Caddick off his pads and Gough, who struck one boundary before perishing, was entirely deceived by the flight of a ball that Warne bowled from way behind the bowling crease. England were all out for 187, having lost 6 wickets for 66 runs in 24 overs. Ward was left not out 23, but that was not particularly to his credit. Having had virtually no experience of shepherding the tail to a realistic total (he opens the batting for Surrey), he did not seem to make much attempt to keep the strike to himself, and so the England tail wilted. This is something the England selectors and Ward himself need to look at.

Lunch was taken, and Australia came out, guns smoking, to take on the England score and pulverise it. By this stage there was no doubt of the advantage of winning the toss. Batting on the

second afternoon would be much easier than on the first afternoon. Matthew Hayden, however, did not find it so. In the second over of the innings, he gave Butcher a straightforward chance at slip, which was readily accepted. Australia 5 for 1. Ponting and Slater decided that making an all-out onslaught on the new ball was the right thing to do, and so it proved for another three overs, during which time 22 more runs were added. Then Ponting followed Hayden's example and edged a catch off Gough to slip. This time it was to Thorpe, but the result was the same: Australia now 27 for 2. Ponting had made 14 off 12 balls, including three fours, but his departure left Australia needing a solid third wicket partnership.

Thanks almost entirely to Mark Waugh, they got it. Michael Slater played a curiously subdued supporting role as the pair put on 78 in 19 overs, with Waugh outdoing his usually very free-scoring partner by two to one. Mark Waugh's innings was a masterpiece. In the Lord's test of 1993, he had been bowled by Phil Tufnell for 99 to become one of only six Test batsmen dismissed on that score at Lord's. Only one of those six, Charles Macartney (99 in 1912) had gone on to score a subsequent Lord's Test century (133 not out in 1926) but now Mark Waugh was to become the second to achieve this recondite feat.

How do you rate a Mark Waugh innings? When he is playing at his best, he combines beauty and power in a way that perhaps only Muhammad Ali or Pele have done among sportsmen of recent memory. His batting is perfect in its shot selection and execution, and his style flows as relentlessly and as gracefully as the Niagara Falls. He is among the best of all time with his strokes through mid-wicket and mid-on: the straight on drive is

Steve Waugh played a subsidiary role to ,his brother, but no less forcefully. The twins put on 107 together, their second century partnership in successive Test innings

generally acknowledged to be the most difficult shot in a batsman's armoury, but Mark Waugh plays it as though it was as easy as taking guard. He seems unruffled by what is going on around him, and by what the bowlers are trying to do to him. As he sailed serenely towards his 100 he had to take evasive action against all of England's quicker bowlers, but he brushed aside their physical assaults as though they were harmless but irritating insects. Cork hit him with a good bumper when he was on 97, and with his score only one run more Caddick hit him on the grille. He just settled back into his stance and waited for the next delivery.

Somewhat typically of the way England played the whole day, Mark Waugh was able to reach his 100 off a Caddick no-ball, which he played to backward square leg. This shot also brought up the 200, in 311 balls just before 5.30. The England players all applauded, which was not only gracious (but then he hadn't survived any contentious appeals; I don't remember anybody even appealing against him on the off-chance of a downright awful lbw decision), but also an acknowledgment that they had been all but powerless to stop one of the great batsmen of his generation when he plays at the top of his game. The only way anybody could see his wicket falling was by a run-out. A few minutes later, the 100 partnership between the Waugh twins came up courtesy of a Mark Butcher wide: on occasion you got the feeling that all the Australian batsmen had to do was to stand there and eventually the England team would give them the lead in extras.

Slater had perished much earlier in the day, caught behind off Caddick's first delivery of his second spell, which only lasted two overs. He had made 25 out of 105. Of the 24 overs, plus plenty of no-balls, bowled in the innings up till then, Slater had only faced 62 balls, barely 40 per cent of the balls delivered, which is a very small percentage by his standards, but still he was curiously muted all innings. When he left at 105 for 3, Steve Waugh joined his brother, who was already past 50. Steve managed with his first ball to give England the first whisper of a chance against Mark. A quick single was thought about, and the hesitation produced a run-out chance for England, but the ball hit Mark's bat as he dived full length to regain his ground.

After tea, taken with Australia on 118 for 3, the Waughs moved inexorably onwards. Mark led the run chase, but Steve played an aggressive supporting role. Steve is always pugnacious, his lack of classic style combining with a totally solid defence to make bowling at him a dispiriting, almost heartbreaking experience. Bowling at Mark is no more likely to bring a wicket, but there is something about being hit for four by a great shot that makes it more acceptable than being bludgeoned to the boundary by Steve. There is no reason to suppose that Steve is any more earnest than Mark when they are away from a cricket environment, but at the wicket any lightheartedness will come from Mark, not Steve.

Atherton brought on Mark Butcher, the bowler of Edgbaston, at five past five, when the score was 180 for 3. Mark Waugh was on 93, and Steve on 26. Ten minutes later, the Australians passed the England total of 187, a four to fine leg by Steve Waugh off Butcher doing the business. Steve seems currently to be out of his sponsorship contract for his bat; he batted with a blade entirely devoid of any markings, although it must have been manufactured by somebody. Mark, on the other hand, was giving Slazenger their money's worth.

The twins were finally separated, when Mark Waugh was dismissed by a brilliant piece of fielding by Darren Gough. In the Lord's Test against the West Indies in 2001 it was a piece of phenomenal fielding by Gough, his outfield catch to dismiss Campbell off Caddick, which turned the Test – and the whole series – England's way, so there was temporary hope that he had done it again. Mark Waugh hit the ball from Cork towards mid-on and set off for a quick single. Gough gathered and threw in one movement and hit the stumps, something England's fielders manage all too rarely. Waugh was out. This was his nineteenth Test century, but still his highest Test score is only 153 not out. There are a number of batsmen who rarely go on to make big scores once they pass their hundred – Colin Cowdrey, Allan Lamb and Graham Thorpe all spring to mind – but it is still a statistical oddity that Mark Waugh should never have gone on to grind his opponents into the mud in the way that pretty well all his team-mates have done at least once. Of the top six in the Australian line-up in this Test, only Damien Martyn has a lower top score in Tests than Mark Waugh, and Gilchrist is now only one run behind.

Martyn came in to replace Mark Waugh as though he had set his mind on changing this odd statistic. Darren Gough was immediately reintroduced into the attack, and showed he was ready for the fray after his run-out. But Martyn cover-drove him for four, and when Gough took a man out of his slip cordon and put him at extra cover, Martyn hit the next ball for four through midwicket.

Steve Waugh did not last long after his twin was out. A slightly leg-side ball from Dominic Cork induced Waugh to attempt a leg glance, but all he managed was to glove it to Stewart, who took a very good leg-side catch, bringing the score to 230 for 5. In comparing Stewart and Gilchrist, people have always looked at Gilchrist's brilliant batting: he is certainly a man who can decide the course of a game from his position at number seven.

However, in wicketkeeping terms, there is little doubt that Gilchrist is still one of the poorer international keepers. He is capable of some great catches, but whereas Stewart did not let through a single bye in Australia's total in this match, and took five catches into the bargain, Gilchrist conceded seven byes in England's first innings, which was in the end less than half Australia's total. Throughout the summer there were moments when Gilchrist looked like a batsman standing in for the real keeper, but there were also moments when he looked the genuine article. Given that Stewart himself is really a batsman-turned-keeper, Gilchrist has some way to go before he can truly be considered a great wicketkeeper/batsman. But as long as he keeps averaging over 50 in Tests, does it really matter if he concedes a few more byes than his peers in other Test teams?

Tonight, Gilchrist had a real struggle to get off the mark. For most of the summer there had been little evidence of England having a clear plan against each batsman. Whenever a new England batsman appeared (i.e. every ten minutes or so), Steve Waugh and his bowlers would reshape their field, sometimes with wholesale movements of players and sometimes with subtle nudges of fielders a couple of yards to the left or right, but always the impression was that the Australians had worked out a way of getting at the new batsman. Whenever an Australian batsman appeared (i.e. every two days or so), England just seemed to carry on as before. If a left-hander replaced a right-hander, then people moved, but otherwise, not much apparently changed. This was no doubt a false impression, but if it seemed that way to the spectators beyond the boundary, how much more so must it have seemed to the new batsman? But this time, with Gilchrist, Andrew Caddick took a long time rearranging his field, and the ploy began to work.

It took Gilchrist half an hour to get off the mark. During that time he survived a very confident appeal from Cork for lbw (though when has Cork not sounded confident in his appeals?), and played and missed many a time. Finally he managed to hit Craig White for three through extra cover to get off the mark, and then duplicated the shot, and the runs scored, to take Australia to 250. In the final over of the day, with Caddick bowling to three slips and two gullies, Gilchrist square-cut him for four to end the day on ten not out, just three scoring strokes in 33 balls faced. Damien Martyn at the other end was on 24 not out, and Australia went in at 255 for 5, a lead of 68. If only England could get rid of one of these two (or preferably, both) early in the morning, then the match might not be beyond them.

Close of play: England 187 (McGrath 5 for 54); Australia 255 for 5 (ME Waugh 108)

Third Day, 21 July 2001

The start of the third day was enlivened considerably by my journey on the Jubilee Line tube that took me to the ground at around 10.15 on that bright Saturday morning (not that you can tell if it's particularly bright when you are in the depths of London's Underground system). I joined the train at Southwark, and took a seat opposite a Chinese girl of about seventeen or eighteen, who was reading a paperback rejoicing in the title *The Book of British Humour*. She stared at its pages intently, without a flicker of a smile ever touching her face. I began to wonder whether British humour was all it was cracked up to be. Then, as the train left Baker Street and headed towards St John's Wood,

Over page: Atherton's last chance to score a Test century at Headquarters begins with an escort of four slips and two gullies.

the driver's voice came over the loudspeaker.

'I know most of you today are going to Lord's for the Test Match. I just want to say that I hope we annihilate the Aussies.' A stage pause. 'Crush the Kangaroos, wallop the Wallabies, demolish the Dingoes.' Another pause. The people in my carriage were all smiling, apart from the Chinese girl, who was still engrossed in her textbook of British humour and determinedly ignoring the practical exhibition of it all around her.

'I'm finishing at one o'clock today,' continued the driver's voice, 'and then I'm going home to watch the Test on television. So please, all of you, make a lot of noise. Cheer loudly.' A little cheer, a somewhat timid dress rehearsal, went round the carriage. 'Except the MCC members,' said the driver as an afterthought. 'They can just clap politely.'

This last remark, as we arrived at St John's Wood, caused a round of applause and we all left the train in a happy mood. All except the Chinese girl, who was travelling beyond St John's Wood, and who would now have the compartment to herself so she could concentrate on the intricacies of British humour without raucous interruptions from the British people.

The British people, and a good number of Australians, arriving at Lord's for Saturday's play had to be there early not to miss the first excitements. In the second over of the morning, the tube driver's exhortation to demolish the Dingoes went unheeded as Mark Butcher dropped a straightforward chance from Adam Gilchrist, who was then on just 13. Australia had made 255 at the time, and a chance to break into Australia's tail at this moment would have been invaluable. But it was not to be, and for the next hour or so Martyn and Gilchrist let rip. At 11.30 the 50 partnership was posted, and the next ball Gilchrist square-cut for four with the speed and precision of a samurai warrior slicing through a falling handkerchief. Martyn hit the first two balls of Cork's first over of the day through the covers for four each. It just all seemed too easy. Craig White, whose bowling was never right all summer, tried going round the wicket to Gilchrist, a tactic that had worked against Lara a year ago, but it made no difference.

Atherton just stood at slip, arms folded, the body language telling everybody that bloody hell, here was another long day in prospect. He took the new ball at the first possible moment, and gave it to Darren Gough. Gough did not strike at once, but Andy Caddick did, having Martyn caught behind for 52, although it may have been that the ball just brushed his sleeve. If only it had been Gilchrist, England might have been through to the tail in no time, but it was not to be. Ian Ward, without doubt one of the fielding stars of the England side, then dropped an admittedly hard chance off Gilchrist in the covers, and to add insult to injury, the reprieved batsman then hit the next two balls for four just wide of Ward. While Gilchrist was marching imperiously to his 50, the new batsman, Warne, managed one four through the covers before becoming Stewart's fourth catch of the innings. Brett Lee now joined Gilchrist, who raced on to his 50 in 78 balls – this after having been ten not out overnight in 33 balls – thanks to two fours hit through Darren Gough's seven-strong off-side field. The second of those went through Mark Butcher's hands like a heat-seeking missile, no more than a quarter of a chance. Gough's own personal 100 came up in his twenty-second over, an economy rate of virtually five an over compared with the innings rate of just four. The Dazzler was barely even a Glimmer at this moment.

About fifteen minutes before lunch, Atherton joined in the game of Double or Drop: once again it was Gilchrist, then on 73, who benefited and once again it was a simple chance. Cork was the unlucky bowler. At this stage it was noticeable that when the scoreboard lit up the name of the 'Fielder', it was almost always the name of the man who missed it, rather than the poor fellow who had to mop up the error. In this morning session, England's fielding, which had in recent series been so brilliant, plumbed the depths. It was bad not only for the runs they gave a side who do not need to have runs given free of charge. It was also bad because it must have sapped the morale of the England side: more runs to chase, less confidence in their own abilities.

Lee, who seemed more of a force as a batsman and fielder than as a fast bowler in this match, added 61 more runs with Gilchrist, until Gilchrist touched one to his counterpart behind the stumps – Stewart's fifth catch of the innings. Even Jason Gillespie hit a couple of fours in his brief innings of nine, and when Lee was last out, bowled by Caddick for 20, Australia had made 401, a lead of 214 over a hapless England. Andrew Caddick ended up with 5 wickets for 101 runs in 32.1 overs – by far the best bowling performance by England. He followed the Australian habit of celebrating his five-for by holding up the ball to the crowd, as a batsman salutes with his bat on reaching 50 or 100, but it seemed a bit flat in the circumstances. England went into lunch with plenty to think about.

After lunch, England began the long climb back to a position of safety, if not victory, which should still have been entirely possible. The first runs from the bat had to wait until the fourth over, when Trescothick played a beautiful straight off-drive off Gillespie for two runs. Two overs later, with only one more run added to his personal tally, Trescothick nicked one to Gilchrist. England 8 for 1. The long climb back seemed even more precipitous.

If there were two men who ought to have been feeling bad about their fielding performances, they were Atherton and Butcher. Their dropped catches had allowed Australia to build a very big lead, as opposed to a merely comfortable one, and now they had to try to rebuild England's prospects with their bats. First wicket down is a notoriously difficult position to fill, and Mark Butcher, a natural opener, would have been nobody's choice for the role at the start of the season. However, after good performances in the First Test, he built on his good start with more solid performances here at Lord's. With Atherton, he took the score steadily along towards 50 and towards tea, until Shane Warne was brought into the attack. Warne is undoubtedly a very great cricketer who, despite a five-wicket haul in the First Test, is not now the force he used to be, but he can still rip the ball out of any rough there happens to be, and can turn it prodigiously from outside the right-hander's leg stump. The players against whom he has had most difficulties recently, VVS Laxman and Sachin Tendulkar of India, have one thing in common: they never swept Warne. It must be very tempting to sweep any leg-spinner who pitches the ball a long way outside the leg stump, but Warne is not any leg-spinner. He has throughout his career not only produced balls that no human being could play unless they knew exactly what was coming (just ask Mike Gatting), but he has also earned a reputation for getting much more bounce than most on all types of wickets. The one thing that playing the sweep requires is a pretty regular bounce. If the ball goes higher or lower than expected, then the horizontal bat will either miss altogether, or else produce a top or bottom edge with potentially disastrous results. In Atherton's case, at half past three on a pleasantly breezy Saturday afternoon in St John's Wood, he missed altogether. Atherton, bowled Warne 20. What a waste!

Graham Thorpe then came in to join his Surrey team-mate, but clearly did not enjoy his brief stay.

A Brett Lee bouncer beat him for pace and smacked into his glove, and Thorpe, the most phlegmatic and unemotional of England's batsmen, could not help but show the pain. However, he batted on until he was undone by the last ball of the same over, adjudged lbw to a ball that could well have been missing off stump. England were now 50 for three, although if Thorpe had not been given out it is quite possible that he would not have been able to continue batting after tea. X-rays subsequently revealed that Lee's bouncer had broken a bone in his hand, which would cause him to miss the rest of the series.

Lee gained press attention for another reason too. Probably out of frustration that his bowling was just not as good as he, and his captain, knew it should be, Lee burst into a chorus of expletives when he rattled first Atherton and then Thorpe with bouncers. Although neither batsman paid much attention to the verbals (whatever they thought of the bouncers themselves), the match referee took a great interest in Lee's over-reaction, and had a little talk with him subsequently.

During tea, I had the chance to talk with Neil Harvey, the great Australian left-hander of the late '40s and '50s, whose one game as captain of Australia had been at Lord's in 1961 when Richie Benaud had been injured. I asked him if he wanted Australia to win. He replied that he always wanted Australia to do well, but he hated to see English cricket in this state. If only England could win a Test or two, he said, it would be good for world cricket and for the Ashes in particular. I am not sure how much Mr Harvey, one of the most gracious and generous men ever to have played Test cricket, was telling me what I wanted to hear, and how much he was speaking from the heart, but I could not help but agree with him. I did not think, however, that he would see his wish come true.

After tea, it almost seemed as though Butcher, Ramprakash and the entire Australian side had taken Neil Harvey's words to heart. Ramprakash, who came into the match with a Test batting average at Lord's in single figures, played at a level of skill and artistry that he had so often promised but rarely delivered at Test level, and Butcher was a revelation. Both men had their share of luck, but where once Butcher's off-side shots looked tentative and technically suspect, he was now hitting with freedom and power. We were reminded of what *Wisden Australia* had said about Butcher's century at Brisbane almost three years earlier: 'Butcher suddenly looked like an accomplished Test opener. Gone was the tentativeness that had plagued his batting... as he played both speed and spin confidently.' But why does he only look like an accomplished Test player about one innings in twenty? That Brisbane innings was the last time Butcher had reached 50 in Tests. He has the talent, he has the temperament. What is missing? The trouble is, we could be asking those same questions about most of England's batsmen, and several of the bowlers too. Consistency at Test level just is not an English virtue.

After batting for almost two hours, and after a partnership of 96 in 29 overs, Ramprakash was beaten by a straight one from Gillespie, and was out, lbw. Nobody seemed to think the decision was anything other than correct. But this was the final alarm of the day for England. With Alec Stewart, whose Test batting average at Lord's is five or six times Ramprakash's, Butcher reached the close of play on 73 not out. Stewart was on 13 and England, 163 for 4, were still 51 runs behind Australia. With good batting the next day, there was no reason why the rest of the England batsmen should not press for a lead of 150 or so, and ever since Headingley in 1981, the Australians have been suspect, at least to English minds, when chasing lowish totals.

Atherton's final Test innings at Lord's ends as he is bowled trying to sweep a Warne leg-break.

Close of play: England 187 and 163 for 4 (Butcher 73 not out); Australia 401 (ME Waugh 108, Martyn 52, Gilchrist 90, Caddick 5 for 101)

Fourth Day, 22 July 2001

This was the day when two sporting dreams faded.

Golf's 'nearly man' Colin Montgomerie, who had been leading for much of the Open at Royal Lytham and St Anne's, slipped off the pace as the one American in the leading pack, David Duval, played brilliantly to win his first Major. And

England lapsed pitifully to defeat at Lord's. Michael Atherton, before play began, had summed up England's chances by saying, 'You never say never, but clearly it's a difficult task.'

Steve Waugh gave his brother Mark the first over. Whether this was merely a ploy to switch McGrath to the other end, or whether he really thought that Mark's gentle off-spin was the secret weapon to bring England to their knees, it was a good psychological move. Mark's first ball to Stewart spun and bounced and sent up a kick of dust. On the second ball, which beat Stewart, Gilchrist asked for the stumping. Not out. The close fielders got a little closer, and Stewart, never the world's greatest player of spin, counter-attacked with his cross-bat off-drive. First round on points to Australia.

Mark Waugh had taken Butcher's wicket twice before in Tests, and it was possible that this was in his brother's mind. However, as Stewart plundered three fours in his second over, Steve decided against prolonging the experiment and let Mark settle back into second slip for the remainder of the innings, while Jason Gillespie took over the bowling duties. As long as Stewart and Butcher managed to stay together, there was some prospect of a meaningful target for Australia to chase. The weather certainly was not going to intervene, so England's only hope was to bat well.

For the first twenty minutes they did just that. Stewart and Butcher added 25 runs in five overs, and England closed in on their first target, the 214 needed to make Australia bat again. Then, with England on 188, Stewart was patently lbw to McGrath, for 28, the eighth Englishman in the match to reach double figures but fail to reach 30. But then, if Ward could only do something, then maybe…

Ian Ward was out first ball, quite brilliantly caught by Ricky Ponting at third slip, the sort of chance that changes the direction of a match and which England, on the previous day's form, would not even have considered a chance. Now the score was 188 for 6, and as the man next to me remarked, 'That's it, I'm afraid.'

Craig White was next man in, coming in on a pair to try to prevent Glenn McGrath from achieving his second Test hat-trick. He did that at least, letting the ball go harmlessly past off stump, but now it all depended on Butcher. So what did he do? After almost four hours of intense concentration and 158 balls successfully kept out, he chased the hundred and fifty-ninth, a very wide delivery from Gillespie, and Gilchrist accepted the offering. 188 for 7. The truth of Geoffrey Boycott's dictum, 'Add two wickets to the score, and see what it looks like then,' was never more obvious. In the space of nine balls 188 for 4 had become 188 for 7 – Boycott plus one, so to speak. The game was up.

Dominic Cork is a pugnacious cricketer, but his pugnacity this time only lasted three balls, before he too was swallowed up by the slip cordon, caught by Shane Warne off McGrath for 2. The score was 193 for 8. Andy Caddick, promoted to number ten after his Edgbaston heroics, stayed with White long enough to bring up the 200 and also, eventually, to make Australia bat again. White was mainly responsible for these heady heights, hitting out in rather the way Ian Ward had done in the first innings – scoring runs for the short term, now that all hope and the need for responsibility had gone. It was fun, it was good batting, but it was ultimately of little value.

What was of value was the dismissal of Caddick, another catch for Gilchrist, and that of Gough, caught by Mark Waugh for 2, to bring the innings to an end on 227. Gough's dismissal was Mark Waugh's hundred and fifty-eighth catch in Test cricket, a new world record, and his team-mates showed their admiration for him in the way they greeted the wicket. It almost overshadowed the fact that it was also Gillespie's fifth wicket of the innings, and he too raised the ball to the crowd as the team walked off. Gillespie's bowling has been one of the big differences between the two sides. He has been very quick, aggressive and above all accurate in both matches, and although he may officially be number two to McGrath in the pecking order, the difference between the Australia of a year ago and the Australia of today – both superb teams, of course – is in the successful return of Gillespie from his horrendous injury when he collided with his captain in the outfield in Sri Lanka.

So Australia were left with 14 to win. It should have been a ten-wicket stroll, but to the surprise of all, not least Slater and Ponting, it was not. In Caddick's first over, Butcher took a very good catch to get rid of Slater for 4 – the only boundary of Australia's second innings – and in the next over, Darren Gough trapped Ponting lbw. If there was anything to be taken by England from this Test, it was the failure of the Australian top order for the second time. The second wicket had fallen at 27 in the first innings and 13 in the second: England had made it to 75 in the first innings and 47 in the second. Neither set of statistics is wonderful, but for a world beating batting line-up, Australia's top three were in terrible form.

The other odd statistic to emerge from yet another Australian win at Lord's was that in the three most recent Lord's Tests only three England bowlers had taken any wickets. Cork had taken twelve, Gough seventeen and Caddick nineteen. All the others – White, Butcher, Hoggard, Vaughan and co – had tried in vain. England's bowling was beginning to look as flimsy as the batting, once you looked beyond the two main pillars of the attack.

Glenn McGrath was chosen as the Man of the Match, despite strong claims from Mark Waugh and Jason Gillespie, but as Steve Waugh said in the post-match press conference, 'the fielding was the difference between the two teams.' So it was back to basics before Trent Bridge: sounder, more positive batting; less generous, more accurate and imaginative bowling; and fielders who can throw and catch. Easier said than done.

Mark Waugh catches Gough off Gillespie to end
England's second innings. This is Waugh's one
hundred and fifty-eighth Test catch, a new world
record.

The Ashes 2001 Second Test
England v Australia
Lord's Ground, London
19, 20, 21, 22 July 2001
Australia won by 8 wickets

England 1st innings

*MA Atherton	lbw b McGrath	37
ME Trescothick	c Gilchrist b Gillespie	15
MA Butcher	c ME Waugh b McGrath	21
GP Thorpe	c Gilchrist b McGrath	20
MR Ramprakash	b Lee	14
†AJ Stewart	c Gilchrist b McGrath	0
IJ Ward	not out	23
C White	c Hayden b McGrath	0
DG Cork	c Ponting b Gillespie	24
AR Caddick	b Warne	0
D Gough	b Warne	5
Extras	(b 7, lb 8, w 2, nb 11)	28
Total	(all out, 63.3 overs, 288 mins)	187

FoW: 1—33 (Trescothick, 11.3 ov), 2–75 (Butcher, 24.4 ov),
3–96 (Atherton, 30.6 ov), 4–121 (Ramprakash, 39.2 ov),
5–126 (Stewart, 42.4 ov), 6–129 (Thorpe, 44.3 ov),
7–131 (White, 48.5 ov), 8–178 (Cork, 58.2 ov),
9–181 (Caddick, 61.3 ov), 10–187 (Gough, 63.3 ov).

Bowling	O	M	R	W	
McGrath	24	9	54	5	
Gillespie	18	6	56	2	(4nb)
Lee	16	3	46	1	(7nb, 1w)
Warne	5.3	0	16	2	(1w)

Australia 1st innings

MJ Slater	c Stewart b Caddick	25
ML Hayden	c Butcher b Caddick	0
RT Ponting	c Thorpe b Gough	14
ME Waugh	run out (Gough)	108
*SR Waugh	c Stewart b Cork	45
DR Martyn	c Stewart b Caddick	52
†AC Gilchrist	c Stewart b Gough	90
SK Warne	c Stewar b Caddick	5
B Lee	b Caddick	20
JN Gillespie	b Gough	9
GD McGrath	not out	0
Extras	(lb 9, w 1, nb 23)	33
Total	(all out, 101.1 overs, 441 mins)	401

FoW: 1–5 (Hayden, 1.5 ov), 2–27 (Ponting, 4.5 ov),
3–105 (Slater, 24.1 ov), 4–212 (ME Waugh, 51.3 ov),
5–230 (SR Waugh, 57.1 ov), 6–308 (Martyn, 81.5 ov),
7–322 (Warne, 83.2 ov), 8–387 (Gilchrist, 96.6 ov),
9–401 (Gillespie, 100.5 ov), 10–401 (Lee, 101.1 ov).

Bowling	O	M	R	W	
Gough	25	3	115	3	(6nb)
Caddick	32.1	4	101	5	(11nb)
White	18	1	80	0	(1nb)
Cork	23	3	84	1	(5nb)
Butcher	3	1	12	0	(1w)

England 2nd innings

*MA Atherton	b Warne	20
ME Trescothick	c Gilchrist b Gillespie	3
MA Butcher	c Gilchrist b Gillespie	83
GP Thorpe	lbw b Lee	2
MR Ramprakash	lbw b Gillespie	40
†AJ Stewart	lbw b McGrath	28
IJ Ward	c Ponting b McGrath	0
C White	not out	27
DG Cork	c Warne b McGrath	2
AR Caddick	c Gilchrist b Gillespie	7
D Gough	c ME Waugh b Gillespie	1
Extras	b 3, w 2, nb 9)	14
Total	(all out, 66 overs, 280 mins)	227

FoW: 1–8 (Trescothick, 5.2 ov), 2–47 (Atherton, 16.4 ov),
3–50 (Thorpe, 17.6 ov), 4–146 (Ramprakash, 46.3 ov),
5–188 (Stewart, 58.2 ov), 6–188 (Ward, 58.3 ov),
7–188 (Butcher, 59.5 ov), 8–193 (Cork, 60.6 ov),
9–225 (Caddick, 65.1 ov), 10–227 (Gough, 65.6 ov).

Bowling	O	M	R	W	
McGrath	19	4	60	3	
Gillespie	16	4	53	5	(2nb, 1w)
Lee	9	1	41	1	(4nb)
Warne	20	4	58	1	(3nb, 1w)
ME Waugh	2	1	12	0	

Australia 2nd innings

ML Hayden	not out	6
MJ Slater	c Butcher b Caddick	4
RT Ponting	lbw b Gough	4
ME Waugh	not out	0
Extras		0
Total	(2 wickets, 3.1 overs, 17 mins)	14

Did not bat: *SR Waugh, DR Martyn, †AC Gilchrist, SK Warne, B Lee,
JN Gillespie, GD McGrath.

FoW: 1–6 (Slater, 1.5 ov), 2–13 (Ponting, 2.3 ov).

Bowling	O	M	R	W
Gough	2	0	5	1
Caddick	1.1	0	9	1

Umpires: S. A. Bucknor and J. W. Holder   3rd Umpire: J. W. Lloyds

* captain   † wicket keeper

Australia's Ashes

The Third Test, Trent Bridge, Nottingham
2–6 August 2001

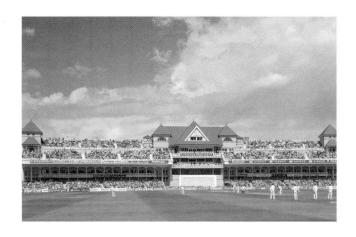

Australia's Ashes

The Third Test

Frank McCourt, in his memoir *Angela's Ashes*, writes that 'when I look back on my childhood I wonder how I survived at all. It was, of course, a miserable childhood: the happy childhood is hardly worth your while.' For English cricket followers, substitute the words 'cricket season' for the word 'childhood' and you have 2001. The misery was completed at Trent Bridge, but it was certainly worth our while.

The day before the England squad was announced on Sunday 29 July, a strange thing happened. The Australians began their game against Hampshire at the very impressive new Rose Bowl ground in Southampton, and were very quickly dismissed for 97, with England reject Alan Mullally taking 5 wickets for 18 runs. OK, so the Australians were resting many of their Test side to give Langer, Katich, Seccombe, Noffke, Miller and Fleming an outing, but the Hampshire side still had to get rid of five of the team who had so easily brushed England aside twice. In reply, Hampshire were 230 for 3 overnight, and the next day Robin Smith (yes, he's still playing very well) scored the first first-class century against the Australian attack all summer.

And while the tourists were having a bad day at the office, the highest scores of the day in the County Championship were by two other Australians. Michael Hussey, whose central contract with the ACB had recently lapsed, scored 329 not out for Northamptonshire against the hapless Essex. This was the highest score ever by a Northamptonshire player, and gave the Midlands side the luxury of having on their books three men who have scored a first-class triple century – Hussey, Mal Loye and David Sales. Sales was out injured for the entire 2001 season, of course, but it is an odd statistic that none of these three had yet played Test cricket. The other big-scoring Australian was Darren Lehmann, who made 222 not out on the Saturday for Yorkshire against Lancashire, the highest score ever made in a Roses match. On the Sunday, he took his score on to 252. So while the main Australian team were collapsing to 97 all out, two discarded Aussies were scoring 551 between them without either being out. The England team knew now, if they were not already aware, that suitable replacements were available if the Australians suffered the same spate of injuries that was depleting England.

Without Hussain, Giles and Thorpe, England

had to regroup again, but the squad announced on the Sunday contained no real surprises. There were not many offbeat selections possible. Mike Atherton had replied with a heartfelt 'I hope so' when asked if Hussain would be fit for the Third Test, but in the event he was left in charge again. Usman Afzaal and Ian Ward also remained in the squad. The only unforced change was the inclusion of Alex Tudor of Surrey in place of Dominic Cork, who had nevertheless scored a hundred for Derbyshire on the Saturday. But no place for Alan Mullally, despite his five-for-eighteen against the tourists, nor for Phil Tufnell, still regarded as the best left arm spinner in the country. Tufnell celebrated his lack of selection by taking the thousandth first-class wicket of his career in Middlesex's county match against Durham, but despite vociferous support in high places, still failed to catch the selectors' collective eye. The full squad of thirteen was: Michael Atherton (Lancashire, captain), Usman Afzaal (Nottinghamshire), Mark Butcher (Surrey), Andrew Caddick (Somerset), Robert Croft (Glamorgan), Darren Gough (Yorkshire), Mark Ramprakash (Surrey), Chris Silverwood (Yorkshire), Alec Stewart (Surrey, wicketkeeper), Marcus Trescothick (Somerset), Alex Tudor (Surrey), Ian Ward (Surrey), Craig White (Yorkshire).

On the Monday, Hampshire completed a remarkable victory over the Australians, by two wickets. It was by no means the full-strength Australian side, with a very depleted batting line-up, but it still showed the English fans something – Australians can come second sometimes. Robin Smith, the Hampshire captain and still remembered as a batsman England discarded too soon, was jubilant. 'This was a fantastic result for Hampshire,' he was quoted as saying, 'but I have also got to praise Steve Waugh for declaring and making a game of it.' Waugh's style of captaincy,

always aggressive, means that occasionally one of his gambles proves to be a risk, and this was one such day. However, the crowd had a wonderful time.

On the same day, Sun Tzu's *The Art of War*, dating back 2500 years but these days a widely-used management handbook, made the back pages of the newspapers thanks to a memo from John Buchanan to each member of the Australian team. Buchanan's memo included a photocopy of Chapter Eleven of the strategic classic, entitled 'The Nine Situations', and went on to look at how Australian cricketers should react to each of those nine situations. He slipped the memo under the doors of each team member in their hotel, but one copy at least found its way into the hands of the English press. It was rumoured that another copy found its way unread into Mark Waugh's waste-paper basket.

The memo revealed Buchanan's thoroughness of approach as he tried to identify the different situations that Sun Tzu had written about in terms of Test cricket. Sun Tzu said: 'The art of war recognises nine varieties of ground: (1) dispersive ground; (2) facile ground; (3) contentious ground; (4) open ground; (5) ground of intersecting highways; (6) serious ground; (7) difficult ground; (8) hemmed-in ground; (9) desperate ground.' While it was easy to imagine England on 'serious ground', 'difficult ground', 'hemmed-in ground' and certainly 'desperate ground', how (and indeed, why) did Buchanan present these situations to his all-conquering tourists? Well, it is obvious that Australia could be described as being on 'facile ground', on which subject Buchanan's memo said: 'We have won two Tests of a five-Test series. Now is no time to ease up, as we have only done part of the job.' Under the heading 'Ground of Intersecting Highways', he wrote, 'We have "joined hands" with the public, sponsors and media about the way the English team plays its cricket, and thus its "ability" to play Australia. Consequently, we have currently gained "psychological control" over England.' Who would have disputed that?

Such was the psychological control that the Australians had by now exerted on the English team and their supporters, that there was no agreement whether this leak was accidental or deliberate. After all, a deliberate leak would just show the Poms that the Aussies had no intention of relaxing even with two of the five Tests in the bag, and there was every chance that they wouldn't understand a word of it anyway: for all the England players would be likely to make of it, it might as well have been written in Sun Tzu's original Chinese. Derek Randall, a Trent Bridge favourite interviewed on BBC television about the affair, noted that the whole concept was far too intellectual for the England team, and only Michael Atherton would have been able to understand the memo. This was obviously a light-hearted remark, but there was nevertheless a grain of truth in it. The England team may not actually be the intellectual inferiors of their Australian opponents, but there seemed to be very little about their training and preparation to cause them to exercise their brains as well as their bodies.

There was a counter-argument that the document had been leaked by somebody in the Australian camp who was not happy with Buchanan's style, and that this just showed there was dissension within that formidable collection of baggy greens. The Australians dismissed all such suggestions as ridiculous, and Steve Waugh, in particular, was very angry that the leak had happened, accusing the English press of the moral equivalent of taking cash from a lost wallet. In all this hypercharged atmosphere (well, the press and the players thought it was hypercharged – the public remained

determinedly less impressed) the truth was bound to be elusive.

The Australians, however, were not to be diverted from their main aim – that of winning the Third Test. They announced the same eleven for the third Test in a row: Steve Waugh (New South Wales, captain), Michael Slater (New South Wales), Matthew Hayden (Queensland), Ricky Ponting (Tasmania), Mark Waugh (New South Wales), Damien Martyn (Western Australia), Adam Gilchrist (Western Australia, wicketkeeper), Shane Warne (Victoria), Brett Lee (New South Wales), Jason Gillespie (South Australia) and Glenn McGrath (New South Wales). There were no fitness doubts, and they marched on to Trent Bridge, on what Sun Tzu would no doubt have described as 'serious ground'.

England's injury problems did not end when the team was selected. On the Wednesday morning, Chris Silverwood and Alex Tudor both reported niggles, Silverwood in his back and Tudor on the left side of his rib-cage. Silverwood was released immediately, and the search was on for another quick bowler to add to the squad. As Hoggard was injured, Harmison was struggling for his place in the county side and Alan Mullally, Martin Bicknell and Ryan Sidebottom were apparently out of selectorial favour, the options open to the selectors were few and far between. The bowling averages showed Mushtaq Ahmed of Pakistan on top, Chris Tremlett, playing for England Under-19s, in second place and the surprise packet of the season, Steve Kirby of Yorkshire, in third place with 30 wickets at 14.53 each. Next were McGrath and Gillespie, with Warne and Sri Lanka's Muttiah Muralitharan also in the top ten, so the options for the selectors seemed to be limited. Glen Chapple of Lancashire, also a useful batsman, one-Test wonder Simon Brown of Durham and Jamie Ormond of Leicestershire may also have featured in the selectors' considerations, but in the end they sent for Richard Johnson, formerly of Middlesex, now of Somerset.

Johnson was playing for Somerset against Kent at Canterbury, in front of the marquees as the St. Lawrence Ground enjoyed baking sunshine for the first day of Canterbury week. He was trying his best on a shirt-front pitch as David Fulton, the first man of the season to 1000 runs, set about compiling his sixth century of 2001, so was probably very happy to be called away from the match, just before lunch, to hurry up to Nottingham. Johnson had been close to England honours a few years ago, but then had to drop out of the tour he was selected for before it had started. Since then, despite becoming the second youngest player ever to take all ten wickets in a first-class innings when he took 10 for 45 against Derbyshire in 1994, his career had drifted. In 2001, he had so far taken 37 wickets at just under 24 apiece, so he was playing a big part in Somerset's challenge for the Championship. It was good for him to know that he had not been entirely forgotten by the England set-up, although being chosen as the replacement for a replacement does not make one's chances of a long Test career all that much greater.

A quick glimpse at the batting averages showed the problems that England faced in that department too. The top four places were occupied by Australians, only one of whom, Damien Martyn, was part of the Test party. Martyn was averaging 119.50, but was followed by Darren Lehmann of Yorkshire (86.50), Michael Hussey of Northamptonshire (72.77) and Stuart Law of Essex (70.92). The highest placed Englishman was the former Oxford University and Northamptonshire player Richard Montgomerie, who was enjoying a glorious year with Sussex. By the beginning of August, he had 1270 runs at 70.55, with six centuries and five fifties. However, he was now thirty, and, like

David Fulton of Kent, was seen as a good county player enjoying a purple patch, rather than as a potential Test batsman. The injured Graham Thorpe had the highest average (61.42) of any batsman selected so far by England, followed by the injured Michael Vaughan (52.77), with Mark Ramprakash the only other member of the Test side averaging over 50. Alec Stewart had 362 runs under his belt at 45.25, and Marcus Trescothick's 473 runs were at a rate of 43 per innings. However, after that, we find Alex Tudor averaging 42.87, some four runs per innings higher than Michael Atherton (546 runs at 39), and five higher than Afzaal (678 at 37.66) and Butcher (560 at 37.33). Tudor's bowling average was only 36.35. Robert Croft, recalled to the side in Giles' absence, had a batting average of 39.85 and a bowling average of 35.84, so that made him an all-rounder too. Ian Ward's batting average was too low to be listed (26.12). The only consolation was that Michael Slater's batting average was 28.87, but to most English people, that merely meant he was bound to come good again any day now.

First Day, 2 August 2001

Thursday morning dawned anything but clear, but the news from the England camp was good, unless your name was Johnson. Alex Tudor reported fit for duty, so Richard Johnson was sent back to Canterbury to resume his travails on that batsman-friendly track. The other man left out was, surprisingly, 24-year-old Usman Afzaal. The England selectors decided to play the extra bowler, as seven batsmen had not been doing much good for England so far this series, but it was a slight surprise that

The bowling of Alex Tudor, who took 5 for 44 in Australia's first innings, the best English analysis of the series, was one of the heartening performances of the summer.

Ian Ward retained his place after such an indifferent Test summer in place of Afzaal on his county ground. Why pick Afzaal in the squad, went the argument, if you are not going to play him even on his home ground?

The other good news was that for the first time in ten Tests England won the toss. Steve Waugh called wrongly, although he was probably not too upset about it. The toss was unlikely to make much difference given the state of the wicket (possibly likely to break up a bit later in the match) and the weather forecast (showers, sunshine and humidity in roughly equal quantities for all five days – although in fact the first day was overcast throughout), so the choice of batting or fielding first would be decided by the psychological point it would make rather than anything else. The Australians would probably have taken the attacking option and put England in: Michael Atherton chose to bat first, and a day of massive highs and deep lows got under way.

By the second ball of the innings, he might have had cause to doubt his decision, as he was given out caught behind off Glenn McGrath. Slow-motion replays showed that the ball hit his arm guard, but Mark Waugh made no mistake at second slip. This was his hundred and fifty-ninth test catch, just two balls (and eleven days) after the hundred and fifty-eighth. It was 0 for 1, not the start that England wanted. Mark Butcher came out to join Marcus Trescothick, and already England were in the same old hole. Australia then created a further frisson of uncertainty in the England batsmen's minds by choosing to open with Lee from the Radcliffe Road end, rather than Gillespie.

English crowds have yet to see Lee at his best, and when he is bowling at less than top speed he does not represent a great threat to Test-class batsmen. He strove mightily, but his opening spell of four overs went for 20 runs, and it was not until

Gillespie came on in his place that Australia managed to turn the screw again. Butcher looked as though he was carrying on from where he left off at Lord's, and Trescothick was starting to play what turned out to be the biggest innings of the match. Watching a Trescothick innings is not good therapy for any England supporter with a heart murmur, but his judgement of what to leave and what to play outside the off stump is better than it looks, and better than most other batsmen's. However, these two had added only 30 (between showers) when Butcher offered a catch to Ponting off McGrath, who as usual was the most impressive of the Australian bowlers. This brought another Mark to the crease, Ramprakash of that ilk. There was one stage during the summer (or maybe more than one) when Marks Butcher and Ramprakash were batting together while Marks Nicholas and Taylor were commentating for Channel 4. All it needed was for Mark Waugh to do the fielding, and no doubt some tabloid headline writer would be looking for the pun on *Full Marks*. Or more likely, the pun would be created by Vic Marks in the BBC Radio commentary box.

Mark and Marcus added 33 more in seven overs before Ramps perished on 14 for the fifth time in six innings against Australia. He had made his runs in 18 balls and hit three good fours, which made it all the more infuriating. Caught Gilchrist bowled Gillespie this time, and once again English cricket's current enigma wrapped inside a riddle failed to build on a solid start. This brought Alec Stewart to the wicket, and he almost at once benefited from a rare Australian fielding lapse. McGrath dropped him at mid-off off Brett Lee when he had made only three, a mistake that proved expensive.

By lunchtime, England had made it as far as 93 for 3, but off only 23 overs, a rate of four an over. Given the batting conditions, the break for rain and the fact that three wickets had fallen, that was a very quick rate: whether it was also a good one was a matter of some debate. Trescothick had made 52 of them, with his trademark hooks and pulls interspersed with powerful square cuts and the occasional – and equally trademark – edge through the slips. He was particularly hard on Gillespie, who eventually captured his wicket, but was in the mean time hit for an average of five an over. The control was exercised by McGrath, whose 18 overs cost only 49 runs, and Shane Warne, who in one spell of sixteen overs either side of lunch took two for 37. His two wickets may not have been England's best batsmen but somebody has to get Tudor and Croft out, and without Warne tying up the Radcliffe Road End for two hours McGrath would not have achieved his umpteenth Ashes five wicket haul. With Shane Warne back to something approaching his best, Australia became a formidable side, with no easy runs for any opposing batsman. His dismissal of Robert Croft, caught by Ricky Ponting at silly point, was his one hundredth wicket in Ashes Tests, making him the eighteenth bowler to reach this landmark.

Once Trescothick was out exactly as Ramprakash had been (c Gilchrist b Gillespie) for 69, the England innings began to stutter. Stewart took over the lead role, adding 25 with Ward who became another Gilchrist victim, and five more with White, who was dropped by Ricky Ponting at third slip in an otherwise uneventful 0. Tudor and Croft added a few more, but with eight wickets down for 168 after only 46 overs it all looked too familiar and too depressing to English eyes. When Andrew Caddick strode to the wicket to join Stewart, there were memories of the First Test, but the pair could not repeat that amazing stand. Stewart spent the next couple of overs watching Caddick thrash a couple of fours, and then got himself out just four short of his 50, caught by Mark Waugh at second slip. Brett Lee was then brought back into the attack, and

with his fifth ball proved too quick for Caddick. England were all out for 185 in just under 53 overs, tea was taken and the partisan Nottingham crowd all thought they had witnessed yet another England shambles.

After tea, England showed the partisan Nottingham crowd that they were wrong. Or at least, if England's innings had been sub-standard, Australia's reply was even more so. However, it began very promisingly for Australia, and for the first dozen overs, everything seemed to confirm the initial opinion – England's innings had indeed been a shambles, and Slater and Hayden were doing a whole lot better. Hayden in particular was ruthless with anything not absolutely on line and length. The left-right partnership as usual made it difficult for Gough and Caddick to keep their line and length perfect, so Hayden waited until the juicy deliveries appeared and fed happily on them. Slater was certainly more restrained, but the way he and his partner ran between the wickets showed they were confident as a pair and determined to press home the advantage they felt their bowlers had gained for them.

As an aside, it is worth noting that Chris Silverwood was named as England's twelfth man as both Johnson (halfway through a county game) and Afzaal (no great shakes in the field) were released. Despite his back injury, which had forced him out of consideration for the final eleven, Silverwood actually fielded for a couple of overs while Craig White (another half-fit cricketer) was off the field. The England selection policy gets curiouser and curiouser.

After ten overs, Atherton brought Alex Tudor into the attack. Tudor is only 23, but since the age of seventeen he has been a player who promises much but does not quite deliver. (How many more players are there that we can write those words about? Far too many in English cricket.) He had

only played three times for England before today, but had a famous 99 not out to his credit, and, more importantly, four for 89 versus Australia at Perth on the 1998/99 tour as his best bowling figures. The Australians knew him and respected him, and must have been disappointed that he was at last fit enough to play against them in England. Tudor has a huge smile on his face most of the time, exudes goodwill to all men and is not a menacing fast bowler in the style of Trueman, Lillee, Snow, McGrath or Gillespie. All the same, when he feels like it, he bowls at a good if not superfast pace and with an accuracy acquired through a determination to make the batsmen think about every ball he sends down. If only he can stay fit, England could have a front-line fast bowler to lead their attack for many seasons to come.

The first three balls Tudor bowled went for eight runs, but he kept his cool. The last ball of his second over did the trick. Hayden, who had made 33 of the 48 on the board, was adjudged lbw although replays showed the ball pitched marginally outside leg stump. Ricky Ponting, who was having a very poor trot in Tests in 2001, was next man in, but the next man out was Michael Slater. He drove with little or no footwork at a widish ball from Darren Gough and dragged it onto his stumps: 56 for 2. Mark Waugh made a hesitant start: his first ball got him a single through mid-off but it was from a shot aimed through mid-wicket which took a leading edge. In the next over, Tudor had a good lbw shout against him, and next ball he was only saved by a late inside edge onto the pad. Darren Gough, bowling an uncharacteristic mix of rubbish and cracking deliveries, was hit for two fours by Ponting, one forward of point and the other backward, before the batsman was surprised by a much better

When Australia really needed runs, for perhaps the only time in the series, Gilchrist came up with a half-century to give Australia a narrow first-innings lead.

delivery and caught behind by Stewart. Suddenly Australia were 69 for 3, only a third of the way to England's total and one third of the wickets down.

England seemed to be producing much more of a gameplan against the Australian batsmen than they had done in the first two Tests, but now they had to separate the Waugh twins, who in both the previous matches had compiled century partnerships. The field placings that Atherton was trying were tailor-made for each batsman, but it depended on good fielding all the time, and sometimes England's ground fielding did not help their captain's cause. Mark Waugh had been a slow starter throughout this tour, and he was finding it very hard to find the gaps today. Unfortunately, when once or twice he did find the gaps, they were between the fielders' fingers.

Alex Tudor's first spell of seven overs yielded just sixteen runs and claimed one wicket. He also must have felt a little aggrieved when an lbw appeal against Mark Waugh was turned down, but all in all it was a fine comeback to Test cricket. He was replaced by Caddick, who almost immediately tempted Steve Waugh to go for the cover drive. The ball was not quite there for it, and the result was an edge to slip, where Michael Atherton held a good catch. Now Australia were 82 for 4, a score that no longer looked any better than England's. Except that at number six for England was a man averaging barely 20 in the series; at number six for Australia there was Damien Martyn, currently scoring at a rate of about 110 per innings. But everybody has to fail some time.

Mark Waugh, even when he is trying to assess the pace and bounce of the pitch at the start of his innings, still knows how to make the most of the loose deliveries. He made Craig White pay for not maintaining line and length by cutting him for four. The ball seemed to be beyond the fielders and at the boundary rope even before he had finished the shot. With 'Junior' Waugh it is the timing, not the power, that makes him so hard to bowl to. However, this was not to be his day. After White completed his second over, Atherton decided enough was enough (although he had only gone for eight runs) and Tudor came back into the attack. This time he made no mistake with Mark Waugh, who flashed rather uncharacteristically at a well-directed delivery, and was caught by Atherton. Now Australia were 94 for 5. Atherton had taken two good catches, had made more than one astute bowling change, and even his notoriously laid-back body language was telling the world that he and England were in charge.

But you get rid of one Australian century-maker and you see another one walking through the pavilion gate towards the middle. Adam Gilchrist, the scourge of England's bowlers all summer, had never had to come in at crisis point in an Ashes Test before, but there was no reason to suppose his team's precarious position would force him to rethink his usual tactics. And they did not. His first ball was straight driven for four.

That, however, was the last ball of Tudor's over, and it brought Damien Martyn up to face Andrew Caddick. The first ball was edged to third man for four, and Martyn was off the mark as well. Australia had now scored two fours in consecutive balls, and the 100 was up. Was it asking too much for these two to rebuild the innings?

Yes it was. The very next ball Damien Martyn was caught behind, 102 for 6, and two balls later Caddick trapped Shane Warne in front of the stumps. Warne, lbw b Caddick 0; Australia 102 for 7. Caddick had taken three wickets for four runs (Martyn's edge through third man) in eleven balls. England, and the full-house Nottingham crowd, were on a roll. The next lamb to the slaughter was Brett Lee, but the light was fading fast. Just five balls later, the umpires offered the light to Gilchrist

and Lee, and they trotted off without a second thought. What had started as yet another England collapse had finished as a very well-balanced first day. About the only thing one could be sure of was that the match was highly unlikely to last the full five days, unless the weather intervened.

Close of play: England 185 (Trescothick 69, McGrath 5 for 49); Australia 105 for 7

Second Day, 3 August 2001

The morning papers were full of England's great fight-back on the previous afternoon and evening, but they were wary of Adam Gilchrist, the batsman of the series so far, who was on 4 not out, and who already had a track record of turning innings, and matches, around in the space of a few overs. As we travelled to the ground, I made a friendly bet with a fellow spectator that England would gain a first-innings lead. Frankly, this was partly to appease the gods of chance, as I was determined to show faith in the England squad. I had predicted earlier in the summer that they would draw the Test series 2–2, so I needed an England first innings lead at the very least to get this particular forecast back on track. I'm not sure how confident I really felt at this stage that England could prevent Australia from passing their score, but at least we all knew that the man on whom it all depended was Adam Gilchrist.

The morning was hot, the sun was bright, and Gilchrist went off like a train; not the train we had caught that morning, you understand. That was the sort that stops where it shouldn't and never quite gets to where it should be at the time it should have done. An English batting train, in fact, not an Australian one. If ever they are looking for a name for a Eurostar train, they could call it after any one of England's top six batsmen as it potters erratically and rather slowly across Kent towards Folkestone, and then rename it Adam Gilchrist as it streaks across northern France towards Paris.

But England kept at it manfully, and Tudor in particular was bowling like a man possessed. Lee, who had kept Gilchrist company for the first 25 minutes of the day, edged one to Butcher, and Australia were 122 for 8. Tudor completed a wicket maiden to Gillespie, the new man in. The Goodyear airship continued its lazy circuits of the sky and my little bet was beginning to look safe.

In many ways the next hour and a quarter decided the match. It certainly decided my bet, because by the time Gilchrist was out Australia had a first innings lead of three. For fifteen minutes or so England kept a lid on Gilchrist, who was never in trouble but was also not really cutting loose. However, when Tudor was rested, having taken one for 13 in 4.3 overs, Darren Gough replaced him at the Pavilion End, and the game slipped away. Gough is England's most experienced and, on form, best fast bowler, but this morning he was not on form. His first ball was cover-driven to textbook perfection by Gilchrist for four, and now they were only 41 behind. The rest of Gough's spell of four overs was equally difficult for England. He bowled just too short, and the runs flowed from both Gillespie and Gilchrist. Gilchrist hit two consecutive half-volleys, both from round the wicket, for four through mid-off. This was meat and drink to a man in Gilchrist's form. Gough switched back to over the wicket after a chat with his captain, and this move resulted in a bottom-edged four behind Stewart. The next ball was a mishit pull towards mid-on, where the ball just fell wide of Alex Tudor, and then there was a no-ball. Gough went for 32 in all in those four overs, but when he gave the ball a little more length, Gillespie in particular was unhappy and tended to fish very uncertainly for

the ball. By drinks the score was 168 for 8. Australia were closing in on England's total.

Four runs later the 50 partnership came up, to polite applause. This was now the highest partnership of the innings. The crowd's reaction made me think of happy days watching county cricket at Canterbury where the spectators, especially those in the members' stands, take special pride in knowing when to applaud as obscure statistics are clocked up. Not for them the simple claps for half-century and century, for individuals and for partnerships. They like to note a highest score of the season by a player, the scoring of the thousandth run of the season, the first time a bowler has taken five wickets against Leicestershire, and any other abstruse figure that they can applaud in passing. They do not seem to worry about the quality of the cricket, just the quality of the statistics. Arguments are not about whether it was the number six or the number seven fielder who made that astonishing pick up and throw in from the mid-wicket boundary; they are more concerned with which scoreboard got it right and which got it wrong. Cricket is a game which attracts all kinds of people into its wondrous clutches, and it would be silly to say that everybody has to appreciate the same things about it. But those who do not see the beauty of the game, and watch merely for the mathematical wonder of it, or even worse for the partisan desire to see one team win in whatever fashion, are missing the greater part of this game's attraction. You cannot enjoy being a partisan England supporter when they play Australia unless you also appreciate the brilliance of the Australian cricket. At least, that's what I told myself as I realised my bet on a first-innings lead was a loser.

Gilchrist brought up his 50 with a boundary off yet another

Over page: Trescothick is very unlucky to be out, caught by Gilchrist off Hayden's ankle. He had middled a full-blooded sweep off Warne.

Gough half-volley, so at 181 for 8, Tudor came back on at the Radcliffe Road End. Early on, he bowled a great yorker at Gillespie, which the batsman managed to dig out at the last moment and the ball squirted through the slips for four. This brought the scores level. At the other end, Robert Croft was brought, very belatedly, into the attack, to cries from supporters all around the ground that they 'should have picked Tufnell'. Tudor, by now quite obviously England's best bowler, then trapped Gilchrist, getting him to edge one to Atherton at first slip. It was now 188 for 9, but Gilchrist's 54 had contained too many easy runs against wayward bowling for it to be called a great innings. However, a batsman can only score off the balls that are bowled at him, and if they are not much good, that is hardly his fault.

Four balls later, Tudor also trapped McGrath, quite brilliantly caught by Butcher at second slip, diving low to his left and taking the ball one-handed inches from the ground. Australia were all out for 190, a lead of five, and Tudor finished with 5 for 44. The grin was wider than ever as he raised the ball to the crowd in acknowledgement of the applause for his achievement. I paid up the bet.

Australia were all out in time to give England ten minutes' batting before lunch. The innings got off the mark with two leg byes from McGrath's first ball to Atherton, and Trescothick, at the other end, hit Gillespie for a lovely four through mid-wicket to give England the lead again. Lunch was taken with England on 11 for no wicket. And then it rained.

The rain at this stage limited itself to the lunch interval. The rather tired fried chicken pieces were not improved by the gentle rain from heaven dropping upon them, but the beer was probably not significantly watered down from its original state by the same shower. After lunch, and after the rain, the two batsmen made their precarious way towards a decent foundation for a winning total. At 36, Atherton decided to leave a ball from McGrath, which cut back into him and hit the pad. It hit him outside the line of off stump, and the reasoning must have been that the ball would not have gone on to hit the stumps, but there was no doubt it was a close call. Hearts, as well as half-eaten chicken pieces, were in the England supporters' mouths.

The dismissal of Marcus Trescothick for 32, the first wicket to fall in the English second innings, proved significant in many ways. Trescothick and Atherton seemed to be batting serenely enough, although Trescothick showed off his remarkable knack of flashing at wide ones outside the off stump without actually getting very near the ball – a habit about which he may be quite relaxed, but which does nothing for the heart rates of the vast crowd of England supporters, spectators and viewers. When the score had reached 46 for 1, Steve Waugh followed the oldest captaincy adage in the book – if you haven't taken a wicket after 40 runs, change the bowling. McGrath and Gillespie (who took the new ball in preference to Lee this time) came off, to be replaced by Lee at the Radcliffe Road end, and Shane Warne from the Pavilion end. The Barmy Army were by now, of course, well lubricated and in full vocal flow, their remarkably tuneless and uncatchy chorus of 'Michael Atherton's Barmy Army, Michael Atherton's Barmy Army,' et cetera ad nauseam, echoing from the stands.

Warne had barely got into his stride when Trescothick connected with a well-struck sweep, which unfortunately for the batsman hit Matthew Hayden, fielding at forward short leg, on the foot and bounced up in the air. Adam Gilchrist leaped forward to take a brilliant catch almost as the ball touched the ground by the batsman's feet, and the appeals were long and loud. The umpires were unsure – had the ball hit the ground before or after hitting Hayden? – and quite rightly referred the case to the third umpire. As soon as the replay was shown on the big screen, it was obvious that Warne had overstepped the line in bowling the ball. Where the umpire had failed to call it, 15,000 throats in the stands compensated with a roar of 'No-ball!' But of course, that was not what the third umpire had been asked to adjudicate on. He merely reported that the catch was indeed fair: the ball had not touched the ground between hitting the sweet spot of Trescothick's bat and landing in Gilchrist's gloves. So Trescothick was given out, although by now even the umpires on the pitch knew that the ball should have been called a no-ball. Trescothick thus joined the ever-swelling ranks of batsmen given out in Tests in England in 2001 off no-balls, and had another remarkable piece of bad luck to follow his freak dismissal in Sri Lanka in March, when the ball lodged in Russell Arnold's shirt off another full-blooded shot.

What should be done about no-balls? Should the third umpire, in this case, have told umpire Venkataraghavan that the ball in question had not been a fair delivery? Under the laws, it seems to be the case that the umpire can make any decision about what has happened on any aspect of a delivery at any time up to the moment the next delivery begins, so in theory Venkat could have called 'No-ball' even at this late stage. There was no precedent for this, though, and the third umpire was not asked to adjudicate on this point. I cannot see why he could not have mentioned it to Venkat, all the same.

However, the situation on no-balls caused by overstepping is bound to be very difficult for the bowling umpires to control, however diligent they are. According to Channel 4's computers, a batsman has about 0.464 seconds to react to one of Jason Gillespie's or Brett Lee's ninety m.p.h. deliveries. Even with Shane Warne bowling at 55 m.p.h.

or so there is still barely 0.8 seconds of reaction time. The batsman, however, is at least able to look at the ball in flight throughout the 0.464 seconds he has in which to make up his mind what to do. The umpire, on the other hand, a man probably at least twenty years older than the batsman and with accordingly slower reactions, has to be looking down at the popping crease as the ball is delivered in order to adjudicate on a no-ball. He then has no more than 0.464 seconds to raise his head, focus on what is going on, see whether the ball pitched outside the line of the stumps and look for the edge, the height of the bounce and the extent of the swing or turn of the ball if he is going to get the lbw appeal, or the caught behind appeal or the bat-pad catch appeal, right. It is a job specification that almost demands failure.

It would be cynical to suggest that there are bowlers who know this and who have calculated that they can afford to overstep a few times because they will not always be penalised for it. If a fair delivery gives a batsman 0.464 seconds' reaction time, then shaving a couple of hundredths off this time by bowling from a foot nearer than is legal is likely to induce further errors in the batsman. Even if the ball is called as a no-ball, the batsman's confidence is affected. In the case of Warne v Trescothick, we would be wrong to imply any deliberate intimidatory bowling, but whichever way you look at it (and too often the umpires are just not able to look at it), the front-foot law is beyond the skills of one man to police. Maybe the game's administrators should think about returning to the old back-foot law.

The move towards electronic aids for the umpires is one which, in general, the cricket public are very wary of. However, once we have started down this path, it is very difficult to stop. If the cricketers are looking for the fairest possible decisions every time, the batsmen especially might be

Atherton, like his opening partner, is caught
Gilchrist b Warne, but in his case the misfortune
was that he probably did not touch it.

in for a shock. At
the moment, the
laws of the game
allow the umpire
to give any benefit

of the doubt to the batsman, so if we take the
doubt away electronically, the bowlers will by definition be the ones to benefit. Batsmen might be
left wondering why they went into the sport at all.
In this Third Test, for example, Matthew Hayden

might have considered himself unlucky in being given out lbw in the second innings to a ball from Alex Tudor that seemed, in the slow-motion replay, to have pitched outside leg stump, but he could equally have considered himself lucky not to have been given out to either of the first two balls he faced in that innings. Darren Gough had two good shouts for lbw, the second ball especially satisfying the television technologists that it should have been given out.

But where technology can be reliably used, as with line decisions like run-outs and stumpings, then it seems logical to extend its use. The no-ball law, if not applied when it should be, can only benefit the bowler, whose delivery is thus deemed fair when it actually is not. His team is therefore not penalised a run, nor is the bowler asked to bowl another ball. What's more, the delivery is a potential wicket-taker. The Laws of Cricket are in all other aspects written to give the benefit of any doubt to the batsman, so failing to impose the no-ball law goes against the grain of the laws twice over.

At Wimbledon, the fairness of serves is judged by Cyclops, an electronic device that beeps when a serve is out. All the players are happy to be judged by Cyclops, and there seems to be little reason why this technology, or something like it, could not be used to help the umpires make the right decision on front foot no-balls. It will always be unfair to ask umpires to perform the almost impossible task of looking down at their feet and up at the batsman in virtually the same moment and making correct decisions within that split second on both axes. There needs to be progress towards a more humane answer to the problem.

The departure of Trescothick was followed immediately by more rain, and this time play was suspended for two hours. It gave us a chance to inspect the Trent Bridge ground and study their mopping-up technology. It never ceases to amaze any cricket follower that the major Test arenas do not have any state-of-the-art solutions to the problem of mopping up rain and getting the teams back in the middle immediately afterwards. Or maybe the teams of young and fit ground staff pulling plastic sheets across the outfield, the two large sit-on sponge rollers, and several smaller hand rollers, buckets and squeegees are state-of-the-art technology, in which case somebody ought to put a bit of money into this particular art. Trent Bridge is not worse than other grounds in this respect, because all county clubs seem to rely on insurance cover rather than ground cover to ward off the evil effects of rain, which as far as the administrators are concerned can be summed up in the words 'loss of money'. But it must surely not be beyond the wit of man to create a ground cover system which would cover all of the playing surface, from boundary to boundary, and which could be moved automatically into place as the first raindrops fall. It would cost money to install, but in the English climate, it ought to recoup its costs very quickly.

What with games of cricket with windball, Coca-Cola bottle bats, and chairs for stumps, and plenty of beer still there to be drunk, the crowds were entirely good-tempered during the rain break. The only brief moment of aggravation came in the darkest corners of the new Radcliffe Road Stand, when a tea boiler failed to boil and a queue of bedraggled people were left with nothing hot to drink. Many people with tickets in the open areas of the Radcliffe Road end spent the rainstorm huddled in the stairwells of the new stand, thermos flasks and plastic cartons of sandwiches spread around them, with that bewildered look of people who have no control over their own lives and who wish they could be somewhere else, anywhere else. The scene conjured up thoughts of an upcountry railway station in Thailand or the Philippines.

The advertisements around the ground were less obviously Thai or Filipino. The npower ad in the outfield is about as gaudy and as hard on the eyes as a week in Ibiza, but the rest of the billboards are more in keeping with the dignity of a Nottingham Test. There are the usual national companies like Fedex, Vodafone and Ricoh, local companies like Russell Scanlan Insurance Brokers of Nottingham, and others that nobody could discover anything about. Who or what is Exito? What do Beko Beko do?

The rain clouds thinned, and the high-tech mopping-up operation allowed play to resume at about 4.50. As the umpires came out the light noticeably faded, and as the players walked onto the field, one of the scoreboard lights came on. By the time Butcher was out, lbw to Lee on the ninth ball after the resumption, a second light had come on, and England, at 59 for 2, were struggling a bit. A few deliveries later, Lee hit Atherton on the helmet grille with a short no-ball timed at 91.8 mph. This ball was sent down after a very obvious bit of field placement, putting somebody down on the square leg boundary, so Atherton could guess a short ball was on the way, and that he really should not attempt the hook. The sparring between Atherton and the fast bowlers did not continue much longer, though, because at 5.20, after only half an hour's play, the players were off again as more rain fell. England were 72 for 2.

Many of the crowd thought that this latest shower would finish play for the day, but they were wrong. By the time play resumed, just twenty minutes later with the crowd a little thinner, there was still time for England to double their total but also to treble the number of wickets lost. The day ended with England on 144 for six, with only Ian Ward standing between Australia and a strong

chance of retaining the Ashes on the Saturday. How did England manage to let it slip away once again? It was not the pitch which, although slightly bowler-friendly, played well throughout. It was not particularly the Australian bowling, which was of its usual high standard but despite Warne's five wickets out of six could not be described as yet another display of leg-spin mastery over the English rabbits. It was not even England's poor batting, although once again nobody built on a good start to his innings to create a big score. It was, in a way, all of the above.

For the first few overs after the teams came back on, Atherton and Ramprakash, who had replaced Butcher, batted well and without real incident, but then, with the score at 115, Atherton was given out caught behind off Warne when clearly he thought he had not touched the ball. Television replays were inconclusive and umpire Venkat, to his credit, thought long and hard about the decision. But in the end his finger went up, and Atherton went, no doubt cursing his luck in receiving two bad decisions in one match.

Worse was to come. Eight balls later, Stewart played on to Warne as he tried to force him into the covers, and as if that was not bad enough, two overs later Ramprakash had a rush of blood to the head. He leaped out to hit Warne back over his head, missed and was stumped. In twenty balls 115 for 2 had become 126 for 5. Ward and White tried to put some semblance of order back into England's innings, but with what proved to be the last ball of the day White pushed at Warne to Steve Waugh at silly point, who took the catch just before it touched the grass. This was another decision that needed the third umpire, and another decision that went Australia's way.

Close of play: England 185 and 144 for 6 (Warne 5 for 25); Australia 190 (Gilchrist 54, Tudor 5 for 44)

Third day, 4 August 2001

The third day turned out to be the last day, and the end of England's Ashes dreams for another summer. England's remaining batting just fell apart, and Australia, for once, did not really stumble when trying to chase a low score. In eight overs and one ball, England disintegrated from 144 for 6 overnight to 162 all out, once again failing to impose themselves on the Australian attack.

Ian Ward, England's last batting hope, was the first man to go. The fifth ball of the morning trapped him palpably lbw to Jason Gillespie, so that was 144 for 7. Croft faced three balls before playing on to the fourth. He has no foot movement at all, which if you are as good a batsman as Damien Martyn against an attack as strong as England's, is generally reasonably safe. Against an attack as strong as Australia's, when you are not as good a batsman as Damien Martyn, it is not good tactics. 146 for 8.

Alex Tudor, who had taken White's place at the start of the day, seemed to know how to stick around, and even played a great square drive for four to bring up the 150, but it was clear that there were unlikely to be any last-ditch heroics. Caddick at the other end sliced a four to bring the lead to 150, but that was the extent of his defiance. He nicked Gillespie to Gilchrist, giving the bowler his hundredth Test wicket, reducing England to 156 for 9. Then the drizzle set in. Could England be saved by the rain?

The answer was no. They were only absent for a few minutes, but when they came back on it was noticeable that Steve Waugh had his arm bandaged. He had been hit a little earlier in the morning by a hard slash from Caddick while fielding at backward point, and although he merely rubbed it at the time, it obviously needed a little treatment. Perhaps, all English supporters thought rather self-ishly, it will limit his batting – in the rather unlikely event that he is even needed to bat.

The innings ended when Tudor tried to hit a Warne leg-break against the spin and top-edged it to cover, where Ponting took a good catch. England were all out for 162 in just 57 overs. England had never, in the first three Tests, lasted until the new ball was due, and so had never given their bowlers much to bowl at. This time Australia were left 158 to win, and we all know how often they have failed to chase small targets. That particular list is always headed by Headingley 1981, but this time England had no Botham, no Willis and certainly no Brearley to turn dreams into reality. They just had wishful thinking.

It was two minutes past twelve on the third day when Australia began their second innings, so there was no danger of a draw unless rain intervened. In six and a half sessions so far, thirty wickets had fallen. England had eight and a half sessions to take Australia's final ten. Both teams started as though they wanted to finish it before lunch. Gough's first ball to Hayden, from the Pavilion End, was a snorter which hit Hayden on the pads and gave Gough, Stewart and the England slip cordon the excuse for a raucous appeal. Not out, said umpire Venkat. Gough's second ball was even better, with the same result – pads, concerted appeals, not out. Hayden must have known he was lucky still to be there, but he managed to get bat on ball at the third time of asking. At the other end, Caddick had to bowl as the rain began again. Hayden and Slater decided they would run everything, rotating strike, upsetting the bowlers' rhythm and line and chipping away at the total. It was smart cricket.

Both Slater and Hayden found the boundary boards within the first couple of overs, but Gough was still able to move one past the outside of Slater's bat, and next ball to bring one back at him.

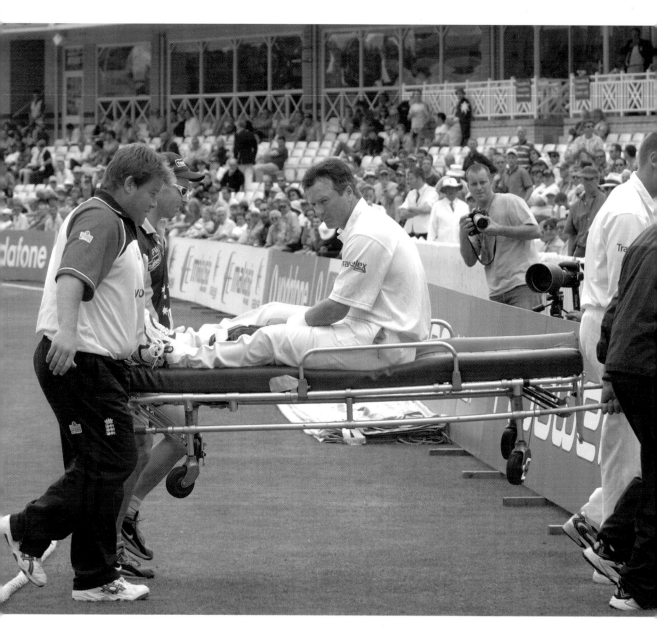

Steve Waugh is stretchered off after tearing his calf muscle taking his first and only run of his second innings. Few thought he would be back for the Oval Test.

As Marcus Trescothick had said earlier about this Trent Bridge pitch, 'You're never in.' Every ball is an adventure and a potential disaster.

The adventure was going Australia's way as they raced to 36 in the sixth over, until Slater drove rather 'halfheartedly' at Caddick and succeeded only in snicking it to Trescothick at third slip. The

next man in was Ponting, a man whose recent run of form must have meant that his Test place was in some jeopardy. For the sake of Australia and his own Test place, he had to stay there until Australia scored the 158 they needed. He began a little cautiously, but Hayden was still going at everything. He got away with a very fast slash through Trescothick's hands when he was on 23; it was perhaps unfair to describe it as a chance as it was high and very quick, but Trescothick got his hands to it

Australia, on the Trent Bridge balcony, celebrate retaining the Ashes.

and no doubt felt he should have caught it. By the time Tudor had replaced Gough, and Hayden had hit him through mid-wicket for four, the 50 was up and Hayden had scored 29 off 24 balls. Atherton tried to revolve the bowling as much as he could to discomfit the batsmen, but it seemed only to discomfit the bowlers. Hayden hit the final ball of the morning session, off Caddick, for four, so they went in at 68 for 1, already almost half way to their target.

Ricky Ponting's hopes of being there at the death were dashed almost immediately after lunch by an unexpected turn of events. Atherton decided to give Robert Croft a bowl, and he managed to slide his second ball past the edge of Ponting's bat to Stewart, who took the catch. Australia were 72 for 2, Ponting had failed again, and who knows, maybe there was time for an England revival. The Australians, on the other hand, were in a confident – one might almost say brash – mood, and they saw no reason why the fall of a second wicket should divert them from their victory charge. Mark Waugh, the new man in, hit the final ball of Croft's over for four, and the Australians continued to rattle along at more than five an over.

That ball turned out to be Croft's final ball of the match, as Atherton took him out of the firing line after only one over. He had bowled two overs in the first innings, so his entire contribution to the game was three overs for ten runs and one wicket, and three runs as a batsman. It must be hard enough for a man like Croft, in and out of the side as conditions as much as his own form decide, to make his mark in any game, but if his captain does not give him any bowling, it is even harder for him to prosper. Croft is not a world-class spinner, but if he is brought into the side at all he should be given a chance to bowl. The same argument could be made on behalf of Craig White (two overs in the match, and seven runs from his bat) whose style of bowling is so different from Croft's that whatever the pitch was doing, one of them ought to have found it to his taste. Australia gave Shane Warne 34 overs in the match, and while nobody would sensibly compare Croft to Warne in terms of class or of what they bowl, it cannot be right that a man

picked primarily for his bowling should be involved in just three of the 84 overs England sent down in the match. If you pick a bowler, use him. If he's not up to the job, don't pick him.

With or without Croft and White bowling at them, Australia wanted to finish the game quickly. Hayden had made 42, including seven blistering fours, in only 51 balls when Tudor induced him to leave one which hit his pad, and the appeal was upheld. The replays showed that Hayden might have been a little unlucky, but he had been incredibly lucky not to have been given out lbw to Gough from the second ball he had faced, and he was shouldering arms. Now Australia were 88 for 3.

Steve Waugh came out to replace Hayden. He was bandaged heavily on his bruised arm, but was not wearing an armguard. This is a very tough cricketer, although in the event not unbreakable. He turned his very first ball towards square leg and set off for the single. At once, he was hobbling. Something had gone in his left calf and although he completed the single, it was obvious that he could not run any more. The Australian physio, Errol Alcott, came out to take a look and quickly summoned the stretcher. To see the Australian captain going off on a stretcher was sad, whichever side you support, because among other things it suggested that we were unlikely to see any more of his batting or his leadership on this tour, and the Australians are a lesser side without him.

The game may have finished for Steve Waugh, but not for brother Mark, nor for Damien Martyn, who replaced his fallen leader. Despite a couple of brief rain breaks in mid-afternoon, the pair kept up the relentless pressure on England as they closed in on the target. Martyn hit three boundaries in one Alex Tudor over, but they were taking no real risks. They just compiled the runs required. By the time the scores were level, the pair had put on 68 in 64 balls. Mark Waugh had 42 from 45 balls, and Martyn 33 from 37. The winning run came, rather ludicrously, from a no-ball by Andrew Caddick. Australia were the winners by seven wickets, and the Ashes were retained.

This was a match which had had moments of great skill and great excitement, and in which England had competed on roughly equal terms for much of the time. Shane Warne was picked as Man of the Match by the adjudicator, Dermot Reeve, but he was not the difference between the teams. The difference is still the way that Australia grind on and on, working together to bring the best out of each other so if one man fails another will succeed: England on the other hand have too many sloppy sessions, too many mini-collapses, too many 142 for 4s becoming 185 all outs, too many bowling spells of four overs for 32, and too many half-chances that don't convert into catches. The gulf between the two sides is large, but there is no real reason, even at this stage, to suggest that England had gone backwards during the summer. England are still the third best Test side in the world, but it is sometimes hard to remember that fact when you are being given a drubbing by the best Test side in the world.

So, on to Headingley, where England might expect to have their captain back, but Australia knew they would have to do without theirs.

The Ashes 2001 Third Test
England v Australia
Trent Bridge, Nottingham
2, 3, 4 August 2001
Australia won by 7 wickets

England 1st innings

*MA Atherton c ME Waugh b McGrath	0
ME Trescothick c Gilchrist b Gillespie	69
MA Butcher c Ponting b McGrath	13
MR Ramprakash c Gilchrist b Gillespie	14
†AJ Stewart c ME Waugh b McGrath	46
IJ Ward c Gilchrist b McGrath	6
C White c Hayden b McGrath	0
AJ Tudor lbw b Warne	3
RDB Croft c Ponting b Warne	3
AR Caddick b Lee	13
D Gough not out	0
Extras b 1, lb 9, w 1, nb 7)	18
Total (all out, 52.5 overs, 225 mins)	185

FoW: 1-0 (Atherton, 0.2 ov), 2-30 (Butcher, 10.5 ov),
3-63 (Ramprakash, 17.3 ov), 4-117 (Trescothick, 28.2 ov),
5-142 (Ward, 36.1 ov), 6-147 (White, 38.4 ov),
7-158 (Tudor, 43.3 ov), 8-168 (Croft, 45.6 ov),
9-180 (Stewart, 48.4 ov), 10-185 (Caddick, 52.5 ov).

Bowling	O	M	R	W	
McGrath	18	4	49	5	
Lee	6.5	0	30	1	(5nb, 1w)
Gillespie	12	1	59	2	
Warne	16	4	37	2	(2nb)

England 2nd innings

*MA Atherton c Gilchrist b Warne	51
ME Trescothick c Gilchrist b Warne	32
MA Butcher lbw b Lee	1
MR Ramprakash st Gilchrist b Warne	26
†AJ Stewart b Warne	0
IJ Ward lbw b Gillespie	13
C White c SR Waugh b Warne	7
AJ Tudor c Ponting b Warne	9
RDB Croft b Gillespie	0
AR Caddick c Gilchrist b Gillespie	4
D Gough not out	5
Extras (b 4, lb 3, nb 7)	14
Total (all out, 57 overs, 243 mins)	162

FoW: 1-57 (Trescothick, 16.3 ov), 2-59 (Butcher, 17.6 ov),
3-115 (Atherton, 36.6 ov), 4-115 (Stewart, 38.2 ov),
5-126 (Ramprakash, 40.2 ov), 6-144 (White, 48.5 ov),
7-144 (Ward, 49.4 ov), 8-146 (Croft, 51.3 ov),
9-156 (Caddick, 53.5 ov), 10-162 (Tudor, 56.6 ov).

Bowling	O	M	R	W	
McGrath	11	3	31	0	
Gillespie	20	8	61	3	
Lee	8	1	30	1	(7nb)
Warne	18	5	33	6	

Australia 1st innings

MJ Slater b Gough	15
ML Hayden lbw b Tudor	33
RT Ponting c Stewart b Gough	14
ME Waugh c Atherton b Tudor	15
*SR Waugh c Atherton b Caddick	13
DR Martyn c Stewart b Caddick	4
†C Gilchrist c Atherton b Tudor	54
SK Warne lbw b Caddick	0
B Lee c Butcher b Tudor	4
JN Gillespie not out	27
GD McGrath c Butcher b Tudor	2
Extras (lb 3, w 1, nb 5)	9
Total (all out, 54.5 overs, 259 mins)	190

FoW: 1-48 (Hayden, 12.6 ov), 2-56 (Slater, 17.1 ov),
3-69 (Ponting, 19.6 ov), 4-82 (SR Waugh, 28.6 ov),
5-94 (ME Waugh, 31.5 ov), 6-102 (Martyn, 32.2 ov),
7-102 (Warne, 32.4 ov), 8-122 (Lee, 39.1 ov),
9-188 (Gilchrist, 54.1 ov), 10-190 (McGrath, 54.5 ov).

Bowling	O	M	R	W	
Gough	15	3	63	2	(1nb, 1w)
Caddick	20	4	70	3	(3nb)
Tudor	15.5	5	44	5	(1nb)
White	2	1	8	0	
Croft	2	0	2	0	

Australia 2nd innings

ML Hayden lbw b Tudor	42
MJ Slater c Trescothick b Caddick	12
RT Ponting c Stewart b Croft	17
ME Waugh not out	42
*SR Waugh retired hurt	1
DR Martyn not out	33
Extras (lb 4, nb 7)	11
Total (3 wickets, 29.2 overs, 192 mins)	158

Did not bat: †AC Gilchrist, SK Warne, B Lee, JN Gillespie, GD McGrath.

FoW: 1-36 (Slater, 5.4 ov), 2-72 (Ponting, 13.2 ov),
3-88 (Hayden, 18.3 ov).

Bowling	O	M	R	W	
Gough	9	1	38	0	(2nb)
Caddick	12.2	1	71	1	(4nb)
Tudor	7	0	37	1	
Croft	1	0	8	1	

Umpires: J. H. Hampshire and S. Venkataraghavan 3rd umpire: D. J. Constant

*captain † wicket keeper

'What's The Point?'

The Fourth Test, Headingley, Leeds
16–20 August 2001

'What's The Point?'

The Fourth test

The evening before the Fourth Test began, we were invited out to dinner. The talk inevitably got round to cricket, and our hostess, a former wicketkeeper for the Manaccan Maidens Cricket Club and somebody who understands and loves cricket, asked, 'What's the point of the Fourth Test?'

The question was quite obviously a heresy, an unbearable thought to a cricket junkie like me, but all the same, an alarmingly logical question. The Ashes were gone. After only three matches, Australia's lead was impregnable. In tennis, if one player wins the first three sets of a five set match, that's it. They shake hands at the net and go off for a shower. In match-play golf, if one player is ten up with eight holes still to play, they shake hands and head straight to the nineteenth. If the Ashes are won and lost, why go on? Why string out the agony?

Well, the obvious answer is that the tickets have already been sold. The first three days, at least, at both Headingley and the Oval were sold out, so there must still be plenty of people who want to watch the cricket even if the overall result is no longer in doubt. And who would deny the populace of Yorkshire and South London the chance of watching cricket being played by one of the great sides of all time? It may be only exhibition stuff, in terms of the significance of the result, but what an exhibition!

Another very good reason to play the Fourth and Fifth Tests, as far as all the England players were concerned, was that there were places on the winter tours to be decided. After three losing Tests, nobody could be sure of his winter's employment, not even the captain whose return from injury had to be tested. The schedule included a series of one-day games in Zimbabwe (politics in that country permitting), followed by Tests and one-day games in India and New Zealand. Losing to the Australians made no difference to England's world rankings, as they had lost to Australia so many times before, but wins against India and New Zealand would go a long way towards confirming England's status as the number three team in the world, while defeat would push us back into the pack again. Cricket is a curious mixture of the individual and the team. Anybody who is not a good team man is unlikely to be picked for a tour, but every player needs to show he has the individual skills to perform at the highest level. Most of England's squad had question marks over their heads as the team reassembled at Headingley, so there was more than just honour to play for.

The Australians, of course, wanted to complete the first ever 'greenwash' of England in England. They were rampant in their baggy greens, and had not drawn a Test in eighteen matches. They intended to continue playing matches in which one side or the other emerged as the clear winner, and they intended it to be them. A five–nil series win, besides being unique in Ashes history, would really show the world how good these Australians are.

The Headingley Test was also to be the three hundredth ever staged between England and Australia, so that was another reason for not cancelling it. Of the previous 299, 144 had been played in England, 155 in Australia. Australia held the overall advantage, with 120 wins against 93 by England and 86 drawn. Even in England Australia held the edge, with 44 wins against England's 40, and 60 draws.

Australia had outplayed England in every department so far in 2001, with the possible exception of the top three batting places. If the top order batting was a concern to Australia, with Slater and Hayden not quite hitting their stride and Ponting seriously out of form, the English batting order was definitely on the critical list. England had three men at the top of the order, Atherton, Trescothick and Butcher, who had averaged around 30 in the first three Tests, a similar position to Australia's. It was a matter of concern that this modest achievement actually represented a major advance for Mark Butcher, whose Test average until now had been in the mid-20s, but the real problem was lower down the order. Australia had four players in positions four to seven who had all scored centuries, with Gilchrist at number seven averaging a Bradmanesque 98.66, but England's middle order

was a shambles. The injuries to three first choice batsmen, Hussain, Thorpe and Vaughan, were a major upset, and there is no doubt that with all three fit to play in all the first three Tests, Australia's triumph would not have been so overwhelming, although it is hard to imagine that they could have changed the course of the series completely. But there were no replacements. When Steve Waugh ruled himself out of the Fourth Test as a result of the calf injury he suffered while batting in the final stages of the Trent Bridge Test, Langer and Katich were ready to replace him, along with Lehmann (top of the county averages in England), Law, Hussey, Maher, Cox, Love, Blewett, Symonds, Di Venuto and all the others available, in form and in England. England have Ramprakash, the eternal enigma; there's Hick, the flat-track bully; Crawley, enjoying a generally terrible season as captain and batsman for Lancashire; Afzaal, whom everybody praises to the roof and then leaves out of the side; Ian Ward, who takes to Test cricket wonderfully well in every aspect except his batting; but we have not yet found another solid middle-order batsman to step in when crisis arises (which it always does).

The batting was not, of course, the only issue. According to many newspapers, the bowling was awful, the fielding ghastly and the wicketkeeping just not good enough. Hussain was even criticised for the cap he wore when tossing the coin, and, while we are at it, for his inability to win the toss whatever he wore on his head. In the national disaster of losing the Ashes, it was often forgotten that no England side would have prospered against this Australian team, not even if we had the May, Cowdrey, Barrington and Graveney middle order of the mid-Sixties, or Gooch, Gower, Lamb, Gatting and co from 1985. The 2001 Australians are that good.

However, just because your opposition are on

paper rather better than you are, it does not mean you wave the white flag even before you start. Some of the tabloid newspapers took to blaming England for not being good enough, but when match after match ended with England in second place they did something far worse for the health of English cricket: they switched their column inches to football, even in the off season. English cricket needs to be in the spotlight, and when the England team cannot provide feel-good stories on a regular basis, the spotlight gets taken away very quickly.

So when it came to the selection process for the Fourth Test, the debate quickly split into two camps. There were those who felt that now that the Ashes were gone, England had to build for the future, kick out the old guard and prepare for a brave new world of English dominance. On the other hand there were those who felt that even though England could not win the summer's series, they could at least restore some pride, and the only way to do that was to pick the very best eleven men available, even if those eleven were not all going to be available for the winter's commitments. The Ashes are, so the argument ran, the most important prize in cricket, and they should

The Sir Leonard Hutton Gates at Headingley, criticised for political correctness and aesthetic incorrectness, were opened by Lady Hutton and son, Richard, the day before the Test.

not be used as a testing ground for candidates to tour Zimbabwe. On balance, this second argument seemed to have the greater validity, largely because the brave new world was always tantalisingly just a season or two in the future, and also because England under Duncan Fletcher and Nasser Hussain had made significant progress which this defeat against the world's top side would not fundamentally change. But if you were a newspaper columnist trying to fill your quota of column inches each day, it was far more profitable to speculate about the young pretenders than to wait for the return of Hussain, Vaughan and Thorpe.

The players who were to be dropped were, by unanimous consent, Craig White and Ian Ward. White put in a late bid for reselection by scoring a career best 186 for Yorkshire against Lancashire as the white rose county made its position at the top of the table virtually uncatchable, but it was too late. Even before the squad was announced, White was told he would not be needed for Headingley, his home ground. As David Graveney said, England need White for his bowling first, and his bowling had not been firing on all cylinders.

The team was announced on Sunday 12 August, and it contained no surprises, unless it was a surprise that it contained no surprises. The thirteen men named for Headingley were:

Nasser Hussain (Essex, captain), Usman Afzaal (Nottinghamshire), Michael Atherton (Lancashire), Mark Butcher (Surrey), Andrew Caddick (Somerset), Robert Croft (Glamorgan), Darren Gough (Yorkshire), Richard Johnson (Somerset), Alan Mullally (Hampshire), Mark Ramprakash (Surrey), Alec Stewart (Surrey, wicketkeeper), Marcus Trescothick (Somerset) and Alex Tudor (Surrey). It was generally expected that Croft would be surplus to requirements, and the final place would be between Johnson, called up for the Third Test at

short notice, and Mullally, bowling superbly, but six years older than Johnson and not much of a batsman.

The Australians had to find a replacement for Steve Waugh, and the race was between Simon Katich, who would thus be making his Test debut, and Justin Langer, who was still not making runs against the counties. It was always expected that the Australian selectors would look forward rather than back, and so it proved: Katich was awarded his first Test cap. Their final team was: Adam Gilchrist (Western Australia, captain and wicketkeeper), Michael Slater (New South Wales), Matthew Hayden (Queensland), Ricky Ponting (Tasmania), Mark Waugh (New South Wales), Damien Martyn (Western Australia), Simon Katich (Western Australia), Shane Warne (Victoria), Brett Lee (New South Wales), Jason Gillespie (South Australia) and Glenn McGrath (New South Wales). Langer was named as twelfth man.

Katich, who was to be seen grinning happily to himself, his team-mates and the television cameras after his selection was announced, thus became the first new specialist batsman to be selected for Australia for three years, since Darren Lehmann was first chosen against India at Bangalore on 25 March 1998. In the same period, England blooded eight batsmen, of whom only two – Trescothick and Vaughan – have shown any likelihood of proving to be of true Test class. We could hope that Usman Afzaal would show he could join them, but what are the future Test prospects of Steve James, Aftab Habib, Darren Maddy, Chris Adams and Ian Ward now?

The PricewaterhouseCoopers ratings, issued on 9 August, showed that Adam Gilchrist was now ranked fourth in the world, with a PwC rating of 813, the highest ever achieved by a number seven batsman. (Gilchrist made his Test debut in 1999, but he does not count as a specialist batsman.) All the same, he still only ranked as the second best wicketkeeper/batsman in the world, after Zimbabwe's Andy Flower. It also showed that the highest-ranked opening pair in the world were Mike Atherton (twelfth) and Marcus Trescothick (eighteenth). This was well ahead of Slater (twenty-first) and Hayden (twenty-seventh). Only Saeed Anwar of Pakistan (thirteenth) and Mark Richardson of New Zealand (sixteenth) among regular Test openers could match either of them. But the downside to this was that Atherton and Trescothick needed to be the best opening pair in the world because every match they had to face the world's best bowler, Glenn McGrath, and the world's fifth best, Jason Gillespie. Remarkably, this did not make McGrath and Gillespie the best opening bowling duo in the world, as South Africa's Shaun Pollock (second) and Allan Donald (third) had a higher combined rating – 1713 to 1686. England's opening pair, Gough and Caddick, had a combined rating of 1397.

As a sideshow to the start of the Test match, the Hutton Gates were officially to be opened by Sir Len's widow on Wednesday 15 August. The Gates created their own furore, thanks to the fact that they showed not only Sir Len playing a characteristic stroke (some said a more characteristic image would have been of him leaning on his bat at the non-striker's end, but this was a churlish comment), but also included two Asian women in saris in the crowd watching him. Several well-known Yorkshire ex-players and committee men went public with their views that the design was an insult to Sir Leonard's memory, as he had never played in the sub-continent and had retired before the population of Britain in general and Yorkshire in particular had grown to include a significant number of people of Asian descent. Others went equally public to say that although much of the above was true, Yorkshire was now a multicultural society, and gates which were expected to be in place for many years ought to reflect the society they will actually keep out of the ground, rather than that which they would have kept out in Sir Len's day. The truth was impossible to resolve, but it became clear that the Yorkshire committee, who had commissioned them, had not been fully aware of what the final design would look like. If a camel is a horse designed by a committee, what is a gate designed by a committee? A white elephant, maybe. Anyway, Lady Hutton and Richard Hutton were there to open the Gates, and the whole affair was soon forgotten as the real business of the cricket took over.

First Day, 16 August 2001

The Thursday morning dawned cloudy and rather muggy. The conditions looked ideal for the bowlers, which did not do much for England's chances, nor for the poor people who had been optimistic enough to buy tickets for the Sunday. If the Test here last year had lasted only two days, what price this one lasting even that long? The answer was 500 to 1, the price William Hill were offering on a one-day finish. Nobody noticed Rod Marsh or Dennis Lillee in the queue for the bookies, twenty years on.

Fortunately for the bookies, but unfortunately for the ticket-holders for the first day's play, the heavens opened at around nine o'clock, before the captains had even managed to toss, and the entire morning's play had to be abandoned. A victory for either side in this one damp day would now have longer odds than Colin Montgomerie winning the equally rain-sodden US PGA Championship starting in Atlanta later in the day.

Both teams had new captains since Trent

Over Page: Matthew Hayden is floored by the ball that also trapped him lbw.

Bridge, the first time that both teams had been led by a different captain in consecutive Tests in mid-series since Headingley in 1968, when Barry Jarman (also a wicketkeeper) and Tom Graveney took over from the injured Bill Lawry and Colin Cowdrey. When Hussain and Gilchrist eventually went out to toss the coin, the result was as usual. Adam Gilchrist called correctly, and decided to bat first. Slater and Hayden put their pads on. The England bowling attack was to be all pace, with Caddick, Gough, Tudor and Mullally sharing the duties, which meant that Croft and Johnson were released. It also meant that when England came to bat, the tail would be a little longer than usual.

Before the match began, there was a brief cere-mony at which Richie Benaud, on behalf of the Australian selectors, presented Simon Katich with his baggy green cap. It was a wonderful moment for the Western Australian widely tipped as a future Australian Test captain, but he was not required to parade his new cap on the field of play just yet.

Gough took the first over. His very first ball was a half-volley which Slater pulled to the boundary, where Mullally misfielded and the ball went through his legs for four. 'Oh, Lord, here we go again,' was the heartfelt cry from the thousands who packed the Headingley stands and the mil-lions watching on television or listening to the radio. And so it seemed for the first few overs. With sixteen runs on the board, Hayden fenced at one which went to gully but dropped tantalisingly short of Trescothick. Not only were England not bowling very well, but the luck was not going their way either. Negative thoughts abounded, and we were not even half an hour into the match.

It was noticeable, though, that Slater was shuf-fling a long way across his stumps, setting himself up as a likely lbw candidate. He took guard a good eighteen inches outside the crease when Gough

and Caddick where bowling, but even this extra distance from the stumps did not significantly reduce the dangers of his style. But first of all he had to make a mistake. Slater had not had a good series since his first innings of the First Test, which in many ways set the tone for the overall Australian batting style for the summer, and he and Hayden certainly needed a big opening partnership to show that the Australian innings did not have to wait until the second wicket fell to get going. The pair began to take the quick singles that show they are feeling good about their partnership, rotating the strike to upset the fielders. One leg bye off Caddick was successfully negotiated despite the fact that the ball just fell at Hayden's feet.

Slater square-drove an overpitched ball from Caddick for four, and the next ball went through Mullally's hands at square leg. At least he pre-vented the four, but the drop might have proved very expensive. It would be unfair to blame Mul-lally alone for the fielding errors: the entire English side looked fragile, whether or not individuals were making mistakes. Tudor in the gully had sev-eral fingers bandaged, Hussain was not fielding in the slip cordon as he usually does, to protect his fingers, and Usman Afzaal is by no means a straight swap for Craig White in the field.

Mullally's miss did not prove expensive in the end. Australia had reached 39 when Caddick began his sixth over. His first ball had Slater lbw. The ball pitched in line with, and would have hit, off stump. Slater had shuffled in front of his stumps once too often. Caddick's second ball, to the new man Ponting, was another snorter, but it was his third ball, the fourth of an excellent over, which caused controversy. Ponting, still to score, sliced the ball to Ramprakash at third slip, who held what he con-sidered a good catch, and those watching consid-ered quite brilliant, low down and just in front of him. But Ponting did not walk, as is his right these days, and the umpire consulted the third umpire, Neil Mallender, who consulted the television screen. After a great deal of consideration and many more inconclusive close-ups with magnifying glasses, Mallender decided there was too much doubt to give Ponting out, and he lived to bat on.

This was, of course, by no means the first controversial decision taken to the third umpire, and at least this time the delivery from Caddick had been completely fair, but it was interesting that the most conclusive evidence that the ball had carried to Ramprakash, a camera angle from behind that seemed to show the fielder had his fingers underneath the ball from the first moment, was not shown until quite some time later. But the decision came home to roost when England batted. Caddick, all fired up by now, hit Ponting on the hand with the last ball of the over. Ponting, however, seemed quite unmoved, although he was no doubt relieved that Caddick had finished his over, one of the most hostile and consistently unplayable of the whole series.

Mullally replaced Gough after six overs, and began his Test summer with a maiden. There was by now a very strong wind blowing across the ground which helped to bring Mullally's deliveries in to the right-handers. At the other end, Caddick carried on snorting fire. Hayden tried pulling him square, but only managed to splice the ball just short of mid-off. Next ball, Caddick and his entire slip cordon went up for a huge lbw shout, and on the replay it certainly looked justifiable. The ball seemed to pitch straight and be on line to take the middle stump, but the umpire disagreed. Would that be an expensive decision, like Ponting's was shaping up to be? No. The very next ball from Caddick hit Hayden on the knee roll with such force that he fell to the ground in pain. When he looked up from his bed of agony just next to silly mid-off, it was to find that the umpirical finger was

in the air, and he was out, lbw to Caddick for 15. Australia were 42 for 2, and once again the openers had failed.

There then followed three and a half hours of cricket, rain and teatime: 45 overs of play, during which Australia dominated the England attack and piled on the runs in conditions that were by no means all in favour of the batsmen. Ponting made the English bowlers pay at last for his lean series so far, and Mark Waugh added yet another high-class and high-scoring innings to his summer tally. Ponting had only to reach 18 to achieve his highest score of the series, which he did very quickly, and he drove on from there. The pitch was certainly not a batsman's paradise. It was obviously quite slow, as both batsmen were early on their shots from time to time, and there was not much bounce in the pitch either. With a surface that made timing difficult for the batsmen but also blunted the fast bowler's armoury by taking all but the most precisely directed bouncers out of the equation, one could be excused for expecting a quiet, attritional period of play. But that is not the way the Australians play, and it is not what the Headingley crowd got. A short delivery from Mullally, for instance, was hit by Ponting over the square leg boundary with a flourish and a power that owed little to pure timing and a great deal to brute force. It was very effective.

The score was 75 for 2 when Alex Tudor was introduced into the attack for the first time, with tea looming. He seemed just to be jogging to the wicket, looking for rhythm, but with his high arm he got a little more bounce out of the pitch. But when he bowled too short, which was rather too often for his team-mates' liking, the batsmen reaped the harvest by scything the ball through square cover for four, or pulling it past mid-wicket for the same result. In the final over before tea, Ponting almost got an edge to a wide one from

Tudor, but it missed the bat. The final ball before the interval went for four byes: the ball swung a long way after it had passed the bat, and Stewart had little chance of stopping it. This may have been an augury for the way the pitch would play or for the way Tudor would bowl, but whichever it was, Australia went into tea on 86 for 2 after 26 overs.

After tea, England bowled 40 more overs without a break. Ponting batted for 35 of those, also without a break, and Mark Waugh for the whole lot. England's bowlers put up what was certainly one of their weakest sessions of the summer, while the Australian pair batted quite wonderfully. Ponting made England pay for his lucky escape before he had scored by hitting twenty fours and three sixes in 154 balls before he was finally out, caught by Stewart off Alex Tudor, for 144. By then the score was 263, and English hearts, not to mention English bowlers' backs, were broken.

The story of an innings of this length and brilliance can normally be broken up into different parts – the overture while the batsman plays himself in, the main thrust of the innings as he builds on a firm foundation, and sometimes a run-scoring crescendo, or a diminuendo as he goes temporarily into his shell to weather a particularly good spell of bowling. It is also a partnership in which one or other batsman plays the lead role as circumstances require: the violins taking over from the piano before handing the theme back a few bars later. The end is either death or glory. But in this innings by Ricky Ponting it would be hard to spot many different stages. After that first uncertain over against Caddick, he played all adversaries as though they were mere net bowlers giving him an early evening workout. The force of his shots did not vary much throughout his stay and the rate at which he scored was metronomically regular. There was, of course, the occasional flurry

of boundaries, but from the way he batted it looked as though any ball bowled to him might well have been dismissed to the ropes. It was just a question of how he was feeling – towards the bowler, the ball, the crowds – as to where the ball ended up. The bowlers did not seem to have any role to play in keeping him quiet. It was a great innings, and all the more so because his performance so far on the tour had been rather feeble. He had started on the road back to form with a sparkling hundred against Sussex at Hove, in the one first-class match the Australians played between the Third and Fourth Tests, and he was carrying on from there.

Ponting's 50 came up off 65 balls and included two sixes and six fours. He reached this first landmark with the sixth of those fours, a drive through the covers off a Tudor half-volley. The score was now 124 for 2. Ponting and Waugh still made the very occasional involuntary or misjudged stroke; although the pitch had eased as the sun came out, it was never absolutely straightforward. Ponting's massive forearms enable him to hit through the off side on either the front or the back foot, or to smash the ball into the stands when the feeling takes him. The third six of his innings was a shot over mid-wicket, lethal in its loveliness, which brought up the century partnership and further dented Tudor's figures.

That particular over went for sixteen runs, and there seemed to be a specific policy on the part of the batsmen to get after Tudor. Perhaps they knew that his confidence, as a comparative newcomer to Test cricket, was fragile, and they needed to prevent a repeat of his first-innings performance at Trent Bridge where he took five wickets and raised the ball joyfully to the crowd as the teams walked off. At this stage both

After a disappointing first three Tests, Ricky Ponting reimposes himself on England's beleaguered bowlers. It was brilliant, ruthless batting.

Waugh and Ponting were racing along. In the 80 minutes after tea, the pair added 103 at virtually six an over. They moved the total from 100 to 150 in only 49 balls, only Mullally being able to stem the tide. Even he did not look threatening: he contained the batsmen to an extent but never looked like getting them out.

The only slight hiccup in the relentless compilation of runs came when Caddick bowled a very fine and very quick over at Mark Waugh. He brought in two fielders short on either side of the wicket, hoping to induce Waugh to mishit a short ball. The first two balls of the over, both short and precisely on line, were well played by Waugh, but the next ball was a more effective bouncer. It hit Waugh full on the helmet, and for a brief moment he was rattled. At the end of the over drinks were brought on, and Waugh signalled for a new helmet. Caddick had broken the one he was wearing. Psychologically it may have been one–nil to the bowler, but in the score book it was still all going Australia's way. Waugh brought up his 50 a couple of overs later from a leading edge which brought him a single off Caddick, but if he was having any luck, he had earned it. Hussain brought Butcher on to see if his golden arm was in working order, which must have pleased Ponting, on 97 not out at the time and looking for a nice friendly bit of bowling to usher him to his century. After one over, which included a wide and which yielded seven runs – but not the crucial three that Ponting needed – Butcher was put back out to pasture. Plan B had not worked, so it was either back to Plan A or switch to Plan C.

There was no Plan C, so it was back to Alan Mullally. Ponting was by now on 99, and he took only one ball of Mullally's left-arm over to reach his goal. He hit it square, and as he ran up the wicket for the single he waved arms and bat in the air in celebration. This was his eighth Test century, made

in 114 balls, and it seemed to have taken the match firmly away from England. It was not long after this that the partnership between Waugh and Ponting became the highest of the series so far, but they were not finished yet. Hussain suddenly thought of a Plan C, and brought Ramprakash on for his first bowl of the match, but although he did not get hit quite as hard or as far as some of the quicker bowlers, he was no more threatening than anybody else. What's more, a statistic that was doing the rounds showed that since 1979 only 49 of the 619 wickets that have been taken in Headingley Tests have fallen to the spinners, the most recent wicket that has fallen to an English spinner being that of Wasim Akram who was lbw to Atherton's bowling in 1996. There was little chance that Atherton would get a bowl this year. The most recent match-winning performance by a spinner is John Emburey's 5 for 82 in 1985 to give England victory against Australia in the first Test of that series. Ramprakash and Emburey both once played for Middlesex, but there the similarity as off-spinners ends. Ramprakash did manage to get a little turn, but that was not good news for England. It only made them realise what a side with a decent spinner in their midst, for example Shane Warne, might do.

By 6.55 the Australians were wreaking havoc on the English bowling attack, and the 200 partnership was up. The Australian third-wicket record at Headingley, 229 between Bradman and Kippax in 1930, when Sir Donald hit an amazing 309 runs in a day, was under threat. Tudor in particular was being caned by Ponting. One four through midwicket, for which Ponting rocked onto his back foot and thumped the ball over the infield and to the ropes, in particular sticks in the mind, but the whole session was an array of glorious batting. Two or three times Ponting hit Tudor for consecutive boundaries, but suddenly, just as we were resigned to an enormous overnight score for two wickets down, Tudor let one go and Ponting edged the ball to Stewart. It was 7 o'clock in the evening, and the score was 263 for 3. The partnership had not quite beaten the record, finishing on 221, and Ricky Ponting walked back to the pavilion to a standing ovation.

His replacement was Damien Martyn, at this stage in the season averaging around 100. If England thought there was any relief in sight, they were mistaken. Within a few minutes of reaching the crease, Martyn was timing it beautifully. A back-foot drive off Caddick through mid-off for four was typical. The Australian batsmen are by and large powerful men, but it is the timing of their shots rather than their force that makes them such dangerous opponents. The English bowling, on the other hand, was not giving the batsmen enough to think about. Tudor, for example, almost sliced Martyn in half with one great delivery which the batsman knew nothing about, but the very next ball was a wide half-volley which Martyn smashed to the boundary.

It was past 7.30 as Caddick came in to bowl the final over of the day. The score was 288 for 3, meaning that Australia had scored 202 runs in 40 overs since tea, a rate of five an over. Mark Waugh and Damien Martyn were closing down for the night. Andrew Caddick had other ideas. His third ball reared up at Mark Waugh, who could not get his bat out of its way. The ball lobbed up gently off the shoulder of the bat to Mark Ramprakash at gully. He had to run a couple of paces forward, and in doing so seemed to aggravate the injury to his ankle (oh yes, even Ramps managed to injure himself during the summer), turning it over again. But the catch was safely held, and Australia went in for the night at 288 for 4, with Mark Waugh out for 72, and Martyn not out 19. It had been Australia's day, even with the two late wickets. Ramprakash no

doubt went straight to the physio's massage table: I assume the England team are all issued with season tickets.

Close of play: Australia 288 for 4 (Ponting 144, ME Waugh 72)

Second Day, 17 August 2001

This was, if you can stomach the thought, the eve of the first day of the English Premiership football season. The newspapers were all full of Manchester United's chances rather than those of the England cricket team. The ever shorter summer break from 'the beautiful game' (ha!) was over, and the sports pages gave themselves back to their first love after a few weeks' dalliance with their summer romance. But at Headingley there was work still to be done, and several major obstacles for England to overcome if they were to end the day still in contention.

Katich took guard for the first ball of the day, his first ball in Test cricket. Caddick had three more balls in his unfinished over from the previous evening, and Katich survived them without undue alarms. At the other end, Martyn set off in exactly the same mode as the night before – determined to reach his double hundred before the first drinks interval. He kept the runs ticking over well, but it was noticeable that he did not use his feet at all. He merely stood tall and used his quick eye and perfect balance to get bat to ball and hit it where he wanted it to go. None of the bowlers looked as though they were likely to get rid of him, although Mullally, bowling at nothing much more than medium pace, was the most successful at containment. When England took the new ball, at 325 for 4, Hussain gave it to Tudor. The result was 30 more runs in four overs.

Katich was playing himself in slowly, getting used not only to the pitch and the bowling but also

to the sensation of playing Test cricket. He had begun to build an innings when Gough bowled him a good length ball which he decided to leave alone. Unfortunately, it was Gough's nip-backer, and it took the top of Katich's off-stump. There is nothing that makes a batsman look quite as foolish as being bowled by a ball which he has ostentatiously left alone. Katich walked off, head bowed, knowing that he had not made the debut he had hoped for. Bowled Gough 15, by the forty-second ball he faced; the score was now 355 for 5.

It was one of the more depressing sensations of the summer, for England supporters and players alike, to see Adam Gilchrist coming out to bat with a massive score already posted. However, at least we all knew we would be in for some exciting batting. In the next six overs Martyn and Gilchrist added 41 runs, and the England attack looked ragged. One straight drive for four by Gilchrist off Gough sticks in the memory, but all one could say was that he looked as good as he had all summer. There was no indication that the responsibilities of captaincy on top of the wicketkeeping duties were affecting his batting. Then, quite unexpectedly, he made a misjudgement. He hit a Gough delivery a little too hard and a little too uppishly, and Trescothick at cover dived forward to take a very good catch. Gilchrist was gone for 19, his first failure of the series. England had reduced Australia to 396 for 6, although 'reduced' is hardly the right word when a team is closing in on 400.

At lunch Australia had moved to 408 for 6, with Martyn on 97 and Warne yet to score. England must have expected a long afternoon in the field in prospect, but it was not to be. The one man who never allows the situation, the wicket or even his own form to get him down, Darren

amien Martyn finished the season with an average excess of 100, only the sixth time this feat has een achieved. His 118 at Headingley was one of e reasons.

Gough, conjured wickets out of nowhere, and Australia were all out for 447 within forty minutes of the resumption. The first to go was Warne, who nicked the first ball he faced after lunch to Stewart and departed for a duck. This was his second consecutive Test duck: despite very good batting form against the counties, Warne was not proving effective at Test level as a number eight batsman. He had at least stuck around long enough for Martyn to reach his second hundred of the series, thanks to a wonderful square drive off Mullally in the first over after lunch. For a man who had never reached three figures in an on-off Test career stretching back almost ten years, Martyn was now making up for lost time.

In the next over 412 for 7 became 422 for 8 as Brett Lee was also dismissed for his second duck of the series, the second man to be caught by Ramprakash in the innings but the first wicket for Mullally. Gillespie hung around for a few more balls, until he was caught by Atherton at slip off Gough. Glenn McGrath hit two boundaries off the six balls he faced, but it was Martyn who was the last man to go. Like Gillespie, he edged the ball to Atherton at first slip, but this one moved so quickly that Atherton could only parry it up into the air for Stewart to take a very good catch on the rebound. Martyn was out for 118, Australia were all out for 447, and Gough had taken five wickets for 103 runs. At 2.25, England had to begin their reply.

As usual, they started well. Atherton and Trescothick overcame the initial threat of McGrath and Gillespie so well that by tea, after eighteen overs, they had posted their 50 partnership and were looking as comfortable as could be expected. The only moment of drama was when Trescothick enjoyed the same experience as Ponting. He had made only four when he edged to slip where Mark Waugh claimed the catch. Trescothick stood his ground, and the third umpire took a long look at every replay at every speed before giving the batsman the benefit of the doubt. At the very slowest of speeds, it did indeed look as though Waugh had taken it on the half-volley, but without the aid of technology neither the batsman, fielder nor umpire would have known that. It was now up to Trescothick to score a century, as Ponting had done after his let-off.

The clouds were gathering in the sky, and the people in fancy dress in the crowd – Roman legionaries and men riding ostriches among some of the more bizarre manifestations of the peculiar habit of dressing up to watch the cricket – were beginning to wonder where they had stored their umbrellas. Perhaps if you dress as a Roman legionary you are not allowed an umbrella, as it would not be chronologically consistent with the outfit, but then again, I don't think cans of lager are chronologically accurate either, and there were plenty of them. Atherton, wearing the usual costume to contend with Gillespie and McGrath, might have wondered whether he could borrow a breastplate from the crowd when one Gillespie delivery rose from only just short of a length and it took all his skill and luck to miss it as it rushed past him on off-stump line.

Atherton's skill more than luck enabled him to seize on a short ball from McGrath and cut it up and over the slips for four; next ball, he took on McGrath's perennial challenge and hooked. The ball went very quickly and entirely safely for another four runs. When Shane Warne came on to bowl for the first time just before tea, it was more in hope than expectation. Warne was closing in on 400 Test wickets at this stage, but only two of them had been taken in his two previous Tests here at Headingley, probably his least favourite Test venue. Warne had dyed his hair a very white blond; he was wearing space-age sunglasses and his trousers sported wide 1970s-style flares. He was

making a clear fashion statement, and the statement was 'I have absolutely no dress sense at all.' Tea was taken after his over, with England on 50 for no wicket.

Immediately after tea, Atherton was out. The third ball of McGrath's first over of the session was good enough to take the edge of Atherton's bat, and Gilchrist made no mistake with the catch. England were 50 for 1. Barely twenty minutes later Trescothick tried to pull McGrath, but all he could do was top-edge it to Gilchrist, so both openers were gone, in their different styles to the same bowler and the same catcher. As a response to the Australian total, 67 for 2 looked less than impressive, and the doomsayers were looking up record defeats in their *Playfairs* and *Wisdens*.

This was the moment when the England captain came out to bat in a first-class game for the first time since he broke his finger in the First Test on 8 July, 40 days earlier. It was also the time when an impostor – the same man who gatecrashed the Manchester United team photo earlier in the year – walked out in full batting kit through the pavilion gates. He was rumbled when his mobile phone went off in his pocket as he walked out, and unlike any other Test cricketer since Ian Botham and Allan Lamb played havoc with Dickie Bird's nerves many Tests ago, he reached into his pocket to answer it. The gag was not nearly as good as when he asked Andy Cole to shove up as the photographer prepared the team photo, and needless to say there was a tabloid newspaper behind the stunt. There were also a large number of incompetent Headingley security men with red faces. They made up for their laxness the next day by refusing admission to a number of people who had every right to be there, including one of the umpires and Henry Blofeld, thereby ensuring that their incompetence

Mark Butcher played the innings of his life to carry England to an unpredicted victory.

was broadcast even more widely than it would otherwise have been.

With only an Essex Seconds game as match practice, it was difficult to imagine that Nasser Hussain would do anything more than play a plucky little knock while ducking and diving to make sure his fingers stayed intact. McGrath did indeed hit him on the fingers early on in his innings, but he did not even take his glove off to have a look. Hussain seems to take his stance very low these days, and this may mean that he has less time to get his hands out of the way of any ball that rears up, especially off a length. It also means that even the balls that do not get up to any particular height may threaten his fingers. But that's the way he plays. Within a few overs, we also saw another way he plays. Attempting to pull Lee, he attacked the ball entirely cross-batted like a baseball hitter, with his front foot planted square on to the bowler, his shoulders making a wide swing as the ball was swatted off the splice for four.

Hussain and Butcher compiled a 50 partnership almost without us noticing the runs piling up, and it was not until after that milestone had been reached that Warne was given another over. He did not really bowl well, in this spell or throughout the match, by his own high standards, but he is always capable of producing the killer ball, and any captain with almost 450 on the board is happy to let Warne bowl for a while even if the wicket doesn't suit him at all. The partnership moved on to 60, the highest third-wicket partnership of the series for England, which was not a feat to be proud of. As the light began to fade, the England duo carried on without any real alarms, helped by the fact that neither Warne nor Lee were bowling particularly well; Lee has definitely been the disappointment of the summer, to his captain as well as to the English cricket public. Only the England cricketers did not seem to mind.

By the time three lights had come on, Gilchrist offered the ball to Katich for his first bowl in Test cricket. But as he marked out his run-up and thought about his field placings the fourth bulb lit up on the scoreboard, and the umpires offered the light. Hussain and Butcher needed no second thoughts, so Katich was left to wonder whether he would be opening the bowling the next morning.

Close of play: Australia 447 (Ponting 144, Martyn 118, ME Waugh 72, Gough 5 for 103); England 155 for 2

Third Day, 18 August 2001

Today England lost eight wickets in doubling (all but one run) their score. They saved the follow-on with some comfort, but it was the same old problem of batsmen getting in and then not going on to make a major score. The total of 309 all out sounds fairly good, and for the first time this series the Australians were forced to take the new ball, but a team of which five batsmen get past 35 should have more than one that reaches 50. McGrath was the destroyer – surprise, surprise – with 7 for 76, but, well though he bowled, England still gave away too many of their wickets.

Nasser Hussain, the first to go, can be absolved of blame. In the third over of the morning he got a ball from McGrath (not Katich, who never got the bowl he had expected the night before) which kept wickedly low, and he was trapped lbw for 46. Butcher, on the other hand, who was not one of McGrath's victims, has only himself to blame. He pushed the ball to mid-on, where he managed not to see Brett Lee closing in on the ball and called Ramprakash for a run. Lee had merely to pick up the ball cleanly and underarm it at the stumps, and Butcher was out by such a distance that even an umpire who knows his handiwork is under continuous scrutiny, on the big screen at the ground and the little screen at home, did not need to call for the third umpire. With Butcher gone for 47, England were 158 for 4 and suddenly in danger of being wiped away by the rampant Australians. English confidence was not necessarily raised by the sight of Afzaal coming onto the pitch as the next man in, a talented player with extravagant strokeplay and a Test top score still in single figures.

He beat his highest Test score by some margin, but still did not last much more than twenty minutes. Afzaal tends to push the face of his bat through, even on his defensive strokes, and the ball tends to spend more time in the air than is safe for a Test batsman. On 14, he got a thick edge trying to force McGrath, but he chose the wrong ball and Warne's safe hands at slip made no mistake. That brought Alec Stewart to the middle, and the Australians brought Warne back into the attack at once, knowing that he has dismissed Stewart ten times in Test cricket. The experiment did not work, but then Warne has never got Stewart out at Headingley (for the record, his two victims at Headingley are Martin McCague in 1993 and Nasser Hussain in 1997).

Stewart and Ramprakash took the score along comfortably to lunch, by which time the partnership was worth 58, by a wide margin England's best sixth-wicket stand of the series. At 232 for 5, England went into lunch knowing that at least the follow-on was as good as saved. After the break they added those vital sixteen runs without any further alarms, and they knew that Australia would have to work very hard indeed for a victory. They were not entirely out of the woods yet, though, and when Ramprakash swished at a loose, if fast, ball from Lee to give Gilchrist yet another straight-forward catch, there was an element of Hansel and Gretel looking for breadcrumbs in England's

progress. Ramprakash had made 40 for the second time of the series. He either makes 14 or 40, or, once, 26, which is of course 40 minus 14. Why can he not go on from a good start?

The rest of the England innings was unsurprising. Another 57 runs were added by the lower order in conjunction with Alec Stewart, who is becoming as adept at helping the tail restore some sort of respectability to England's total as he was in posting a respectable score when he batted at the top of the order. Tudor's only runs were from a Surrey cut, the ball aimed expansively into the off side but actually scuttling through the batsman's legs to backward square leg. He then fished at one from McGrath outside his off stump, and was caught by Gilchrist.

Caddick became the target of a very quick bouncer from Brett Lee. It was timed at 90.2 miles per hour, and hit him on his left armguard. At that speed, as we have seen, the batsman has under half a second to assess length and direction and choose his way of playing the ball. Better batsmen than Caddick would have been troubled by it. The next ball, the one you bowl when you know you've got the batsman a little rattled, clean bowled Caddick. Unfortunately for Lee, it was a no-ball. Great theory, imperfect execution, which made Lee determined to bowl even faster. The next ball hit Caddick on the body, but the the one after that was poorly directed, well wide of the off stump. Caddick gave himself even more room and whacked it to the cover boundary for four. Lee was not impressed. The final ball of the over was such a short bouncer that it soared over Caddick's head (and Caddick is 6'5" without boots or helmet). An overhead smash in the style of Greg Rusedski was attempted, to no avail.

In the next over, Stewart reached his fifty with a boundary off McGrath. After four of the England top order had been out in the forties, it was a great relief to see somebody at last reach fifty. Stewart did not stop there. He knew that he was among the rabbits, and that it was time to take risks. McGrath decided to come round the wicket to him, and gave himself a seven-two offside field. Stewart's response was to step back and hit the ball for six over extra cover, the shot of a very good batsman with a great eye. The crowd went wild. McGrath did not. In the next over, Stewart pulled Lee for four, fighting against fearful odds as though he were d'Artagnan despatching yet another wicked soldier with a rapier to the heart. It was stirring stuff, but it could not last very long.

Caddick was the next musketeer to perish. Another quick ball from Lee hit him on the arm-guard, but he was given out caught behind. This was one of the very few bad umpiring decisions in the Ashes series: the appeals from Lee and Gilchrist could not be described as anything more than half-hearted, but umpire Venkat still put up his right index finger in his distinctive style, like a rather pessimistic weather man testing for the direction of the wind. Caddick had to go.

Gough, who took his place, began with an all-run four – just what his 38-year-old partner would have appreciated after two and a half hours at the crease – and as the light grew significantly darker, finished his scoring with a four over mid-off off McGrath. Retribution was almost immediate: he then skied a ball to cover, where Michael Slater took an easy catch. It was 299 for 9, and enter Alan Mullally, with a bat devoid of sponsors' marks. He and Steve Waugh seem to be the only two batsmen not paid by one company or another to use their equipment. In no other sense could you couple the names of Mullally and Steve Waugh as batsmen.

Stewart brought up the 300 with the first ball of a Lee over, leaving Mullally to survive the remaining five, but before they could be bowled the umpires consulted and offered the light, and off

they all went. The band of Jimmy Savile lookalikes in the crowd also went off, no doubt for a drink. There followed a two-hour interruption which proved one thing only: that the new electronic scoreboard at Headingley, with its red numbers, is impossible to read when the light is good, but shines as bright and unmissable as an advertisement in Times Square when the sky above is almost pitch black.

It was 5.13 when England's last wicket finally fell. Mullally was well caught by Simon Katich at forward short leg from a ball that came up at him more than he expected. This gave McGrath the exceptional innings figures – even by his own high standards – of 7 for 76 off 30.2 overs, and more importantly, his three hundred and fiftieth Test match wicket in his seventy-fourth Test.

The Australians set about their second innings in their usual way, like an express train trying to beat the timetable. After three overs the score was seventeen for no wicket, with Slater in particular tucking in to some very average bowling from Gough and Caddick. Caddick even committed the unforgivable sin of bowling two no-balls in succession, the second of which Slater played on to his stumps. So Caddick had achieved the very rare feat of both being bowled by, and bowling somebody with, a no-ball in the same match.

Luckily Slater did not make England pay for this let-off in the way that Ponting had in the first innings. When he had made only 16, with the score at 25, he played at a ball well outside the off stump, did not move his feet and dragged the ball onto his stumps. This brought in Ricky Ponting, who was also following team orders to get on with it. He had made only four when he was dropped by Atherton at slip off Gough, a fast

Nasser Hussain, back in the side after weeks without any first-class cricket, played two decisive innings to help create his team's triumph.

and high chance, but one which any Australian slip fielder would have held. If Ponting had made 0 and 4 in this Test, instead of 144 and 72, his Test future would have been very precarious. On such pieces of luck are careers made and broken.

Hayden was taking his time to build an innings, but Ponting was now firmly established in the driver's cab of the runaway train. By the time the 50 came up, Ponting had made 20 in 24 balls, Hayden just 11 in 47. By the close, which came at 6.30 when bad light stopped play once again, Australia had reached 69 for 1, with Ponting on 30 and Hayden on 12.

Close of play: Australia 447 and 69 for 1; England 309 (Stewart 76*, McGrath 7 for 76)

Fourth Day, 19 August 2001

The day began in bright sunshine, so it was a pity that it should have been so spoiled later by bad light and rain. In retrospect, however, the weather helped set up a thrilling final day's play. That was of little consolation to the large Sunday crowd. When England's opening batsmen were offered the light at 6.01, after 2.3 overs batting in murky conditions, it cannot have been coincidence that this meant that precisely 25 overs had been played during the day, exactly enough to ensure that the spectators could not claim back any of their admission money. After two overs, there were three lights on the scoreboard, the umpires conferred but did not offer the light. Two balls later, they conferred again. After the next ball, with the light no worse, they decided to offer the light, and the batsmen eagerly sought the safety of the pavilion. The crowd, wrongly, suspected collusion between the Headingley authorities and the umpires to do them out of a refund. The day thus ended on a sour note, which was no fault of the players themselves.

Ponting began the day as he had finished on Saturday, determined to score at least a double hundred before lunch. Hayden pottered along happily in his wake. The only move that any England player made that stopped the flow of runs was when Trescothick managed to spill several sweets from his pocket as he chased the ball, and wasted a moment or two picking them all up again. If only all the England players could have been told to fill their pockets with sweets or other foodstuffs, and to drop them at regular intervals, it might have broken up the batsmen's rhythm long enough to slow them down and then get them out. It's a long shot, but one worth storing away for the future.

Ponting reached his 50 in only 52 balls, in bright sunshine. Forty-four runs came off the first eight overs of the day, the majority from Ponting, who was hooking, driving and even in one instance upper-cutting the ball square to the boundary. The sunshine, and the strokeplay, could not last. As quickly as it had appeared, the sun went behind a cloud, the umbrellas came up, and at 11.40, the players went off. The break lasted only 40 minutes, but both men were unsettled, and 124 for 1 became 129 for 2 when Ponting, who could well have been given out the ball before, was adjudged lbw to Gough for 72. The partnership had made 104 in 20 overs. Hayden was still there on 26.

Not for long, though. Three overs later, Mullally got his reward for a good spell of bowling, tempting Hayden to give a catch to Stewart and make it 141 for 3. By lunchtime, the score was 146 for 3, with Mark Waugh on 4 and Damien Martyn still to score. After lunch, it was clear that Mark Waugh was taking on the Ponting role: he hit Mullally over mid-off for four and was clearly intent on scoring quick runs. Damien Martyn was oddly subdued at the other end, and the pair had only added 30 when Caddick, with the first ball of a new spell, trapped him lbw for just 6. The score was now 171 for 4.

The weather, which had been playing hide and seek with the players all day, now moved into serious mode. There was just time for Mark Waugh to play the ball gently down to Gough at fine leg for a single, only for him to see another four added to his total as Gough's wild throw was missed by Stewart and his back-up fielders and rolled over the boundary. The static in the air was clearly visible in Alan Mullally's hair as he prepared to bowl: wisps of his blond locks were standing on end as the electrical storm drew closer. After only three balls of this hair-raising over, the rain came down, the players went off and the covers went on. And that was that for the next three hours and forty minutes.

The thunder and the rain decided the match. When play was once more possible, at 5.50, there were in theory twenty overs left to play. Adam Gilchrist took the bold course and declared, leaving England 315 to win in a maximum of 110 overs. He was perhaps conscious of the torrid time the media had given him after the tourists' match against Essex, when he had carried on batting until the game was dead, and even more conscious of the determination of the Australians under Steve Waugh to win every match they play. If the score in the series had been 2–0 rather than 3–0, would the Australians have declared, or would they have batted on to make the game, and therefore the Ashes, absolutely safe? This was a bold declaration to go for the 5–0 'greenwash', but it seems unlikely they would have taken the risk of losing if the Ashes had not already been safely retained. However, Australia's plans were dealt a heavy blow when more bad light restricted the evening's play to just those infamous 2.3 overs. Instead of going in overnight with England perhaps at 40 for 1 (a score from which England would only be able to build an innings defeat in the next Test at the Oval), they found they had given England a whole day to score those 315, on a pitch that was of little or no use to Shane Warne. Even so, the media overnight gave England little chance. Michael Henderson in the Daily Telegraph voiced the majority opinion when he wrote, 'One would have to say that, if the Australians get 90 overs in, they will expect to win.' Nobody was castigating Gilchrist for too generous a declaration at the end of that murky Sunday.

Close of play: Australia 447 and 176 for 4 declared (Ponting 72); England 309 and 4 for 0

Fifth Day, 20 August 2001

This was Mark Butcher's day. The Surrey left-hander, who began the year clinging on to his place in the county side (and not always with success) found himself in the England side only after injuries to at least two of his county colleagues, Thorpe and Ramprakash, not to mention Michael Vaughan of Yorkshire. But he seized the opportunity and much to the surprise of the English public, and probably to himself and the selectors as well, found himself at the top of the England batting and bowling averages as the Fourth Test began. He was still hardly a household name, though, as Monday August 20 began. By the time the sun set, he was a national hero.

The day began inauspiciously. Atherton hit a boundary off McGrath's first ball of the day but was undone by an unplayable ball before the over was completed. It was one of those deliveries, a ball which lifted from a length just outside off stump, which they say only the best players would have got a touch to, but that was no consolation to Atherton, c Gilchrist b McGrath for 8. This was the cue for the entry of Mark Butcher. The wicket was

still playing tricks – one good length ball from Gillespie flew over Gilchrist's head for four byes – but somehow Butcher and Trescothick survived the first half hour. Then, just as it looked as though the pair might create a lasting partnership, Gillespie induced a loose drive from Trescothick, and Hayden in the gully took the catch. Hayden was one Australian who fielded brilliantly all day: he may have had a disappointing series with the bat, but his fielding was well up to the highest Australian standards.

We worry about Trescothick: he plainly has the temperament for Test cricket, and the talent, but his style involves such little use of the feet that all bowlers must feel that if they give him enough balls wide of the off stump he will eventually commit suicide. He leaves the ball brilliantly, appearing to play at some that he has no intention of trying to hit, and this can infuriate bowlers who think he is beaten every time. Good left-handers do this a lot: John Edrich did, and Mark Benson of Kent, now an umpire, used to drive county bowlers to distraction with his play-leave shot, but it is a dangerous tactic in Test cricket, and many England fans would rather see Trescothick using his feet a little more to get in line. Still, he has established himself rightfully at the top of England's batting order, and it will be interesting to see how he stands the different conditions in India and New Zealand in the winter.

With Trescothick gone, Nasser Hussain came to the wicket. Having made a solid 46 in the first innings, including a partnership of 91 with Butcher for the third wicket, the captain had to do even better this time round. And he did. If this game will be remembered as Butcher's match, it should not be forgotten that it was also the match in which Hus-

Shane Warne does not like Headingley. His only victim was Ramprakash, the last wicket to fall before England's victory.

sain, having had no cricket for two months or so, and with a pretty awful eighteen months' batting just behind him, came back to lead England to victory as much by his batting as by his captaincy. Hussain and Butcher are good friends (after the match everybody was claiming to be Butcher's friend) and they batted together as though they were enjoying each other's company as much as the runs they were scoring. In recent Tests 33 for 2 has been the starting point for an England collapse rather than a winning total, but Butcher played like a man who had money on an England win by tea time.

The rest of the morning was all England's. Butcher seemed to target McGrath in his attempts to put Australia off their stride. This is a dangerous tactic, as batsmen all over the world have failed to upset the McGrath metronome, but Butcher was on a different level today, and McGrath and his colleagues found that their own performances dropped as the left-hander got into his stride. To say that the Australian attack was below par all day is not to take anything away from England's performance – it is a compliment to their batting, because it was their brilliance that disheartened the bowlers and made it even easier for England. We had seen this all summer from the Australians, whose batting had so often induced calamitous errors in England's bowling and fielding, and now it was good to see the boot on the other foot. Hussain's six off Gillespie was a wonderful example of this: the ball was not really there to be hit out of the ground, but that is precisely what Hussain did. The ball bounced on the tarmac beyond the boundary and out of the ground.

Gillespie, who had been such a powerful foil to McGrath all summer, ended with figures of 2 for 94 in 22 overs, treatment as rough as he had experienced in Test cricket for some years. He looks like the Count in the classic silent film *Nosferatu*, with his dark looks, his moustache and goatee beard, and with the ball in his hands is a frightening sight to any batsman. But he is no vampire in reality: the blood-sucking ends when he returns to the pavilion, where he is as popular with his opponents as among his own team-mates. The entire summer's series was played in very good spirit, with almost no disputes between the teams or individuals within them, and this is very largely because the aggression that the Australians show on the pitch is carefully channelled by Steve Waugh and the team manager John Buchanan, so that it never spills over beyond the boundary.

Butcher reached his century after lunch, but not without alarms which almost duplicated his first-innings suicide. On 97, he played the ball to mid-on and set off on another daft single. McGrath gathered the ball, but his throw was poor, and Butcher was able to regain his ground and his composure. When he did reach his 100, the Australians all made a point of congratulating him. As Gilchrist said later, 'We could see it was something special. I've never seen so many of our guys go in and congratulate a guy.' Butcher said afterwards that lunch had consisted of 'coffee and a couple of cigarettes', which is not perhaps the healthy diet that many sportsmen would advocate when there is a Test match to be won, but it worked for him. It was probably his craving for another cigarette that drove him to score the required runs at such a rate.

The 200 came up in an almost English fashion, with Lee bowling a no-ball. Lee had been very quick all day, his fastest being a 94.6 m.p.h. express round the wicket to Butcher, but not effective. His bouncers were usually easily ducked, and whenever his length and direction strayed, the batsmen took full toll. Hussain's 50 came up with a great square cut off Lee for four, confirming that the captain's batting form had returned at last. The partnership had lasted for three and a quarter hours when Butcher, on 114, was hit on the instep by a fast full toss from Lee: the resulting appeal was turned down. With the first ball of the next over, Gillespie hit Hussain on the pad, and once again the appeal was turned down. The 'Hawkeye' evidence on television implied that both appeals could well have been given out. In Butcher's case, it was an expensive escape, but not in Hussain's. The very next ball, he was given out caught behind, although this time the television evidence was that the ball did not actually touch bat or glove on its way through to Gilchrist. Two wrongs do not make a right, but at least if the ball did not touch his glove, it couldn't break his fingers again. Hussain left the ground to a standing ovation, out for 55. His partnership with Butcher had put on 181, beating the previous record third-wicket partnership for England against Australia at Headingley, 153 set by Bill Edrich and, of all people, Alec Bedser in 1948. It was also the second highest third-wicket partnership ever in England against Australia, behind only Gower and Gatting's 187 at Trent Bridge in 1985.

Records are all very well, but there were still 101 runs to be made. Ramprakash, another reborn England batsman, came in to join Butcher. There was just time before tea for Ramprakash to off-drive Lee for four, one of the shots of the day, on the up but perfectly controlled and perfectly placed wide, and for Butcher to pass his previous Test highest score, 116, which he had managed twice. Tea was taken at 222 for 3, so umpire Shepherd no doubt spent the whole twenty minutes with his feet up off the ground.

The weather was a feature of the day – bright and perfect for batting – and it remained so in the crucial overs after tea. Mark Butcher carried on exactly as before, not so much playing each ball on its merits as dominating the bowlers so that each ball was of less merit than it might otherwise have been. Lee in particular struggled to find any answer. Butcher even engineered four leg byes off his helmet from one less than perfect delivery. The 250 came up, and England were now closing in on the target. For the first time it was clearly England's game to win: only by feeble batting could they lose. The groundwork laid by Butcher and Hussain, and now by Ramprakash, was surely the basis for victory. Not even the introduction of Mark Waugh into the attack made a difference. The younger Waugh twin had taken Butcher's wicket twice before in Tests, so perhaps the idea was to see if a man closing in on his 150 could be upset by some gentle off-spin. He wasn't, and the Waugh experiment lasted just one over.

The 50 partnership came up in under an hour off just 74 balls. Gillespie replaced Waugh and Butcher and Ramprakash moved up a gear, Butcher hitting him on the up through the covers as though he was the man who taught Brian Lara how to play. Gilchrist, to his credit, was trying to maintain attacking fields, but by now it was clearly too late. When Butcher reached his 150, it was with yet another blistering four through the covers. He became the first Englishman to score 150 in a Test since John Crawley (remember him?) hit 156 not out against Sri Lanka at The Oval in 1998. He also passed the previous highest score of the series, Gilchrist's 152 at Edgbaston. And there were still runs that needed to be scored.

When England had made 289, and the partnership was worth 75, Ramprakash was brilliantly caught low down and left-handed by Mark Waugh off Shane Warne. Somehow the wicket was totally unexpected, although English crowds have learnt to expect a wicket almost every time that Shane Warne turns his arm over, and Ramprakash stood there while the third umpire was asked to check whether the ball had carried. In the end he was

given out, although there were some who still thought the ball had been taken on the half-volley. Still, it did not matter what others thought. The umpires thought he was out, c ME Waugh b Warne 32.

Usman Afzaal now came in, with four balls of Warne's over to survive. He did so, despite the final ball turning so much that not even Gilchrist could stop it going for four byes. At the other end Butcher decided it was time to bring the game to a close. The first ball of Gillespie's over was on-driven for four. The second ball was misfielded by Martyn, and four more went on to Butcher's total. The 300 was now up. The third ball of the over was square-cut for six! This was a great shot, safe and exciting at the same time, and it was the straw that finally broke the Australian camel's back. Butcher had scored 14 off three balls of the over, and there were now just eight needed to win. So he took a single, and gave Afzaal a chance to share in the fun. He did: a beautiful if extravagant square cut for four meant that England had scored 19 off Gillespie's over, and there were only three more runs needed to win.

The second ball of Warne's next over was the one: Butcher hit it for those magic three runs and England had won. Their total of 315 for 4 was the second highest score they had ever made to win against Australia in the 301 Tests between the sides, and the thirteenth highest winning fourth-innings total in Test history. What was more poignant was that Butcher's score of 173 not out was exactly the same score that Don Bradman had made in 1948, also at Headingley, when Australia had successfully chased 404 to win against England. Many people rated Butcher's innings the better of the two.

It was a euphoric moment for English supporters. Yes, we knew that the win had only been possible because Australia were not willing to settle

for a draw – the mistake England had made against Pakistan at Old Trafford – and we knew that Australia still had the Ashes. All the same, it was a moment to savour in a summer which had in all other respects showed us how far behind the superb standard set by the Australians we still were.

After the match, Adam Gilchrist was philosophical about the defeat. 'You have got to try to dangle the carrot, but it turned out to be a good batting wicket. We've been beaten a couple of times in the past eighteen months, and it's always taken a fantastic innings to do it.' Nasser Hussain agreed. 'Australia are playing their cricket the right way, and I commend their team and their captain. Today was the day we have been waiting for all summer.' For Mark Butcher, it was the day he had been waiting for, hoping for, all his life.

Nobody was asking 'What's the point of the Fourth Test?' now.

Butcher trots off the pitch waving a souvenir stump.
His was a truly great Ashes innings.

The Ashes 2001 FourthTest
England v Australia
Headingley, Leeds
16–20 August 2001
England won by 6 wickets

Australia 1st innings

MJ Slater lbw Caddick		21
ML Hayden lbw b Caddick		15
RT Ponting c Stewart b Tudor		144
ME Waugh c Ramprakash b Caddick		72
DR Martyn c Stewart b Gough		118
SM Katich b Gough		15
*†AC Gilchrist c Trescothick b Gough		19
SK Warne c Stewart b Gough		0
B Lee c Ramprakash b Mullally		0
JN Gillespie c Atherton b Gough		5
GD McGrath not out		8
Extras (b 5, lb 15, w 1, nb 9)		30
Total (all out, 100.1 overs, 449 mins)		447

FoW: 1–39 (Slater, 11.1 ov), 2–42 (Hayden, 13.6 ov),
3–263 (Ponting, 59.3 ov), 4–288 (Waugh, 66.3 ov),
5–355 (Katich, 84.3 ov), 6–396 (Gilchrist, 90.5 ov),
7–412 (Warne, 94.1 ov), 8–422 (Lee, 95.4 ov),
9–438 (Gillespie, 98.5 ov), 10–447 (Martyn, 100.1 ov).

Bowling	O	M	R	W	
Gough	25.1	4	103	5	
Caddick	29	4	143	3	(6nb)
Mullally	23	8	65	1	(3nb)
Tudor	18	1	97	1	
Butcher	1	0	7	0	(1w)
Ramprakash	4	0	12	0	

Australia 2nd innings

ML Hayden c Stewart b Mullally		35
MJ Slater b Gough		16
RT Ponting lbw b Gough		72
ME Waugh not out		24
DR Martyn lbw b Caddick		6
SM Katich not out		0
Extras (b 5, lb 7, nb 11)		23
Total (4 wickets dec, 39.3 overs, 182 mins)		176

Did not bat: *†AC Gilchrist, SK Warne, B Lee, JN Gillespie, GD
McGrath.

FoW: 1–25 (Slater, 8.2 ov), 2–129 (Ponting, 28.2 ov),
3–141 (Hayden, 31.4 ov), 4–171 (Martyn, 38.1 ov).

Bowling	O	M	R	W	
Gough	17	3	68	2	(2nb)
Caddick	11	2	45	1	(4nb)
Tudor	4	1	17	0	
Mullally	7.3	2	34	1	(5nb)

England 1st innings

MA Atherton c Gilchrist b McGrath		22
ME Trescothick c Gilchrist b McGrath		37
MA Butcher run out		47
*N Hussain lbw b McGrath		46
MR Ramprakash c Gilchrist b Lee		40
U Afzaal c Warne b McGrath		14
†AJ Stewart not out		76
AJ Tudor c Gilchrist b McGrath		2
AR Caddick c Gilchrist b Lee		5
D Gough c Slater b McGrath		8
AD Mullally c Katich b McGrath		0
Extras (b 2, lb 3, nb 7)		12
Total (all out, 94.2 overs, 428 mins)		309

FoW: 1–50 (Atherton, 18.4 ov), 2–67 (Trescothick, 22.4 ov),
3–158 (Hussain, 54.2 ov), 4–158 (Butcher, 55.5 ov),
5–174 (Afzaal, 60.5 ov), 6–252 (Ramprakash, 83.5 ov),
7–267 (Tudor, 86.2 ov), 8–289 (Caddick, 89.4 ov),
9–299 (Gough, 90.5 ov), 10–309 (Mullally, 94.2 ov).

Bowling	O	M	R	W	
McGrath	30.2	9	76	7	
Gillespie	26	6	76	0	(1nb)
Lee	22	3	103	2	(5nb)
Warne	16	2	49	0	(1nb)

England 2nd innings

MA Atherton c Gilchrist b McGrath		8
ME Trescothick c Hayden b Gillespie		10
MA Butcher not out		173
*N Hussain c Gilchrist b Gillespie		55
MR Ramprakash c Waugh b Warne		32
U Afzaal not out		4
Extras (b 14, lb 16, nb 3)		33
Total (4 wickets, 73.2 overs, 329 mins)		315

Did not bat: †AJ Stewart, AJ Tudor, AR Caddick, D Gough, AD Mullally.

FoW: 1–8 (Atherton, 2.6 ov), 2–33 (Trescothick, 9.6 ov),
3–214 (Hussain, 54.3 ov), 4–289 (Ramprakash, 71.2 ov).

Bowling	O	M	R	W	
McGrath	16	3	61	1	
Gillespie	22	4	94	2	(1nb)
Warne	18.2	3	58	1	
Lee	16	4	65	0	(2nb)
Waugh	1	0	7	0	

Umpires: S Venkataraghavan and D. R. Shepherd   3rd umpire: N A. Mallender

*captain † wicket keeper

Remembrance of Times Past

Fifth Test, The AMP Oval, Kennington, London
23–26 August 2001

Remembrance of Times Past

The Fifth Test

I love the Oval. The first Test match I ever saw, live, was there. It was against the Aussies, too, in 1956 when I was still in short trousers. I saw Denis Compton, and Laker and Lock and May and Cowdrey, Cyril Washbrook and the Reverend David Sheppard and best of all Frank Tyson. I saw Neil Harvey and Ian Craig, Keith Miller and Ray Lindwall, Benaud and Davidson and Colin McDonald who was caught at gully by Tony Lock off Tyson with as brilliant a piece of fielding as I have ever seen. I've been to many other Tests there too, some of wonderful memory, like the 1962 match against Pakistan when Ted Dexter (172 not out) and Colin Cowdrey (182) tore the Pakistan attack to shreds, or 1968 when Derek Underwood and a horde of spectators with squeegees mopped up the Aussies in the final, very wet day, or 1985 when in the glorious sunshine David Gower (157) and Graham Gooch (196) batted virtually all day, compiling a second-wicket partnership of 351 against a powerless Australian attack. The Oval always brings back great cricketing memories, but this is the new millennium and things have changed.

The Oval itself has changed. No longer the Kennington Oval nor even the Foster's Oval, a pseudonym it used for a few years, the place is now known as the AMP Oval, for reasons best known to the Surrey CCC committee. The pavilion, which looks like an ocean liner tied up in a dock three sizes too small for it, seems to have a new internal layout every season, so that only those with Geography 'A' Level can find their way around it. The ground itself is a South London antidote to Lord's – more informal, more crowded, livelier, more commercial and dirtier. Your average cricket watcher at the Oval wears a T-shirt and shoes when there's a need to be formal: otherwise it's bare chests and flip-flops. It's remarkable how two grounds in the same city can be so different in every respect.

The final two Tests of the summer were played back to back, a schedule almost unheard of in England. This meant the selectors had to delay their announcement of the squad for the Oval until a few minutes after Mark Butcher had sealed England's victory at Headingley with those final three runs off Shane Warne. The side that they came up with was notable for its omissions rather than its inclusions. Fourteen men were asked to come to the Oval:

Nasser Hussain (Essex, captain), Usman Afzaal (Nottinghamshire), Michael Atherton (Lancashire), Mark Butcher (Surrey), Andrew Caddick (Somerset), Robert Croft (Glamorgan), Darren Gough (Yorkshire), Richard Johnson (Somerset), James Ormond (Leicestershire), Mark Ramprakash (Surrey), Alec Stewart (Surrey, wicketkeeper), Marcus Trescothick (Somerset), Alex Tudor (Surrey) and, last alphabetically but by no means least in the eyes of the English public, Phil Tufnell (Middlesex).

The selection process coincided with the Cricket Writers' Club annual choice for the Young Cricketer of the Year. The search for candidates was an illuminating one. The obvious front-runner was Owais Shah, who had done well in the One Day Internationals but had then been studiously ignored by the Test selectors despite a very good season's batting average. Others with a good case for selection included Nicky Peng, the young Durham batsman; Rob Key of Kent, who was part of a revitalised Kent batting line-up in 2001; James Foster of Essex, widely tipped as Alec Stewart's latest successor behind the stumps for England; Ian Blackwell of Somerset; Ian Bell of Warwickshire, currently England's Under-19 captain; and Richard Dawson, the young Yorkshire off-spinner. The trouble was that while this was my list, you could bet that every cricket writer would have a different set of front-runners for his or her vote, and there was nobody who was pressing for immediate inclusion in the Test side.

The leading scorers of the summer continued to pile on the runs during August. Richard Montgomerie of Sussex hit a century against the Australians (which was trumped by one each from Adam Gilchrist and Ricky Ponting), while David Fulton of Kent hit three in a row, two against Somerset while the Third Test was under way, and one more against Northamptonshire between the

showers. The two against Somerset were both not out – 208 and 104 – and by the time he had made 188 against Northants, he had scored 500 runs without being dismissed. He went on to make 197. Suddenly his name was being seriously suggested for the Test squad, even though he fulfilled neither of the conditions that were being bandied around – he was not already an experienced Test player, nor was he young enough, at 29, to be part of the next generation of England players. What's more, he was an opener, and the one part of the England team that was by general acclaim not in need of repair or replacement was the opening partnership. Putting a promising opening bat into the England team out of position had already failed in the case of Ian Ward.

It is always difficult to know whether a prolific county player will make the switch to Test cricket successfully. There have been many cases of brilliant county players underachieving at Test level. You could start the list with Graeme Hick and Mark Ramprakash and work backwards. English county cricket is littered with them at the moment. Even the Australians have players who excel at State level but do not make the step up to Test cricket. Jamie Siddons, of Victoria and South Australia, the most prolific run-scorer in the history of Australian domestic cricket with 10,643 runs between 1984 and 2000, never played a Test. Some argued that if county cricket was to mean anything at all, then those who succeeded best at that level had to be given a chance at Test level. Yes, but in the case of David Fulton – nice guy, great natural talent, safest pair of hands in southern England – his success at county level had been for just half or three-quarters of a season after six or seven years of relative failure. The case for including him was not strong enough. Just to add to the confusion, two of England's more publicised rejects, Graeme Hick and John Crawley, chose the day before the Test to hit very big scores for their counties. Crawley was finally dismissed for 280 at about the time the captains went out to toss at Headingley, by which time Hick was also back in the Edgbaston pavilion, for 201.

There was no room yet for Michael Vaughan or Graham Thorpe, both of whom could be pretty sure of places on the winter tours but could not yet be sure of their own fitness. Vaughan had played a county game for Yorkshire while the Fourth Test was under way, but at the end of it admitted that he was very stiff and was not sure he could last a five-day Test match. Thorpe had not played at all since Brett Lee broke his hand, so even though the Test was on his home ground he was not considered. Throughout the Ashes series, England had not once been able to pick their first-choice top six batsmen. This was not an excuse for the loss of the series, but it was a factor in the margin of Australia's win.

Owais Shah duly won the Cricket Writers' Club vote for Young Cricketer of the Year, but did not make the squad; this was perhaps inevitable as nobody had played badly enough in the previous Test to warrant exclusion. Shah, like the rest of England's young batting lions, would have to wait to see whether he had earned a winter in the sunshine of India, the bracing winds of New Zealand or, politics permitting, the blazing heat of Zimbabwe. The only man to be dropped was Alan Mullally, who had bowled well within himself in the Headingley game but never looked like taking five wickets for eighteen runs as he had done in the tourists' game at Southampton. It turned out that in the course of the Fourth Test he had injured his ribs, and so he was forced to stand down, even if the selectors had wanted to persist with him.

Into the fourteen for the first time came James Ormond of Leicestershire and Phil Tufnell of Middlesex. The selection of the 35-year-old left arm spinner Tufnell was greeted with general enthusiasm. The Oval is always the ground where the spinners are expected to come into their own, the ground where Saqlain Mushtaq and Ian Salisbury are match-winners for Surrey. As Tuffers was bowling with all his old guile and success for Middlesex, it was no real surprise to see him included, along with Robert Croft, in the squad. Whether he would play, either with or ahead of Croft, was more doubtful, but the smart money was on him making the final eleven. After all, there were very few bowlers in England who could rightfully claim they had won a Test with their bowling, but Tufnell was on that shortlist. His enthusiasm had sometimes got the better of him in the past, but the word around the county circuit was that he was bowling as well as he had ever done. He had taken 55 wickets at 24 in the season so far, but like all good tailenders had scored fewer runs than he had taken wickets – just 43 had come off his multi-edged bat. The tail would be longer with him in the side (his career batting average was marginally lower even than Mullally's) but the game would also be more alive and more competitive for his presence.

The inclusion of the right arm fast medium Leicestershire swing bowler Ormond was a little more surprising. Coventry-born Ormond got the news of his inclusion on his twenty-fourth birthday, so he had double cause for celebration. He made his county debut against Oxford University, aged seventeen, in 1995, and toured Sri Lanka with England A in 1997/98, since when he had been mentioned in one or two of the more fanciful squads thought up by bored journalists looking for ways to fill their allotted column inches. In tandem with the ageless Phillip DeFreitas he had been a consistent spearhead for Leicestershire's attack, but it must have been the fact that he was still able to stand upright at this late stage in the season, as

The AMP Oval, Kennington, London

much as his penetrative swing bowling, that earned him his first Test call-up.

England had now either used or mentioned in despatches a huge array of fast bowlers during the summer – Gough, Caddick, Cork, White, Tudor, Sidebottom, Johnson, Silverwood, Hoggard, Mullally and Ormond all made at least one Test squad, while the likes of Steve Kirby, Glen Chapple and Martin Bicknell must have come very close. Bicknell of Surrey, two months younger than Andrew Caddick and almost three years younger than Phil Tufnell, must have been wondering what he had to do to get into the England side. At this stage in the season he was England's leading wicket-taker, having overtaken 38-year-old Devon Malcolm, and

he had just scored his maiden first-class hundred to save a game against Kent that had looked hopeless when he arrived at the crease. Bicknell had played two Tests in 1993 but had then dropped out through injury, and although he was just one of many whose fitness let him down from time to time early in his career, in the past four or five years he had been pretty well omnipresent in Surrey's championship and cup-winning teams. *Wisden* selected him as one of their Five Cricketers of the Year in its 2000 edition, since when he has, if anything, been playing even better. Surrey, with the backbone of their batting ripped out by the England selectors

Justin Langer, who was knocked cold by a Caddick bouncer that smashed into the side of his helmet, waits to be helped off the field.

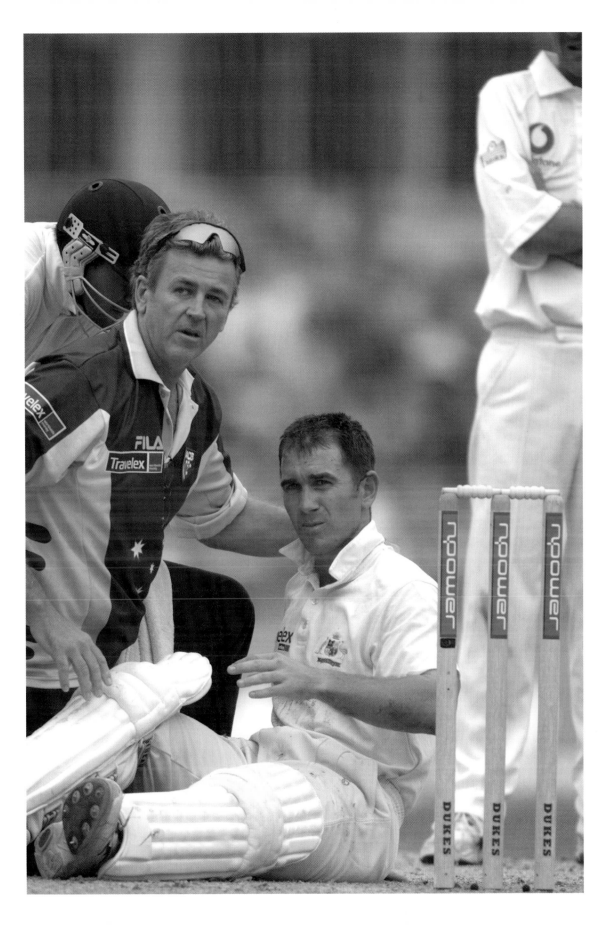

all summer, must have been pleased not to lose both their opening bowlers as well, but that was no consolation for the unlucky Bicknell.

As if to show that the England revival at Headingley did not mean that much had changed, Alex Tudor cried off the day before the match with a hip injury, apparently picked up during the Fourth Test. Tudor's run of two Tests in a row, the longest he had ever managed, thus came to an end, and there were now big questions surrounding his fitness, both physically and mentally, for the fray. Memories of Chris Old, the man who broke down whenever he was in the same room as a cricket ball, came flooding back. The raw talent is there by the gallon, but in Tudor's case the determination to overcome injuries and pain in order to represent his country do not seem to be sloshing around in similar quantities. He should look to Steve Waugh for inspiration.

Was Steve Waugh going to be fit for the final Test? Everybody who saw him stretchered off at Trent Bridge would have thought that was what the Romans called a *num* question: one which expects the answer 'no'. But two weeks later he was listed as 50:50 to play, and given the determination of the Australian captain to lead from the front, it seemed quite probable that he would come back into the side. If he did, who would drop out? It would be a little unfair on Katich, who had done nothing really wrong at Headingley, to be denied a second chance, but if he stayed, then who should go? The answer was simple: fairness has nothing to do with selection for the Australian eleven, and if Waugh came back, then Katich would drop out. His chance would come again.

That dilemma would be eased if Steve Waugh were not fit, as Australia could pick the same eleven that played at Headingley, but the problem of a shaky opening partnership would not be solved. Michael Slater set the cat among the

pigeons on the Wednesday by telling an Australian radio station that he had been dropped, and implied that his replacement as opener was the one man whose tour had been even more awful than his own, the occasional opener Justin Langer. The impression given by these odd remarks was that Australia were very undecided, perhaps even rattled. Long gone was the confidence shown by the way they had announced their First Test eleven three days earlier than they needed to, just to show the English they were on top of their game. In its place was the first sign of minor disarray. It would be wrong to suggest that the wheels were coming off the Australian juggernaut, but optimistic Englishmen thought they detected a couple of hubcaps working loose.

Steve Waugh announced later in the day that Slater had indeed been dropped, and that his omission was not entirely due to loss of form. There had been reports that Slater's understanding of the Australian team ethic had been rather sketchy of late, with a missed team bus and other misdemeanours mounting against him. Slater, like Mark Butcher, had been having personal problems over the past nine months, and there was no doubt that his form had suffered. He was not a member of the Limited Overs team, despite the pace at which he plays his cricket, and although the management were full of the usual statements about how he was dropped just for this one Test, and how he had every chance of regaining his place back in Australia, there was a serious possibility that Slater's Test career was over, at the age of 31 and after an unbroken run of 40 Tests. His replacement for this match, Justin Langer, was no more than a makeshift choice, so the longer-term issue of who will open the Australian batting remains to be decided.

The other man in danger of losing his place in the side was Brett Lee. His summer had been undistinguished, and there was talk of Colin 'Funky' Miller replacing him at the one ground where spin is a valid option. The interest then would centre on what colour hair Miller would be sporting. But in the end Lee kept his place, and the rumours of Steve Waugh's remarkable recovery proved true. It was indeed poor old Simon Katich who was left out, so his first bowl in Test cricket, which almost happened at Headingley, would have to wait for a month or two at least. The revelation of Colin Miller's latest hair colour took less time. He came out onto the pitch on the first afternoon on twelfth man duty, and revealed that this week, or at least for that day, his hair was a very bright sick-bucket lemon-lime colour.

The teams announced as the captains went out to toss were: for England, Atherton, Trescothick, Butcher, Hussain, Ramprakash, Afzaal, Stewart, Ormond, Caddick, Gough and Tufnell; and for Australia: Hayden, Langer, Ponting, Mark Waugh, Steve Waugh, Martyn, Gilchrist, Warne, Lee, Gillespie and McGrath

For England, James Ormond of Leicestershire became England's six hundred and seventh Test cap in 125 years. That meant England would be batting with a number eight, Ormond, whose career average was a smidgen under twelve, and a number eleven, Tufnell, whose career average was under ten. For Australia, Justin Langer was picked to open the batting for only the second time in his 42 Tests. The only other time he had opened for Australia was against the West Indies at the WACA, his home ground, in early 1993. He made 10 and 1, opening with David Boon, and Australia lost by an innings and 25 runs. England had to hope those omens were good.

There was another good omen, for those who believe that history repeats itself. This was the thirty-third Test between England and Australia at the Oval, and of the previous 32 England were currently ahead by fifteen wins to five, with twelve matches drawn. On no other ground do England have such dominance over Australia, and indeed their record at the Oval is even better than Australia's notorious dominance of England at Lord's. At Lord's, even including the 2001 victory, Australia lead by only thirteen wins to five, with fourteen drawn. Australia had not won at the Oval since 1972, eight matches ago. In 1997 England stole victory here by nineteen runs, and both Caddick and Tufnell had five-wicket hauls. England play well at the Oval. History is on their side.

First Day, 23 August 2001

With the proper captains Waugh and Hussain both back in charge, and opposing each other for only the second time in the series, the question was: would Hussain lose his ninth Test toss in a row? Of course he did! Steve Waugh called correctly and chose to bat. There was no doubt that it was a good toss to win, and Hussain must have been ruing his luck as he led his team out into the field. The weather was good, and apparently set fair, and England knew they had somehow to prevent Australia compiling a huge total on a pitch that looked to be as true a batting surface as had been seen all summer.

Australia's new left-handed opening partnership began with caution. Andy Caddick, in his fiftieth Test, began with a maiden, and Gough at the other end was also in a mean mood to begin with, his first spell of seven overs going for just ten runs. But the pitch was very slow, and it soon became clear that the batsmen would have to get themselves out if England were to prosper. They almost did that very thing when, with only ten runs on the board, Hayden played the ball to short leg and set off for a run, only to discover that Afzaal had fielded brilliantly. If his throw had been as brilliant as his fielding Afzaal would have claimed his first run-out in Tests, but it was wide, and Hayden scrambled back to safety.

Langer soon realised that this was the pitch on which to play himself back into form. It was very slow and there was a suspicion that the wicket-keeper and slips were standing too far back: a couple of times the ball was edged, but fell short of the slip cordon. Langer took full advantage of any England lapse, driving a no-ball from Caddick crisply through the covers for four. James Ormond came on for his first bowl in Tests when the score was 31 for no wicket, and immediately got the ball to swing. His first over went into the scorebook as a maiden, though it did include four byes off his second ball, which did not swing in as Stewart was expecting and anyway bounced under his gloves, further evidence of the keeper standing too far back. The days of Godfrey Evans standing up to Alec Bedser, a bowler of similar pace to Ormond, seemed very distant.

Australia continued to play carefully in conditions which were perfect for batting, if very hot and clammy. When the drinks break was called on the pitch at midday, the score was just 40. The broadcasters in their tiny quarters were complaining of the heat, but at least they were able to get drinks more often than once an hour. One of the oddities of the new, vast Oval pavilion complex is that the television and radio commentators have tiny little boxes in which to sit all day, and there is no doubt that it is not the favourite venue of the broadcasters. This is partly because the proliferation of companies with different bits of the broadcast rights means that where once there was a box for BBC Television and BBC Radio, now there have to be sub-divisions for Channel 4, Sky, BBC *Test Match Special*, BBC Radio Five Live and a horde of lesser channels, all of whom have some contractual right to be there for at least some of the time.

Broadcasting the Tests is an integral part of the Test match experience for the viewers, listeners, players and, perhaps most importantly, umpires. No longer are the commentators, cameramen and technicians just a peripheral addition to the game: they have become players as well as spectators.

The 50 partnership came up at 12.25, and at the same time the clouds gathered. This was Ormond's chance: conditions were perfect for his type of swing bowling. But the chance could not be taken, because just five minutes later the drizzle began, drizzle that was entirely unforecast and a great disappointment to all, players and spectators alike. Luckily it caused only a fifteen-minute delay, and when the players came back out the conditions were still very muggy. Caddick's first ball after the resumption, to Hayden, gave rise to a huge shout for lbw, and up in the commentary boxes 'Hawk-eye' was telling the world that it would have hit. But the umpire's verdict, which is the one that counts, was not out, and Hayden breathed again. If he had been out then, for 25, his Test career might have been in tatters like that of his erstwhile partner Slater, but luck was with him. He needed a little less luck to survive another appeal later in the same over when he put in a big stride but then left a ball that came back in from outside off stump onto his pad. This time 'Hawkeye' agreed with the umpire: not out, but living dangerously.

That was the way play continued through to lunch, which was taken after 24 overs with the score at 66 for no wicket. Ormond had Langer playing and missing a couple of times, and another edge towards the slips did not quite carry to Atherton, but England could not make the breakthrough. Ormond was bowling well: the pitch was not helping him but the conditions were. The question he was hoping to

Mark Waugh hits Gough for six: the picture that proves he too can play the cross-batted heave effectively.

answer in the negative was whether he would be yet another of those England fast bowlers who get one or two Tests, usually at the Oval, and then never play again. Oh my Igglesden and my Bicknell long ago!

After lunch, Langer and Hayden moved up a gear. The first 50 had taken them 116 balls to piece together, but they went from 50 to 100 in only 76 balls, and to the 150 in a further 64. The century opening partnership was the Australians' first of the summer, and for Langer it was his first partnership of any size since coming to England. His 50 came up with a big six off Tufnell over mid-on towards the scoreboard at the Vauxhall End, this three minutes after Hayden had also reached his 50 off Tufnell. In the first hour after lunch the pair added 70 runs.

Light rain returned shortly thereafter, and the players went off with the score at 146 for no wicket, with Langer on 67 and Hayden on 60. The total also owed something to the Extras column, then at 19 and looking good for a big score. England bowled sixteen no-balls during the day, a continuing drain on their efforts to contain and dismiss their opponents. At least they kept the wides column blank.

When they came back on half an hour later, Langer brought the 150 up with a lovely cover drive off Tufnell for four, and normal service appeared to be continuing. An over later Hayden tried a slog sweep, very flat towards the midwicket boundary. Unfortunately for him, but happily for England, he hit it exactly where Trescothick had been placed. The catch was a good one, low down, and Hayden departed, clearly annoyed with himself for missing out on greater riches, but all the same with 68 more Test runs under his belt. Hayden c Trescothick b Tufnell 68, Australia 158 for 1.

He was replaced by Ricky Ponting, another man who had played himself back into form over the summer courtesy of the English bowlers. Almost immediately he was the subject of a vociferous lbw appeal by Tufnell, and it must have been very close. Umpire Willey, however, turned it down. At this point, Hussain tossed the ball to Ormond and asked him to bowl a bit of off-spin. Ormond's skills as an off-spinner had been kept hidden to such an extent that even the authoritative *Playfair Cricket Annual* did not seem to know of them, and clearly another Jim Laker, the scourge of the Aussies in 1956, he is not. Yet suddenly here was our own Colin Miller, a bowler who could bowl fast or slow, according to his mood, but without the hair colouring. By the end of his first over, which showed him to be a flattish, quickish off-spinner, it was not just Miller we were comparing him to. What about Ian Botham, who bowled off-spin in a Test at Lord's once when he was feeling bored? Or Bob Appleyard of Yorkshire, who took 200 wickets in a season with the same mix of slow and fast, or Tom Goddard of Gloucestershire who switched from fast medium to become one of the great off-spinners of all time? Or even Gary Sobers! Perhaps we were getting carried away, but Ormond was doing his long-term prospects no harm by showing off his versatility. The Australian batsmen were duly reverential to this new talent, at least for a couple of overs, until it occurred to them that since the retirement of Lance Gibbs almost thirty years ago there has not been an orthodox off-spinner anywhere who has been able to turn a Test Match. Ormond, adequate though his off-spin may be, is merely another Hick, Vaughan or Ramprakash who can bottle up an end for an over or two while the better bowlers catch their breath.

For what it was worth, another off-spinner appeared in England colours at this moment – twelfth man Martyn Ball of Gloucestershire, a chubby chap picked for his availability rather than his fielding skills. He came on for Michael

Atherton, who was having ice treatment on a thigh injury. Fortunately for England's overall standard of fielding, Atherton was not off for long; when England batted, Steve Waugh, with a three-inch tear in his calf muscle, did not go off for treatment at any stage. Mental and physical toughness go hand in hand, and Australia showed all summer that they had more of both.

From then until tea, Ponting and Langer made untroubled progress towards the huge total that Australia had promised themselves. One top-edged sweep by Ponting off Tufnell did not quite carry to Michael Atherton, but that was as near as England came to another wicket. Ormond had another go in his quicker mode, and Ponting pulled consecutive balls for four. Langer spotted Tufnell's quicker arm ball and hit it through the covers for four more, bringing him to 87, the score that Australians dread, and the total to 200. But Langer did not linger on 87. Another single took him to 88, and then it was tea time, at 203 for 1 with Ponting 26 not out.

After tea, Langer made his way to his century in four balls: four, dot, four, four. A wonderful sweep off Tufnell took him to 96, and the next ball he cut for the four he needed to take him to his 100. He was a very happy man: his support for the team he could not get into for most of the summer had been widely appreciated, and now he was thrilled to support them the way he knew best, by scoring runs for them. This was his eighth Test century in all, and he became the sixth Australian to hit the magic three figures this summer. Of the top seven in this side only Hayden had missed out. Langer relaxed a little after all this excitement and let Ponting do the scoring. One Ponting square slash off Gough went to the boundary so quickly that no England fielder moved. It was all Australia with no relief in sight.

Langer scored two more runs, and then shaped up to face Andy Caddick. Caddick does not claim comparison with Frank Tyson of 1956, but the ball he delivered to Langer could have come from Mike Tyson for the impact it made. Langer thought about hooking the ball, but failed to judge how much and how quickly it was climbing at him, and as he turned his head aside it hit him full on the helmet, over the temple. Langer went down and stayed down. The physio and the doctor came rushing on to the pitch, and Langer stirred, shook himself and rose unsteadily to his feet. He took off his helmet to reveal a trickle of blood by his left ear. He was given some water, but was obviously in no position to carry on batting. He was helped off the field and up the stairs to the Australian dressing room. From there he went to hospital for a precautionary scan, but – to everyone's relief but nobody's surprise – quickly announced that all was well and he would bat again if needed the following day. These Aussies are a tough bunch without a doubt.

With Langer retired hurt, Mark Waugh came to the wicket, with the score at 236 for 1. He made it absolutely clear from the start that he wanted some of these runs that seemed to be on offer everywhere, and began hitting boundaries so crisp and so powerful that he even disturbed the pigeons who otherwise spent the entire day pecking at the grass seed on the edge of the square. Within twelve overs another 50 had been added, and there seemed to be nothing that would slow down the relentless progress of the Australian batsmen. The crowd tried at one point, by throwing onto the pitch a large number of soft red balls that had been given out during the game by some optimistic advertiser, but this did not cause enough of a hold-up to put Ponting and Waugh off their stride.

They were eventually put off their stride when Ormond

Over page: Steve Waugh acknowledges the ovation for his hundred, made on one leg, and in particular its final run, completed on none.

came back into the attack. Hussain was clearly not going to excuse him any punishment just because he was a new boy, and in his quicker mode Ormond persuaded Ponting to edge one to Atherton at first slip. This, though we did not know it then, was Atherton's final catch in Test cricket. Australia were 292 for 2, a crisis indeed, and Ponting was gone for 62, made off just 102 balls.

It was now ten minutes to six, and two lights were shining on the scoreboard. Would Steve Waugh come out to bat, or would he send out somebody else so that he could rest his injured calf for another day and be raring to go in the morning? Silly question. This was very likely to be Steve Waugh's final Test in England (the twins were now 36 years and 82 days old) and he did not want to miss a moment of it. He also wanted to take a close look at the wicket, which was showing signs of taking spin later in the match. Dust flew up as the ball sometimes broke through the surface: Shane Warne was no doubt sitting in the Australian dressing room with a very big smile (if not a pizza or a cigarette) on his lips.

Steve Waugh took some time to get off the mark, thirteen minutes to be precise, before he took a single that showed running would not be easy but that would not stop him. A little later in the day he ran a three. He was making no excuses and expecting no quarter for his injury. The 300 was posted by Mark Waugh, a beautiful extra cover drive off Ormond's slower ball (but still in his quick mode, if you see what I mean). It was all timing, as the best of Junior always is. The timing was a little less perfect next ball, when a direct hit on the stumps by Phil Tufnell, of all people, had the brothers struggling. The adjudication, quite correctly, was not out, but only by an inch or two.

The only thing that finally brought the inexorable slaughter

Previous page: Glen McGrath, the best bowler in the world

to a temporary close was the light. With eight overs still to play, the light had deteriorated to such an extent that even the Waugh brothers took the offer of the light from Peter Willey at just before 6.30. The score was 324 for 2, Mark Waugh not out 48, Steve not out 12. Mark Waugh had overtaken David Boon during the afternoon to become Australia's fourth highest Test run-scorer of all time, and Australia had taken away from England all hope of another Test victory.

Close of play: Australia 324 for 2 wickets (Langer 102 retired hurt, Hayden 68, Ponting 62)

Second Day, 24 August 2001

On the opening day Australia had plodded along at a mere 3.95 runs an over, while losing as many as two wickets. On the second day they picked up the pace, scoring a further 317 runs at 4.53 an over, while rather carelessly losing another couple of wickets. And they still had time to get rid of Atherton before stumps were drawn. On this beautiful sunny Friday, the Waugh twins in particular tore apart the English bowling, and English hearts, bringing back memories in mirror-image of the way Gower and Gooch had shredded Australian hopes on an equally sunny day here at the Oval in 1985. The only thing to be said about the day was that Mark Waugh, who made an exquisite 120 before generously giving his wicket away, was not even the most prolific batsman of that name in first-class cricket that day. His homonym Mark Wagh of Warwickshire was 266 not out at the end of a day's batting against Middlesex at Lord's, and on the Saturday he went on to make 315. Mark Waugh, the Australian version, has never made a higher score than 229 not out, but that was when he and brother Steve (who made his career best 216 not out at the same time) put on a world-record 464 for the fifth wicket for New South Wales against Queensland. With the two brothers together on a belter of a pitch, the England players cannot have felt too confident that the world third-wicket record would not have fallen to them as well.

It didn't, but that was not because of Mark Butcher. The hero of Headingley became, for a while, the villain of the Oval by dropping Mark Waugh off Caddick's first over with the new ball when a really easy chance was offered to him at second slip. The ball before, Mark had scored the two needed to bring him to his sixty-third Test score of 50 or more, and even the poker-faced Caddick could not disguise his disappointment. Butcher had taken some brilliant catches in the slips during the summer – the one that dismissed Glenn McGrath at Trent Bridge in particular sticks in the mind – but he has also made a couple of howlers. This was the second time he had floored an easy catch in the first few minutes of a day's play, and on both occasions England paid for the miss.

Hussain gave the new ball, which had been due the previous evening, to Ormond rather than Gough on the basis that the ball might swing; he had also spotted that Steve Waugh's injured calf meant that he was not using his feet as much as usual. England were not helped in the execution of this clever bit of captaincy by a series of misfields: Afzaal and Hussain himself were among the guilty men, on top of Butcher's disastrous drop. At 340 for 2, a Waugh straight drive broke the bowler's stumps, but Caddick could not get his fingers to it, and the non-striker made his ground back to safety. There seem to have been more cases of the straight drive that breaks the stumps in this series than in many of recent years, but none have resulted in that unluckiest of dismissals – the backing-up batsman run out as the ball grazes the

bowler's fingers en route to the stumps. Why are batsmen hitting straighter, and why are bowlers not bending down to field? One or two of the drives have been so hard that nobody who wanted to bowl again that year would put his hands in the way, and some have sent the umpire scurrying for cover, but we might still have expected one batsman during the summer to be seen trudging back to the pavilion cursing his luck and his partner's straight drive.

Throughout the first part of the morning Caddick bowled as well as he had done all summer, but without luck, and Steve Waugh limped heavily. One ball from Caddick over the top of middle stump almost cut him in half, but he kept his bat and gloves out of the way. Still the runs kept coming at a hectic pace: Mark Waugh brought up the 350 with a square pull over Phil Tufnell's head for four, and the next ball was caressed – if caresses can happen at 90 miles an hour – through extra cover off the back foot for four more. By the time drinks were taken, the score was 368 for 2. The brothers refuelled for further remorseless attack on the tiring English bowlers. It's funny; it's usually the bowlers who are described as 'the attack', but in this case, on this day, it was most definitely the men with bats in their hands who were attacking.

Mark Waugh decided that Phil Tufnell, who had just managed his first maiden in 25 overs of toil, needed to be removed from the game. This was shrewd thinking, as the only man who might have got among the Australians, even at 370-odd for 2, was Tufnell. The one potential danger had to go. And go he did, with one mighty straight six landing several rows back into the pavilion. The ball was not really there for the straight hit, but Junior fetched it from just outside off stump and thumped it on the full into the membership. The 100 partnership, their ninth together in Tests and their third of the summer, came up in 189 balls.

Steve joined his brother in the fun, as the total passed 400, by going down on one knee and whacking the ball from outside off stump into the crowd beyond mid-wicket. His 50 came up off the next ball, but it was obvious by now that he was batting on one leg. Even so, England were so much on the defensive that only Atherton (the man with the calf strain) was in the slips, and the Waughs were toying with the bowling. I remember watching Barry Richards in a charity game hit a hundred in no time. By the end of his innings he was turning his bat sideways and playing each ball with the edge. Still he hit sixes and fours at will. The Waugh twins found batting just as easy today, although there were very few edges.

Before lunch, Ormond had a twirl with his off-breaks, and so did Ramprakash. It made no difference: it was 440 for 2 when they broke for Butcher's cup of coffee and a couple of cigarettes (his example would no doubt be followed by fellow fitness fanatics Warne and Tufnell, but the rest of the players would have had the usual salad, pasta or just a look at the racing pages), with Mark on 92 and Steve on 77. After lunch, Mark made his move, to bring up his second century of the series, his sixth in all against England and twentieth against all opponents. It had taken him 161 balls, all of which he seemed to have under his complete control. The score was now 467 for 2, about as disheartening a total as England could imagine. And it was to get worse before it got better. What proved to be Mark Waugh's final scoring shot was a six over mid-wicket: with most batsmen this would be achieved by means of a hefty and perhaps inelegant pull over the outfield, but Mark does it his own way. He gave himself room to play Gough's slower ball into the off side, only to change his mind and pummel it into the cheap seats, where they cheered the sheer audacity of the shot. Mark was now on 120, Steve still on 98. That was it for Mark Waugh,

though. Giving himself room to play what looked like a one-day shot off Gough, he missed and was bowled: 489 for 3.

As one brilliant strokeplayer left the field, another took his place: the man for the crisis was Adam Gilchrist, promoted above Damien Martyn whose average was only in the low hundreds, obviously not good enough for the situation. All the Aussies so far had made at least 60, and there were still two centuries waiting in the pavilion for more jam. Once Gilchrist had got off the mark with a ball that bobbled past the unsuspecting Afzaal, the interest focused on how long it would take the limping captain to reach three figures.

It took him well over half an hour. The score passed 500 and still he was on 99. Then at last he hit the ball to mid-on, where a slight misfield gave him the opportunity: he dot-and-carried himself towards his goal 22 yards away and threw himself like a rugby winger for the line. Still prone on the ground, he waved his bat in the air to acknowledge the crowd. There was no doubt, though, that he would eventually get up and carry on batting. Steve Waugh on one leg is a better batsman than most men on two.

At 533 for 3, in the hundred and thirty-fifth over, Usman Afzaal got his first bowl in Test cricket. Afzaal, who bowls left-arm spin, had claimed nine wickets so far in 2001 at just 53 runs each – cheap at Kennington Oval rates. His first ball was a leg-side full toss, but his third ball was a wicket-taker: so wide that Gilchrist, on 25, should not have been tempted, but he was and he hit it straight and low to Ramprakash at cover. All this did was to bring in Martyn, who was instructed by his captain to get a move on. Unhappily for England, he followed that instruction to the letter. Only the pigeons in the outfield were

Mark Ramprakash hit his first home Test century on what is now his home ground. Unfortunately it was not enough to save the match.

unmoved as he tore apart the rest of the England bowling, taking fourteen off one over from Ormond and being almost as severe on everybody else. By tea time the score was 580 for 4, with Martyn on 25 and Waugh 137. Despite Steve Waugh's 30 minutes of abstinence, Australia had added 140 runs in the session, at 4.8 runs an over.

Tea did nothing for Waugh's mobility. He took a single off Caddick's first ball after the interval, but hobbled to the bowler's end and dropped his bat in pain as he got there. He was soon so immobile that England could slow down the scoring by cutting off the fours in the knowledge that Waugh could only run the easiest of singles. So Martyn took to the reverse sweep to find the gaps, and the 600 was brought up by a shot that even aficionados would have to describe as an extra cover wallop from Waugh. His next shot brought him his 150, and within a few minutes Martyn had reached his 50, in 43 balls with eight fours. It was a fathers and sons school game, except the fathers were giving no quarter.

Hussain tried everything, apart from Trescothick who successfully avoided his captain's eye every time he was searching for another man to serve up the cannon fodder. In the end, with Australia on 641 for 4, Waugh did the merciful thing and declared. In what was almost certainly his final Test innings in England, the bane of English attacks for over a decade had made 157 not out with an injury that would have kept most men in hospital for a week, and the entire Oval crowd stood to cheer him to the rafters (if the rebuilt Oval still has rafters). It was magnificent. In later years people will tell their grandchildren they saw Steve Waugh at the Oval, just as they will tell them they saw Mark Butcher at Headingley. The English bowlers will be less pleased to recall that they had to bowl at him: Caddick (no wicket for 146), Tufnell (1 for 174), Ormond (1 for 115) and Gough (1 for 113)

were the main victims of the Australian penchant for cruel and unusual punishment. Gough might have been consoled by the knowledge that, while he had been flogged to all quarters, his Yorkshire team-mates had clinched their first County Championship title for 33 years, beating Glamorgan by an innings, even though Gough himself had only played two games for Yorkshire all season. Craig White was the hero, hitting his second score of over 180 in the month to give Yorkshire the high ground.

England, very much on the low ground, were left with eighteen overs to negotiate. Australia, not unexpectedly, went on the attack from the start, so runs were not hard to come by if the ball was not in exactly the right place. For an hour England prospered. Trescothick was by far the more aggressive of the openers, but Atherton, in his understated style and making profitable use of that inside-to-out, lazy, pendulum scissor shot of his, kept his end safe. McGrath, who bowled mainly at Atherton, bowled his opening spell of four overs for five runs. At the other end Gillespie went for 35 in his first four overs. Trescothick made 30 of the first 35 runs scored. In the ninth over, Warne took over from McGrath, to see what the dusty pitch could offer him.

Of course it offered him help. At 58, he bowled a ball to Atherton which pitched well outside leg stump. Atherton thought he had it covered and left his bat raised, and the ball fizzed past him to clip off stump. Yet again a top-quality Test batsman was made to look like a beginner by another wonderful Warne delivery. Atherton, b Warne 13, the lowest score of the match so far. None of the other bowlers seemed to think much of the Oval wicket, including Lee who was hit through the covers to bring up Trescothick's 50, the seventh of the match, in just 49 balls. The final over of the day was bowled by Ponting, trying out his off breaks.

He raised a little dust but no alarms. Trescothick (55*) and Butcher (10*) ended the day together, with England at 80 for 1, needing another 362 to avoid the follow-on. A long day in the sunshine beckoned.

Close of play: Australia 641 for 4 dec (SR Waugh 157*, ME Waugh 120, Langer 102 retired hurt, Hayden 68, Martyn 64*, Ponting 62); England 80 for 1 (Trescothick 55*)

Third Day, 25 August 2001

It was noticeable throughout the summer that wickets tended to fall at the beginning of sessions, especially at the beginning of the day. Arrive late for the first over of the day, and the chances were that you would miss a wicket, or even two. This has happened more often to English than Australian batsmen, partly because England's batsmen are not as good as their Australian opponents, and also because at least two simple catches have been dropped by England's slips at the start of play. Today it was Trescothick's turn, 55 not out overnight, and 55 out to the fifth ball of the day, bowled by a Shane Warne delivery that did less than Trescothick expected – the double bluff that Warne uses so brilliantly. This brought Hussain to the wicket far earlier than he would have liked.

Without wishing to give away the ending, I can reveal that Warne finished the day with six wickets for 155 runs. This was a true representation of the way he bowled, and of the way the Australian batsmen had given him the freedom to bowl. He was not at his best, with far too many full tosses, half-volleys and balls going harmlessly wide for this to be described as one of his great days. But in amongst the lesser deliveries were a number of completely unplayable balls, and when a side has 442 runs to play with before their opponents even save the follow-on, it is the unplayable balls that

count. All the England batsmen were able to hit the loose balls, but only one of them could claim that he was master of the good balls too. That was, amazing to relate, Mark Ramprakash.

At the beginning of the year, you could have got any odds you like against the only two men to score centuries for England in the Ashes series being Butcher and Ramprakash. Neither was in the running for a place in the Test side, let alone a big score. Even if you had known in advance that the two centurions were to be Surrey players, you would have gone for Thorpe and Stewart, or even Ian Ward, ahead of either of these two rejects and has-beens. Yet in 2001 they both showed that rejects can be recycled, and that a has-been is always better than a never-was, because he might be again. Ramprakash's innings at the Oval in 2001 will, we all hope, mark the beginning of the 'proper' Test career that everybody has been hoping for, and expecting, from this very talented underachiever. I saw him hit a double century at Lord's for Middlesex against Surrey a few seasons ago; it would be hard to imagine a more complete, more stylish, more error-free innings than that one. The Surrey bowlers were not mugs, but Ramprakash could not be stopped. He showed all the batting talent in the world that day, but until today he had rarely brought that talent to the Test arena.

He came to the wicket with the score on 104, after Butcher gave Warne his three hundred and ninety-ninth Test wicket by playing the ball softly to Langer at short leg. Steve Waugh spent most of the day under the helmet at short leg or silly point because he could not move very much, but now it was Langer who held the catch. At 104 for 3 there were only 338 to go to save the follow-on. Ramprakash began quietly, while Hussain continued the good form he had shown in the Fourth Test, playing Warne with very soft hands and as late as he could safely manage. Warne wheeled away

practically all morning, and the only significant blow struck for England against him was by Hussain, who drove a half-volley straight into the backside of the swivelling Steve Waugh at silly point. Waugh would have a sore left buttock for the next few days which might make the flight home uncomfortable, but if he was flying Qantas you can bet they'd not begrudge him an extra cushion.

Without really noticing it, Ramprakash and Hussain brought up the 50 partnership, with Hussain very much the dominant partner. Steve Waugh gave brother Mark an over or two, and Hussain lofted him over his head for four. Lunch was taken with England on 158 for 3, Hussain one run short of his 50, and Ramprakash settling in on 12. After lunch, Hussain and Mark Waugh carried on as they had left off, and Hussain reached his second consecutive Test 50, no mean achievement against the Australian bowling attack. His was the eighth 50 of the match, and as it turned out, the lowest of them all. He tried to play Mark Waugh with soft hands, but they were too soft and the ball rolled back rather than forward to dislodge the off bail. Hussain, b ME Waugh 52, England 166 for 4. Enter Usman Afzaal, hoping to show that there is more to his cricket at the top level than just talent and cockiness.

Mark Waugh was promptly removed from the attack, having done his job, and Shane Warne, rested and pizza'd since his last spell, came back on. At 188, the great wrist spinner led a loud appeal against Afzaal, who had strayed out of his ground long enough for Gilchrist to whip off the bails; the third umpire was consulted and eventually Afzaal was given the benefit of the doubt. Warne's four hundredth Test wicket would have to wait a few more overs. Afzaal celebrated his let-off by carrying on as

Hussain's lbw in the second innings, to Warne for just 2, was the wicket that made England's defeat inevitable. The Australian fielders know it.

before, the flowing strokes more often than not connecting sweetly with the ball. In no time the 200 was up, and then suddenly he had overtaken Ramprakash and was racing towards a first Test 50. When the score reached 216, the half-century partnership, Afzaal was on 42 not out. The risks were paying off.

When Warne and McGrath both took a breather, batting suddenly looked as it should be: pretty straightforward on an easy-paced strip. When McGrath came back again, the batsmen had to work for their runs, but Afzaal, a real twitcher at the crease, worked hard enough to earn his 50. He got there with a single, square on the off side, and we all said, 'Now he has to go on to make a hundred.' I have to admit that none of us thought he would, and all too soon we were proved right. Afzaal, who will have many more chances to score a Test century, seemed so excited at reaching this first mini-milestone that his concentration just upped and left. He had made a mere four more when McGrath tempted him with a short ball to hook, and Gillespie took a very good catch at deep square leg. 255 for 5, Afzaal gone for 54, only one more recognised batsman, Alec Stewart, and 187 more runs needed to save the follow-on.

Stewart lasted until tea, but not without alarms. The last ball before the interval was bowled by Warne and pitched well outside leg stump. Stewart, despite the repeated advice of the media hacks not to sweep Warne, did just that and missed. The ball ripped back past off stump, past the startled Gilchrist and all the slips, almost all the way to the boundary for three byes. Tea was taken at 259 for 5.

After tea, only Ramprakash looked at ease. Stewart looked happy enough against McGrath, Gillespie and Lee, but could not play Warne except when he bowled full tosses. As the day wore on and the heat did not falter, Warne tired and the full tosses became more frequent, but the unplayable

balls were still mixed in there for the unwary batsman to ignore at his peril. Ramprakash eventually
reached 50 as well, his thirteenth 50 in 42 Tests. He
became the tenth batsman of the match to do so
and the fourth Englishman – the first time that so
many England batsmen had reached 50 in one
innings this series. The previous best was just two,
at Edgbaston and again at Headingley. When
Ramps got past 55 a few balls later, he became the
highest scorer of the innings and that was the
heart of the matter: the England players were
reaching fifty while the Australians were reaching
one hundred.

The new ball was taken and the 300 came up,
still with five wickets down, although Ramprakash
almost ran himself out in a carbon copy of
Butcher's *auto da fé* at Headingley. Luckily for the
batsman, this time the fielder, Lee, missed the
stumps. Gillespie was bowling as meanly as ever
with the new ball, and hit Stewart on the hand
hard enough for Dean Conway to be called onto
the pitch with the pain-killing spray. There was
some concern for a time as to whether Stewart
would be able to keep wicket in Australia's second
innings, but we should have known that would not
be a problem. Australia would not need a second
innings.

Stewart's dismissal came at 313, when he had
made 29. He was adjudged by umpire Willey to
have nicked a ball from Warne that went on into
Gilchrist's gloves. This was Warne's four hundredth
wicket in Tests, so the Australians celebrated even
more than usual. Stewart, on the other hand, did
not like the decision and walked off reluctantly.
Warne had become the first spinner ever to reach
400 Test wickets, and eleven of those wickets had
been Stewart's. The full list showed that the England keeper had also been both Warne's hundred
and fiftieth and his two hundred and fiftieth Test
wicket, so he was becoming used to trudging off

while the Australians mobbed Warne. Stewart's dissent cost him an immediate penalty: Talat Ali, the
match referee fined him 20 per cent of his match
fee for 'standing his ground for a short period
before walking off and indicating that he did not
agree with the decision'. The next day, the ECB sent
an official request through to Channel 4 for
footage of the dismissal so they could look at Stewart's reaction again. Unfortunately, the 24 cameras
had been concentrating on Warne's celebrations
rather than Stewart's slow walk back, so the evidence was inconclusive. The relationship between
broadcasters and the ECB has now become so
intertwined that the producer of the television
coverage has to ensure not only that his team are
putting together a clear and entertaining coverage
of the day's play – Elvis impersonators, airships,
pigeons and all – but also that they do not miss any
of the incidents that the authorities might need for
official purposes. The third umpire takes his infor-
mation straight from the Channel 4 edit truck, and
has no access to anything except the footage the
editor chooses to feed to him. Sometimes, as in the
case of Ramprakash's non-catch of Ponting at
Headingley, this can be unintentionally mislead-
ing.

Alec Stewart is England's buttoned-up man. He
wears his sleeves long, his shirt buttoned up to the
collar, and his trousers immaculately ironed and
perfectly white for each new day of cricket. He is
tidy in his actions as well as in his thoughts and
plans. He announced during the Test that he was
pledged to play for another two years for Surrey,
and would therefore be available for England also
over that period. The one exception was to be the
India tour before Christmas 2001. His official
reason for opting out was that he needed to have a
break after so many successive winters away from
his family on Test duty, although many people suspected that there was another equally powerful

reason behind his decision. The match-fixing enquiries, to which his name was linked before he was exonerated, had begun in India, and there were dark mutterings of the risk of violence against anybody who, like Stewart, had told all they knew to the investigation commission and then dared to come to the sub-continent. If Stewart was worried about his own safety he was unlikely to let others know it, but it is quite likely that his family's fears strengthened a decision already made.

Stewart went, and next ball Caddick followed him. The verdict was officially lbw b Warne, but there was a suspicion of inside edge onto the pad. If so, then he was caught at slip as well, so it was out whichever way you saw it. That brought Little Jimmy Ormond in to face his first ball in Test cricket, up against Shane Warne on a hat-trick. Situation desperate but not serious, and still 129 to avoid the follow-on. Ormond prevented the hat-trick and went on to play some good shots. When the rapidly tiring Warne bowled loosely, both Ormond and Ramprakash went after him. One over went for seventeen runs, of which four were bonus overthrows from Brett Lee. When England got to 350, it was the first time in the series they had reached such giddy heights. Australia had reached that level in every match except the low-scoring Trent Bridge Test.

England lost their eighth wicket at 350 when Ormond became the third batsman bowled by Warne in the innings. He had made 18 and had not disgraced himself at all. Warne now had 6 for 136, and with just Gough and Tufnell to come, things looked bleak for England. Gough, however, does not know the meaning of the word 'bleak' (well, he probably does, but he just didn't think of it now). The final hour of play was England's. They moved to 409 without losing another wicket, and, more importantly, Ramprakash reached his first Test century in England, with a swept four off Warne. It

had taken him 196 balls and he was understandably thrilled. The Australians, too, acknowledged the hundred with generous applause, and Ramprakash kissed the three lions on his helmet. He had secured for himself some warm winter employment. England ended the long hot day needing just 33 more to avoid the follow-on, and Australia with two wickets still to capture.

Close of play: Australia 641 for 4 declared; England 409 for 8 (Ramprakash 124 not out, Trescothick 55, Afzaal 54, Hussain 52, Warne 6 for 155)

Fourth Day, 26 August 2001

The Sunday was very overcast and humid, perfect conditions for bowling. Some had speculated overnight that Australia would bat again even if England did not save the follow-on, to give their bowlers some rest after the exertions of Saturday and to grind England's hopes into the increasingly dusty Oval surface. The weather had come to Australia's aid. In the much cooler conditions of Sunday, a day's bowling was less of an ask. Waugh was certainly going to enforce the follow-on if he could.

He could. The first Englishman to go, in the sixth over of the day, was Ramprakash, who tickled one that he could and should have left alone, and Gilchrist made his ninety-ninth Test match dismissal. Ramprakash had made 133: it was an innings, like Butcher's, to resurrect a Test career, but unlike Butcher's it was not an innings to win a match. The crowd rose to him. We love a plucky loser. Phil Tufnell, the number eleven's number eleven, lasted fifteen minutes and even hit a boundary before Gough was deceived by a ball from Warne that

Over page: The victorious Australian party with the Ashes Trophy (as opposed to the Ashes themselves)

did not bounce at all. Gilchrist took the ball at his toes and made a very smart stumping. England were all out for 432, having missed their target by just ten runs. Warne finished with 7 for 165, and Gilchrist became the fastest ever wicketkeeper to 100 Test victims (93 caught and seven stumped). For a man who they say is too tall to keep wicket and who lets through more byes than most, this is a remarkable achievement.

England's second innings got under way in murky light. Michael Atherton came out with Trescothick for what was expected to be his final Test innings. Steve Waugh asked Brett Lee to open the bowling, in the hope that he might at last turn in a performance worthy of his reputation. Lee bowled very fast, but without unduly disturbing the England openers. It was McGrath who did that. In the sixth over of the innings, with two lights on the scoreboard and a mist rolling in from the Thames, McGrath induced Atherton to touch the ball to first slip, where Warne took the catch. Atherton c Warne b McGrath 9 is not much of a final score, but we knew it was indeed his final score when the whole crowd stood as Atherton walked back to the pavilion, and the Australians and Trescothick applauded too. As he reached the foot of the pavilion steps, Atherton stopped briefly to raise his bat and acknowledge the applause.

Atherton was not, perhaps, a great cricketer, but he was a great competitor and a great influence on England, both as captain and as opening batsman, at a time when cricketing greatness was very thin on the ground in England. It was a dignified and moving exit from Test cricket, a chance for us all to remember and appreciate things past, and it was a privilege to have been there.

Steve Waugh's injury was now upstaged by brother Mark, who split the webbing between two fingers of his right hand while taking a ball low in the slips. So Mark was off for the day, and perhaps

the match, which left Steve with one less bowling option. In the event, it did not matter, as by 12.40 four lights were shining on the scoreboard and the teams came off. The weather then closed in for the day; by one o'clock it was raining hard and the car lights in the Harleyford Road shone like miners' lamps through the deepening gloom. Play was not officially called off until 4.40, but long before that most of the crowds had gone home.

Close of play: Australia 641 for 4 dec; England 432 (Ramprakash 133, Trescothick 55, Afzaal 54, Hussain 52, Warne 7 for 165) and 40 for 1.

Fifth Day, 27 August 2001

Sod's law, for the English team, would have it that Monday dawned bright and clear. A weather-beaten draw was no longer a possibility; if England were to get out of this particular hole, they would have to do it themselves. But they had batted brilliantly at Headingley to pull off an unlikely win, so there was no reason in theory why they should not bat through the final day to secure a draw at the Oval. Mark Butcher was still at the wicket, with Hussain and Ramprakash and others still to come. Don't worry, be happy!

Be happy, at least, that we had the privilege of watching a truly great cricket team, lacking only a reliable opening pair and a third seamer, take apart a pretty good team. England are not yet a powerful side, and are certainly not a great one, but still they justify their third place in the world rankings. It's just that the team in first place is a couple of leagues ahead of all the rest, and today that team dismantled the England batting as though it were a half-done jigsaw puzzle that needed to be started again.

The first piece removed was Mark Butcher. Steve Waugh, under the helmet, caught him off

Shane Warne when the score was 46. Trescothick fell two runs later, unable to keep down a ball from McGrath and lobbing back the easiest of caught and bowleds. Two more runs, and the third piece was put back in the box: Nasser Hussain, lbw to Warne. Five runs later, Afzaal, playing loosely again, was quite stunningly caught by Ponting at second slip, and 40 for 1 had become 55 for 5. England's hopes, and the match, were gone. Ramprakash and Stewart had a go at rebuilding the picture, but they had done no more than put in a couple of pieces of figurative sky before Ramprakash was caught by Hayden off Warne, so lunch was taken with six wickets down and Stewart and Caddick needing to repeat their century partnership at Edgbaston to give England any chance at all.

It was not to be. Even though England's notoriously fragile tail brought the score up from 55 for 5 to 184 all out, and only Tufnell made no useful contribution to the total, the Australian juggernaut was not to be diverted. Stewart made 34 before being bowled by a Warne special that pitched well outside leg stump, and England were 126 for 7. That was the last ball of the over, and to the first of the next over more bails went flying as Brett Lee claimed his only wicket of the match, to Caddick's disappointment. The memory of his first-baller in the first innings was almost but not quite obliterated by the Somerset man's 17 in the second: close but no cigar. Jimmy Ormond showed that his first innings had been no fluke by battling for almost an hour and a half for another 17, while Darren Gough flailed his bat mightily and constructively at the other end, but then Gilchrist snaffled Ormond up behind the stumps, as he had done to so many others so many times before during the series.

When this ninth wicket fell, the Australians formed their usual celebratory huddle, and Shane Warne pointed out to Glenn McGrath that they had both taken four wickets in the innings, with one more wicket to fall. 'Yes,' replied McGrath, 'and we've both taken thirty-one wickets in the series so far. And look who's coming out to bat.'

Phil Tufnell, for it was he, lasted just two balls before being caught Warne, bowled McGrath. It was a fitting end to the summer's cricket, with the two main destroyers of England's batting finishing off the England innings clinically and unselfishly: there was no danger that Warne would drop the catch. Warne was voted Man of the Match for his eleven wickets for 229 runs, and McGrath was chosen as Man of the Series for his 32 wickets at a shade under 17 each. At the end of the match, the PricewaterhouseCoopers rankings confirmed what we all assumed, that Steve Waugh was the world's number one batsman and Glenn McGrath the world's number one bowler. England have not had a number one in either batting or bowling since Graham Gooch headed the batting list in 1991. If the past is another country for England's cricketers, the present is another country too, and the country is Australia.

The papers were full of the debate over whether or not the Australians should and would be allowed to take the Ashes back to Australia. Figuratively they were doing so, of course, but physically they were not. After seven successive series wins, the Aussies felt they had a strong case for taking the trophy home, and there were many in England who agreed. But the Ashes urn itself belongs to the Marylebone Cricket Club, who are not keen to let the single most important item in their collection of memorabilia out of their sight. This was not a new problem: ever since the 1930 series, the first one played in England after the Ashes had come into the possession of MCC, there have been calls for the Ashes to be held physically as well as morally by the country that won the series. The answer has always been the same. In 1930 Dame Sybil Thorndike was asked to present a 'Consolation Cup' to the Australian captain Bill Woodfull after Australia had regained the Ashes that year, and there is newsreel footage of the ceremony, with Dame Sybil struggling to hand over a vast trophy to the bemused Woodfull. MCC would argue that if the Australian authorities do not know where that enormous 'Consolation Cup' is now,

then they are damned if they are going to let the tiny Ashes urn out of their clutches, as these colonial chappies would only lose it, don't you know.

The Australians, as ever, were one jump ahead. Steve Waugh and his team-mates got the bails used in the final Test, burned them and took the ashes back to Australia. They will be placed in a suitable trophy, and Australia's Ashes will be born. It is now up to England to win them back.

The Ashes 2001 Fifth Test
England v Australia
The AMP Oval, Kennington, London
23, 24, 25, 26 and 27 August 2001
Australia won by an innings and 25 runs

Australia 1st innings

ML Hayden	c Trescothick b Tufnell	68
JL Langer	retired hurt	102
RT Ponting	c Atherton b Ormond	62
ME Waugh	b Gough	120
*SR Waugh	not out	157
†AC Gilchrist	c Ramprakash b Afzaal	25
DR Martyn	not out	64
Extras	(b 10, lb 13, w 1, nb 19)	43
Total	(4 wickets dec, 152 overs, 624 mins)	641

Did not bat: B Lee, SK Warne, JN Gillespie, GD McGrath.

FOW: 1–158 (Hayden, 42.2 ov), 2–292 (Ponting, 72.5 ov),
3–489 (ME Waugh, 123.1 ov), 4–534 (Gilchrist, 134.3 ov).

Bowling	O	M	R	W	
Gough	29	4	113	1 (7nb)	
Caddick	36	9	146	0 (7nb, 1w)	
Ormond	34	4	115	1	
Tufnell	39	2	174	1 (5nb)	
Butcher	1	0	2	0	
Ramprakash	4	0	19	0	
Afzaal	9	0	49	1	

England 1st innings

MA Atherton	b Warne	13
ME Trescothick	b Warne	55
MA Butcher	c Langer b Warne	25
*N Hussain	b ME Waugh	52
MR Ramprakash	c Gilchrist b McGrath	133
U Afzaal	c Gillespie b McGrath	54
†AJ Stewart	c Gilchrist b Warne	29
AR Caddick	lbw b Warne	0
J Ormond	b Warne	18
D Gough	st Gilchrist b Warne	24
PCR Tufnell	not out	7
Extras	(b 3, lb 13, w 1, nb 5)	22
Total	(all out, 118.2 overs, 514 mins)	432

FoW: 1–58 (Atherton, 12.4 ov), 2–85 (Trescothick, 18.5 ov),
3–104 (Butcher, 30.1 ov), 4–166 (Hussain, 50.1 ov),
5–255 (Afzaal, 71.6 ov), 6–313 (Stewart, 86.2 ov),
7–313 (Caddick, 86.3 ov), 8–350 (Ormond, 94.5 ov),
9–424 (Ramprakash, 113.3 ov), 10–432 (Gough, 118.2 ov).

Bowling	O	M	R	W	
McGrath	30	11	67	2	
Gillespie	20	3	96	0 (3nb, 1w)	
Warne	44.2	7	165	7 (1nb)	
Lee	14	1	43	0 (1nb)	
Ponting	2	0	5	0	
ME Waugh	8	0	40	1	

England 2nd innings

MA Atherton	c Warne b McGrath	9
ME Trescothick	c & b McGrath	24
MA Butcher	c SR Waugh b Warne	14
*N Hussain	lbw b Warne	2
MR Ramprakash	c Hayden b Warne	19
U Afzaal	c Ponting b McGrath	5
†AJ Stewart	b Warne	34
AR Caddick	b Lee	17
J Ormond	c Gilchrist b McGrath	17
D Gough	not out	39
PCR Tufnell	c Warne b McGrath	0
Extras	(lb 2, nb 2)	4
Total	(all out, 68.3 overs, 283 mins)	184

FoW: 1–17 (Atherton, 5.3 ov), 2–46 (Butcher, 14.2 ov),
3–48 (Trescothick, 15.5 ov), 4–50 (Hussain, 16.6 ov),
5–55 (Afzaal, 23.5 ov), 6–95 (Ramprakash, 36.2 ov),
7–126 (Stewart, 48.6 ov), 8–126 (Caddick, 49.1 ov),
9–184 (Ormond, 68.1 ov), 10–184 (Tufnell, 68.3 ov).

Bowling	O	M	R	W	
Lee	10	3	30	1	
McGrath	15.3	6	43	5 (1nb)	
Warne	28	8	64	4 (1nb)	
Ponting	2	0	3	0	
Gillespie	12	5	38	0	
ME Waugh	1	0	4	0	

Umpires: P Willey and R. E. Koertzen 3rd Umpire: M. J. Kitchen

* captain † wicket keeper

Winter Talk By The Fireside

Francis Bacon, the Elizabethan politician and philosopher (but not a known lover of cricket) wrote that dreams and predictions 'ought to serve but for winter talk by the fireside'. This winter England have Test tours to India, before Christmas, and New Zealand in the New Year. Our dreams and our predictions are not usually the same thing (especially when we are talking of English cricket), but that will not stop us having them. Remembering also that Bacon was also the originator of the phrase about curing the disease and killing the patient, what should English cricket have learnt from the Ashes series against Australia?

Let us begin with the obvious: Australia are better than England at the present time, and indeed have been for a decade or so. They seem to be still improving, and are now, by the end of 2001, by a considerable margin officially the best team in the world. They clearly have many of the best players in the world – six of their top seven batsmen ended the summer in the top twenty rankings – but which comes first, the style of play and the attitude which breeds success, or the players to create that style and attitude? In Australia's case, immense effort has

been put into producing the players over the past ten to fifteen years, and the determination of their captains and managers to play positive, aggressive cricket has enabled the talented players who have come through to Test level to show off their skills in a way that they enjoy, and the crowds enjoy too. In England, we are way behind: only this year is an Academy getting into shape, under the leadership of the Australian Rodney Marsh. As yet there is no physical base for this central plank of England's cricket development, so for at least one year, and probably two, our brightest and best are going off to Adelaide for the winter to learn excellence the Australian way. This is clearly making the best of a bad job, as the likelihood of there being a bricks-and-mortar home for the Academy in England in the foreseeable future is slight. There is every danger that the siting and building of the National Cricket Academy will become a national soap opera, maybe a farce rather than a tragedy, along the lines of the National Football Stadium at Wembley (or not). The cricket authorities would argue that the Academy can exist without a home, providing that facilities are found as and when necessary. We shall see.

The cricketers chosen to be the first intake of the Academy, and who will thus spend the winter of 2001/02 in Adelaide, have a very different profile from the players who make up the bulk of the Australian Academy's intake. In Australia, the students at the Academy are just that – students who are hoping to make the grade in cricket. In England, all the cricketers named already have county contracts, two have Test caps and two more have toured with the senior England party in previous winters. Whereas the Australian academicians are almost all aged between eighteen and 21, the ages of the England squad range from eighteen to 25. The Australians are looking for mental strength above all, taking for granted the basic levels of skill and fitness required to get chosen in the first place. What are the criteria for selection to the England Academy? In his official statement announcing the winter sides, the Chairman of Selectors, David Graveney, said, 'In picking the National Academy Squad, the selectors chose a group of players that we believe will be very quickly pushing for places in the international set-up.' In other words, it's an A tour without the fixtures.

The players chosen were: Ian Bell (Warwickshire, current captain of England's Under-19 side); Stephen Harmison (Durham, a fast bowler who has been selected for England squads without yet winning a Test cap); Simon Jones (Glamorgan, a right arm fast bowler, son of the former England fast bowler Jeff Jones); Derek Kenway (Hampshire, a promising 23-year-old wicketkeeper/ batsman); Robert Key (Kent, a pugnacious opening bat of great promise); Steven Kirby (Yorkshire, a fast bowler who is already, aged 24, with his second county); Nicky Peng (Durham, a batsman and the youngest in the party, still only eighteen when the party was

Michael Atherton's last exit at The Oval. He acknowledged the crowd's ovation without actually looking at them.

announced); Chris Schofield (Lancashire, a leg-spinner who played two Tests under an ECB central contract in 2000); Andrew Strauss (Middlesex, an opening bat who ended the season in sparkling form); Graeme Swann (Northamptonshire, an off-spinning all-rounder who has toured with England and played a single One Day International); Chris Tremlett (Hampshire, the tall, young and very quick fast-bowling son of Tim and grandson of Maurice); Alex Tudor (Surrey – what is an established Test player doing at the Academy?); Mark Wallace (Glamorgan, another wicketkeeping prospect); Mark Wagh (Warwickshire, established 25-year-old batsman and occasional bowler who won his county cap in 2000); and Matthew Wood (Yorkshire, a 24-year-old who had a good season with the bat in 2001).

They are a motley if talented crew who will no doubt benefit from their winter in the Adelaide sun, but was their selection really part of a long-term policy rather than a quick fix? What about those who do not make the grade? Will they just go back to their counties with their secure jobs and their sponsored cars, and play at the workaday level until they earn a benefit, or will they be regarded as not good enough for county cricket if they are never going to challenge for an England place? I suspect the former. It is essential that the Academy set standards and goals for its graduates, so that they will not be content with the daily round of county cricket without a realistic prospect of Test cricket as well. Michael Atherton has retired from Test and county cricket in one fell swoop, and David Gower gave up the county game as soon as it became obvious that he was terminally out of favour with the England selectors. These are men who were not content just to earn a crust in county cricket; if they could not play with the very best, they did not want to play at all. This is the attitude we need to instil into more of our cricketers, so that county cricket does not merely encourage mediocrity.

The quality of county cricket is not improving. The new two-division system is having an effect that few would have forecast when it was put in place. With three of the nine sides in each division being either relegated or promoted, one third of the teams change divisions every year. This means that a team that has one slightly off season can find itself down among the lower regions for a season or two, and a county that has the rub of the green in the Second Division can flounder out of its depth in the upper echelons the following year. With the weather taking such a large role in English cricket as well, a club has only to have a couple of games washed out and a few of its stars awarded central contracts by England to find itself in trouble on the playing field. In 2001, the defending champions Surrey strengthened their squad Manchester United-style by importing Mark Ramprakash and Ed Giddins, but thanks to a combination of Test calls (six players totalling 26 Tests between them during the summer), injuries and a certain amount of under-performance, their season finished with one trophy, the B&H Cup, relegation from the First Division of the Norwich Union National League and a flirtation with relegation from the First Division of the Championship until they beat the newly crowned champions, Yorkshire, by an innings in September thanks to a maiden championship century by Ben Hollioake. It would have been ironic if they had been relegated, as Ramprakash had said that the chance of First Division cricket was one of the main reasons for his move across London. Meanwhile his old club Middlesex just missed promotion from the Second Division at the end of 2001. The long-term effect of all this movement will surely be that the difference between the quality of play in the two divisions will not be great. The County champions will be a better cricketing side than the team who finishes bottom of the Second Division, but it is likely to be shades of grey in between.

This does not sharpen up the cricket. The way to do that would be to make promotion and relegation very difficult indeed: if there was just one up and one down each year, players would be more determined to play for a First Division club, and competition would become much fiercer. Perhaps a better way of achieving this competitive edge would be to abandon the County Championship and introduce instead a regional championship, of, say, eight teams, beneath which the county and other local sides would provide a pyramid for aspiring cricketers to work their way up. If there were only, say, 100 professional cricketers in the country, instead of nearer 300 at present, they would have to show their worth every day, and those who are not quite good enough would soon discover that fact, and not just play on making useful contributions from time to time while they wait for the benefit to roll round. There are far more professional cricketers in England than in any other nation, but that has not made us better. All it has done is complicate the selectors' decisions: is Jim Blank of Whereshire really a Test-class player or is he just enjoying a purple patch at county level? That is why in England in 2001 there were 70 cricketers who had appeared at least once for England in a Test. This compares with just 35 Test-capped Australians.

It can be very difficult to pick out the Test players from the rest. For every natural talent that any old fool could spot, your Athertons, Thorpes and Goughs, there are twenty who look as though they might be the real thing, but who only flatter to deceive. And then there are the David Steeles and the Trescothicks, whose county form would not make one think they were of Test calibre, but who in the event exceed those expectations. County cricket only complicates the issue. The first time I saw Atherton play was for Cambridge University against Essex in 1989, and Mark Waugh was playing for Essex. He was dismissed for 92, lbw b Atherton! It was easy to pick out those two as stars, even though Atherton scored very few runs. It was more difficult to spot the other Test players-to-be on show – Steve James of Cambridge University and Glamorgan, and Mark Ilott of Essex. Who'd be a selector!

I've seen Alex Tudor many times playing for Surrey, and he always manages to look like somebody with all the talent in the world, which he then only applies on odd occasions. He has some way to go before he can match the consistency of a McGrath, a Donald or even a Gillespie, and I suspect that as long as he continues to do most of his bowling on county pitches which tend to favour bowler more than batsman he will be like practically all of his peers on the county circuit, a man who does not need total consistency to achieve good, even match-winning, analyses. This makes for lazy bowling and it is no coincidence that the English county circuit is no longer a breeding ground for either Test batsmen or Test bowlers. County batsmen can compile runs against workaday bowlers, and good bowlers can take wickets against run-of-the-mill batsmen. The cricket is designed for people with a reasonable talent but no real flair to succeed. Conformity rules, in a sport where non-conformist original thought has always been the way forward.

In 2001, there were almost no bowlers of international quality playing regular county cricket. The overseas stars, with the exception of Saqlain at Surrey, Muralitharan at Lancashire (for half a season) and Andy Bichel at Worcestershire, were all batsmen or batting all-rounders, and the England

bowlers, such as Caddick and Gough, were centrally contracted and played no more than a couple of games for their counties. No wonder lesser talents like Fulton, Montgomerie, and even England discard (or is he?) Graeme Hick had good seasons.

We cannot blame the counties for this state of affairs. They quite rightly put their own interests first, which means that the pitches and the playing squads are prepared to win trophies, not to provide England with players who will then scarcely be available for their own counties. However, self-interest and the national interest are not so far apart. If cricket is to attract new fans to watch at all levels, then it has to be worthy of banner headlines and plenty of column inches on the back pages of the tabloids, as well as in the sports supplements of the broadsheets. That only happens when the national side is strong. The profile of the average county membership is reflected in the fact that at the end of the 2001 season Kent CCC announced a new sponsorship deal with Saga, the holidays to insurance group which deals exclusively with the over-50s. 'Its membership has many parallels to our customer base. We see this as a marketing opportunity as well as a chance to provide direct support to the development of our county cricket club,' said a Saga spokesman. While not wishing to knock a very successful company, it seems odd that county cricket should want to identify itself as being of particular interest to the middle-aged and above.

A strong national side helps the county sides: every county chairman would agree with that, so club versus country should not be an issue. The problem is that the chairman of Leicestershire, for example, might be happy for six Surrey players to be used by England, and for two of them to score Ashes centuries and thus raise the whole level of interest in cricket in the land, but the chairman of

Surrey, although proud of his players' efforts on England's behalf, would no doubt wish that they had been a little more available for Surrey's attempt to win the Championship for a third year in a row. The chairman of Essex, after an awful county season, would no doubt agree with his Surrey counterpart that injuries suffered by players on England duty are another – broken – bone of contention.

What can the cricket authorities do to stop injuries occurring, or at the very least to keep them to a minimum? The first thing to note is that cricket is played with a hard ball, and although it is not a contact sport per se, injuries are bound to occur. The second factor is that cricket has become more directly confrontational ever since the 1970s when the West Indian fast bowling attack was feared as much for its ability to produce injury as for the brilliance of its skills. Mike Gatting, Paul Terry and Andy Lloyd were just three names on the injured list, and today we hear commentators extolling the brilliance of a bouncer that in the days before helmets might have killed the batsman. Bodyline may be dead, but its spirit lives on. That is why the re-emergence of truly world-class spin bowlers like Shane Warne, Muttiah Muralitharan and Saqlain Mushtaq is so encouraging, because they prove that cricket is still a game of subtlety and artistry and not merely the bludgeoning of batsmen into submission by speed. Having said that, the greatest fast bowlers, like Glenn McGrath, Courtney Walsh, Fred Trueman and Malcolm Marshall, are and were all masters of subtlety and artistry as well as speed. Although sometimes they will hit a batsman, their bowling is intimidatory in the sense that that batsman never knows which ball is going to get his wicket, rather than which ball is going to break his arm or his nose.

The law-makers and the umpires have a responsibility here too. There seems to be too much desire to tinker with the laws and not enough desire to apply them fairly. If the game is not to be dominated by fast bowling, one of the more important issues is that of time-wasting. Some people would argue that the crowds want to see excitement and a result, and if that requires a consistent barrage of fast bowling at a rate of ten overs an hour, so be it. Nobody will complain as long as the game ends in a win. That argument is the same one that says that supermarkets are a good thing because they give every customer a wide choice, good quality and cheap prices, and if that causes village stores to shut down, no matter, as the greater good has been served. Fast bowling is the Tesco of cricket, because it provides an efficient service, usually of the highest quality, and it brings results. If it means that customers actually only witness 70 overs a day, compared to around 120 a day in county cricket forty years ago, does that matter? Spin bowlers can still survive, but they have to be exceptional, like Warne, Murali and Saqlain. This surely is a good thing: there are no easy ways to the top in any sport, and a cricketer who has to prove himself against the odds must indeed be a wonderful player.

This argument has a certain force, and few would suggest that Tesco has had a purely baleful influence on shopping in Britain (especially not Lord MacLaurin). However, fast bowling is just one part of the glory of cricket, just as supermarkets are just one part of the glorious retail trade, and to keep it that way we need the clear application of controls to ensure the survival of all aspects of the game, including good spin bowling. The great advantage of sport over real life is that sport does not exist beyond the framework of its rules. Legislators can change a sport quite easily; it is less easy to legislate, for example, in favour of village stores, because the consequences of such restrictions are impossible to foresee. It is often equally hard to anticipate the players' reaction to a new law: coaches and strategists will always find ways that the authorities had not imagined to get round a new piece of cricketing legislation, so the best answer usually is not to tinker with the laws at all. What was good enough for 'W.G.' and Bradman should be good enough for us. The new laws against unfair play, with the award of five penalty runs for breaches of the spirit of the laws, may well help prevent sledging and time-wasting, and thereby incidentally help keep spinners in business and the volume on the stump microphones up. But we can be sure that some of the more Machiavellian cricketing strategists are even now staying up late to work out how to earn enough penalty runs to win a match before it has started. It will happen.

That would, of course, be entertaining, and cricket, like all professional sport, is entertainment. Spectators expect a good show as well as skilful cricket (or even in preference to skilful cricket), and this is where television comes in. The relationship between cricket and television has changed rapidly over the past ten years or so; where once it was there to report on events, now it is helping to shape them. Channel 4, who now have most of the rights to Test Matches in England, admit that it was a proud moment when the BAFTA for Best Sports Programme was won in 2000 by their cricket coverage, but to win that award they had to create a programme, not merely an outside broadcast coverage. A disgruntled viewer wrote to Channel 4 recently, saying that he was no longer watching a cricket match, he was 'subjected to a television programme'. Channel 4 staff would take this as a compliment, not as a criticism, but by turning cricket into a television entertainment – very successfully, it must be said – the programme's producers are creating a hybrid

that is not quite cricket and not merely television either.

Watching cricket on television is by far the most common way of following the game these days. Even at a Test we watch the big screen to relive the moments of tension or doubt, and at county games where there is no television we miss the instant replay. But television is merely a clever technology. It is not infallible, and is not there to help the players, the umpires or the administrators. It is there to provide entertainment. The relationship that is now building between, for example, Channel 4 and the ECB, is very cordial but there is a danger that it will distort the game. Channel 4's 26 cameras, fifteen miles of cable, effects microphones, super slo-mo replays and all the other pieces of electronic wizardry are used according to the wishes of the programme director, not the ECB. The ground and match authorities have no control on the positioning of cameras, and the cameras are not officially part of the match. The third umpire is looking at the same pictures that we see at home or in the pub, and should reach the same decision that any one of us who has a reasonable grasp of the laws could make. Disputed catches, run-outs and lbws can be replayed on television as often as you like, but even the 'Hawkeye' technology, the 'Red Zone' and the see-through batsmen cannot replace the human skills and frailties of the umpires. Nor should they. At present the players are at the mercy of the decisions of two men in white coats, appointed by the relevant cricket authority and standing with the players on the field. If this were to change so that the players were increasingly at the mercy of a television director whose first priority must be to make a BAFTA-winning programme rather than to see fair play on the cricket pitch, then the game would suffer permanent damage.

If television technology is to be used more and more within the game to control the game, then the cameras need to be controlled by the match authorities, not the television companies. And that costs a great deal of money. For run-outs and stumpings, OK, the positioning of a camera or two square to the wicket is easily done, and the decision is easy to make even in two dimensions. But for lbws, catches which did or did not carry and a host of other less predictable events, the umpire on the field has to be the ultimate arbiter, not the television company. When the match referee made an official request for videotape of Stewart's dismissal in the Oval Test, so that he could judge the extent of his dissent (this on the the day after Stewart had been fined twenty per cent of his match fee for the crime), the television company reported that the tapes all showed Warne's reaction to his four hundredth Test wicket, rather than Stewart's to his dismissal. This was good camera work from Channel 4's point of view, but not from the ICC's. This is but one small example of the conflict of interest. The only thing we can be certain of is that there will be more, and on more important issues, in seasons to come.

That is not to suggest that there should only be 'official' television coverage of Test cricket. The Channel 4 coverage is much better as a shop window for cricket than the BBC's more staid approach used to be. Other times, other methods. I have been a fan of the stump mike ever since we overheard Stephen Boock, the New Zealand left arm spinner of a decade or so ago, describe himself as 'you big girl's blouse' when he was out for another duck in a Test. I like 'Hawkeye' (although I'm not sure I believe it all the time), and I think the snickometer is a remarkable gadget. Simon Hughes' analysis is not only astute, it is a fascinating way of opening up the mysteries of cricket to the armchair viewer. And of course, there is always Richie Benaud. The man who was one of the great captains of cricket is now indisputably one of the great commentators on the game. 'Good shot for three,' that is his catchphrase, as EJ Thribb would say. Listen to others try to emulate him. 'Good shot for three,' they say; 'oh no, it's just reached the rope. Good shot for four.' Benaud has all the facts at his fingertips (especially if his fingertips are within range of his laptop) and he interprets those facts brilliantly. Between his spots on air he barely ever leaves the commentary box, and he brings his own sandwiches every day. He is an obsessive, of course, but a witty, observant and outgoing obsessive, which is what the ideal commentator should be. He does not believe that the game was by definition better in his playing days; he is loud in praise of the cricketers of today if they deserve it. He brings the game to life in his understated way, and everyone else in the commentary box struggles to keep up with him. Next season, Michael Atherton will probably be in there with him, another cricketer trying to prove that commentary is easy. The only thing the ex-cricketers usually prove is that it is certainly easier to play the game from the commentary box, and probably easier to commentate on it from the middle of the pitch where nobody can hear you unless the stump mikes are turned up to the full. Becoming an entertainer after years of opening the batting is not an easy transformation to make.

If the question that remains after the Ashes series is still 'Whither England?', then the immediate answer is 'India and New Zealand'.. The same team has been chosen for both tours, despite the gap between them (so that the players can spend Christmas at home) and despite the vast difference in playing conditions in the two countries. By issuing just one contract to cover both tours, the ECB is firstly disqualifying both Alec Stewart and Darren Gough, who both said they wanted to miss

The Ashes trophy, a many times life size glass replica of the original urn. Steve Waugh holds up the trophy: a job well done by a great captain leading a great side.

side shaped for Indian pitches and climates. England will probably also be taking to New Zealand one or two players who will have poor tours of India (somebody always has a bad trot on tour) and who would be dropped if it were not for the cost of their contracts. This seems like a deliberately perverse policy just to show some of the players who is in control, but we shall see. Will we really need three spinners in New Zealand? Is it the India leg, and secondly condemning England to play in New Zealand with a side shaped for Indian pitches and climates. England sensible to do without the talismanic Darren Gough, who by the New Year will have rested after the rigours of the 2001 season and of his benefit year?

The sixteen men entrusted with the very difficult task of taking on India at home, and then having a go at the improving New Zealand side, are: Nasser Hussain (Essex, captain); Usman Afzaal (Nottinghamshire); Mark Butcher (Surrey); Andrew Caddick (Somerset); Robert Croft (Glamorgan); Richard Dawson (Yorkshire); James Foster (Essex); Ashley Giles (Warwickshire); Warren Hegg (Lancashire); Matthew Hoggard (Yorkshire); James Ormond (Leicestershire); Mark Ramprakash

(Surrey); Graham Thorpe (Surrey); Marcus Trescothick (Somerset); Michael Vaughan (Yorkshire) and Craig White (Yorkshire).

The only uncapped players in the squad are off-spinner Richard Dawson and wicketkeeper James Foster, the two youngest players in the side. The oldest is Warren Hegg, who will turn 34 during the New Zealand tour. No fewer than four finished the season with injury doubts, but even so there were few surprises. The batting looks strong. We have four people who scored Test centuries in the summer of 2001, Trescothick, Vaughan, Butcher and Ramprakash, and two more, Hussain and Thorpe, who did so on England's tours to Pakistan and Sri Lanka the previous winter. If they can all stay fit and in form, two very big ifs after the rigours of an Ashes summer, then we should be able to compile big scores away from home.

The bowling is more of a concern. Without Darren Gough, the opening attack looks flimsy. Who will support Caddick? The front runner must be Matthew Hoggard, but with only Ormond, essentially a swing bowler, and Craig White to support these two, fitness will be paramount in a country where English cricketers have always found it a problem. There's always Butcher and Trescothick to bowl a bit of gentle medium pace as well, but neither of them are potential Test Match winners with the ball. Alex Tudor has joined the Academy, and Ryan Sidebottom is in the one-day squad, but what's happened to Richard Johnson or Chris Silverwood or Alan Mullally or Dominic Cork or any of the other names bandied about during the summer? It may make sense to pack the side with spinners for India, but the three specialists who have been chosen are not likely to give Tendulkar or Ganguly, or even Stephen Fleming, many sleepless nights; nor are Vaughan and Ramprakash, the part-time off-spinners. There are no Muralis, no Warnes, nor even any Vettoris making

their way through English county cricket at the present time, and if Chris Schofield and Graeme Swann are considered to be Academy students rather than Test cricketers, then we must make do with what we have. Let us hope the whole team proves us wrong.

Only seven of the senior side, Hussain, Foster, Hoggard, Ormond, Ramprakash, Trescothick and White, were in the one-day side expected to go to Zimbabwe. They were an odd seven to choose, as of these only Hussain has played in even as many as 50 One Day Internationals. The most experienced of them all, Graham Thorpe, has been left out. Ashley Giles and Robert Croft would also have strengthened the one-day side, but we have to assume that the selectors knew what they were doing. As Graveney explained, 'With regard to the Zimbabwe ODI series, the selectors intend to use this squad to explore various options. There are a number of senior players who have been omitted but they will remain part of the thinking for the next World Cup.' By which time the split between Limited Overs cricket and first-class cricket may have widened still further.

It seems very likely that by the end of the first decade of the new millennium, the two forms of cricket will be as far apart as Rugby League and Rugby Union, with only a few players attempting both codes at the highest levels. Specialisation is gathering momentum in all sports – look at the different players who dominate hard court and grass court tennis tournaments, for example – and there is no reason that cricket should be left out of this trend. Already there is quite a difference between the counties in the First Division of the Cricinfo Championship and those in the top division of the Norwich Union Limited Overs league. Almost all national squads have players who specialise in one-day cricket. Michael Bevan has for several seasons been the best one-day cricketer in the world, but he cannot get near the Australian Test team any more. Players like Neil Fairbrother, Alan Mullally and Mark Ealham have been significantly more successful in the shorter version of the game, while the likes of Nasser Hussain, Mark Taylor and Justin Langer are considered Test players pure and simple. The two codes will drift apart, and it is up to the authorities to ensure that support for the longer version does not fall away as a result, as already happens on the sub-continent. It is a difficult problem, and one that English cricket alone cannot solve, but it will move increasingly to the forefront of the administrators' in-trays as the third millennium gets into its stride.

What else did I learn as I chased around the country watching the 2001 Australians? I learnt that the most comfortable seats at a Test match ground are at Trent Bridge, where, however, the worst food of any Test match ground rather takes the edge off the day. I decided that the bas-relief tribute to Sir Leonard Hutton at the Oval is a far better work of art than the new gates at Headingley, and that Brett Lee still has a way to go before he is a threatening Test bowler again. I had my belief reinforced that a player's form in one-day cricket is no pointer to his form in the longer game, and that something must be done to improve the mopping-up of cricket grounds, especially the outfields, after rain. I rejoiced in the batting of Gilchrist and the Waugh twins, the one for the first time and the others, sadly, for probably the last time. I enjoyed the revival in the careers of our top Marks, Butcher and Ramprakash. We can only hope that their Test hundreds were not just a couple of flashes in the pan, but the start of solid second (or in Ramprakash's case, fifth or sixth) Test careers for England. It was almost frightening to watch the power

of Ponting and Martyn, and the persistent and unflagging accuracy of Glenn McGrath. Shane Warne is still extraordinary – though you know he can turn the ball a couple of metres, it is still a surprise when he does. How a man can do what he does on a diet of pizza and cigarettes will continue to confound the sports fitness experts, and how much longer he can go on doing what he does will continue to confound the surgeons who have worked on his shoulder over the years. Behind the bleached-blond hair and the angelic smile is a very hard and dedicated competitor.

I learnt a little about sports injuries, and about recovering from them quickly like Steve Waugh or slowly like Graham Thorpe. I still found advertisements around the grounds that made no sense, and logos which must have been created by designers whose hatred of cricket is so strong that they want to blind those who watch the game by forcing them to look all day at these hideous scars on the pitch, or at least make them want to throw up (if the Trent Bridge chicken pieces haven't done that already). I've seen people in all sorts of fancy dress – two dozen Elvises at the Oval, several Jimmy Saviles and the usual swarm of Roman gladiators and bearded nuns at every other ground – but the best fancy dress all summer was Colin Miller's amazing Technicolour hair. I've enjoyed it all, from Katich's century at Arundel to Ramprakash's century at the Oval and all points between. It has been a great summer, not because the cricket was evenly matched (it wasn't, most of the time), but because we saw wonderful cricket played by some of the greatest cricketers of this or any age. Look back on the Ashes 2001 and smile: we may not see another team as good as these Australians for a long time to come.

Appendix

The Statistics

2001 Test Series Averages

Australia Batting and Fielding

Name	Mat	I	NO	Runs	HS	Ave	SR	100	50	Ct	St
SR Waugh	4	5	2	321	157*	107.00	56.81	2	-	2	-
ME Waugh	5	8	3	430	120	86.00	56.87	2	1	9	-
DR Martyn	5	7	2	382	118	76.40	73.74	2	2	-	-
AC Gilchrist	5	5	0	340	152	68.00	90.66	1	2	24	2
RT Ponting	5	8	0	338	144	42.25	83.04	1	2	7	-
ML Hayden	5	8	1	234	68	33.42	57.35	-	1	4	-
MJ Slater	4	7	0	170	77	24.28	61.15	-	1	1	-
SM Katich	1	2	1	15	15	15.00	31.25	-	-	1	-
JN Gillespie	5	4	1	41	27*	13.66	42.70	-	-	2	-
GD McGrath	5	4	3	11	8*	11.00	36.66	-	-	1	-
B Lee	5	4	0	24	20	6.00	37.50	-	-	-	-
SK Warne	5	4	0	13	8	3.25	54.16	-	-	6	-
JL Langer	1	1	1	102	102*	-	54.83	1	-	1	-

Australia Bowling

Name	Mat	O	M	R	W	Ave	Best	5	10	SR	Econ
GD McGrath	5	194.2	56	542	32	16.93	7–76	4	-	36.4	2.78
SK Warne	5	195.2	41	580	31	18.70	7–165	3	1	37.8	2.96
JN Gillespie	5	174	42	652	19	34.31	5–53	1	-	54.9	3.74
B Lee	5	120.5	18	496	9	55.11	2–37	-	-	80.5	4.10
ME Waugh	5	13	1	69	1	69.00	1–40	-	-	78.0	5.30
RT Ponting	5	4	0	8	0	-	-	-	-	-	2.00

2001 Test Series Averages

England Batting and Fielding

Name	Mat	I	NO	Runs	HS	Ave	SR	100	50	Ct	St
MA Butcher	5	10	1	456	173*	50.66	56.36	1	1	4	-
MR Ramprakash	4	8	0	318	133	39.75	47.81	1	-	3	-
N Hussain	3	6	1	177	55	35.40	48.62	-	2	-	-
AJ Stewart	5	9	1	283	76*	35.37	65.81	-	2	13	-
ME Trescothick	5	10	0	321	76	32.10	61.49	-	3	4	-
MA Atherton	5	10	0	221	57	22.10	45.66	-	2	7	-
J Ormond	1	2	0	35	18	17.50	41.66	-	-	-	-
U Afzaal	3	6	1	83	54	16.60	60.58	-	1	-	-
AR Caddick	5	9	2	101	49*	14.42	60.47	-	-	1	-
D Gough	5	9	3	82	39*	13.66	50.61	-	-	-	-
IJ Ward	3	6	1	68	23*	13.60	40.23	-	-	-	-
DG Cork	1	2	0	26	24	13.00	83.87	-	-	-	-
GP Thorpe	1	2	0	22	20	11.00	38.59	-	-	1	-
C White	3	6	1	38	27*	7.60	42.69	-	-	1	-
PCR Tufnell	1	2	1	7	7*	7.00	41.17	-	-	-	-
AJ Tudor	2	3	0	14	9	4.66	29.78	-	-	-	-
AF Giles	1	2	0	7	7	3.50	28.00	-	-	-	-
RDB Croft	1	2	0	3	3	1.50	21.42	-	-	-	-
AD Mullally	1	1	0	0	0	0.00	0.00	-	-	-	-

England Bowling

Name	Mat	O	M	R	W	Ave	Best	5	10	SR	Econ
RDB Croft	1	3	0	10	1	10.00	1–8	-	-	18.0	3.33
MA Butcher	5	14	4	63	4	15.75	4–42	-	-	21.0	4.50
AJ Tudor	2	44.5	7	195	7	27.85	5–44	1	-	38.4	4.34
D Gough	5	155.1	24	657	17	38.64	5–103	1	-	54.7	4.23
U Afzaal	3	9	0	49	1	49.00	1–49	-	-	54.0	5.44
AD Mullally	1	30.3	10	99	2	49.50	1–34	-	-	91.5	3.24
AR Caddick	5	177.4	24	748	15	49.86	5–101	1	-	71.0	4.21
DG Cork	1	23	3	84	1	84.00	1–84	-	-	138.0	3.65
AF Giles	1	25	0	108	1	108.00	1–108	-	-	150.0	4.32
J Ormond	1	34	4	115	1	115.00	1–115	-	-	204.0	3.38
PCR Tufnell	1	39	2	174	1	174.00	1–174	-	-	234.0	4.46
C White	3	46.4	7	189	1	189.00	1–101	-	-	280.0	4.05
MR Ramprakash	4	8	0	31	0	-	-	-	-	-	3.87

Australia in England 2001
Complete First-class Tour Averages

Batting and Fielding

Name	Mat	I	NO	Runs	HS	Ave	SR	100	50	Ct	St
DR Martyn	9	14	5	942	176*	104.66	71.58	5	3	3	-
AC Gilchrist	8	10	2	663	152	82.87	88.99	3	2	28	4
SM Katich	5	7	3	288	168*	72.00	64.71	1	1	7	-
ME Waugh	9	15	6	644	120	71.55	59.68	2	2	12	-
SR Waugh	7	11	2	583	157*	64.77	64.49	3	-	5	-
RT Ponting	9	15	1	844	147*	60.28	89.50	3	5	11	-
ML Hayden	10	17	1	636	142	39.75	65.97	1	3	6	-
MG Bevan	1	2	0	67	34	33.50	63.20	-	-	-	-
JL Langer	6	11	2	285	104*	31.66	47.02	2	-	5	-
WA Seccombe	4	5	0	157	76	31.40	51.81	-	1	8	2
SK Warne	8	10	2	237	69	29.62	74.29	-	2	13	-
MJ Slater	8	13	1	341	77	28.41	62.79	-	2	1	-
AA Noffke	3	3	0	69	28	23.00	48.59	-	-	1	-
CR Miller	5	4	1	68	62	22.66	128.30	-	1	2	-
B Lee	8	7	0	127	79	18.14	63.50	-	1	-	-
GD McGrath	7	6	3	53	38	17.66	58.24	-	-	1	-
JN Gillespie	8	9	3	94	27*	15.66	31.97	-	-	3	-
DW Fleming	5	6	0	49	20	8.16	50.00	-	-	-	-
NW Bracken	1	2	2	10	9*	-	50.00	-	-	1	-

Bowling

Name	Mat	O	M	R	W	Ave	Best	5	10	SR	Econ
NW Bracken	1	24	5	61	5	12.20	3–29	-	-	28.8	2.54
GD McGrath	7	234.5	74	624	40	15.60	7–76	4	-	35.2	2.65
SK Warne	8	263	56	784	42	18.66	7–165	3	1	37.5	2.98
DW Fleming	5	138	32	390	19	20.52	6–59	1	-	43.5	2.82
MJ Slater	8	3.2	0	23	1	23.00	1–23	-	-	20.0	6.90
SM Katich	5	24	2	106	4	26.50	3–21	-	-	36.0	4.41
DR Martyn	9	9	1	53	2	26.50	2–38	-	-	27.0	5.88
JN Gillespie	8	228	54	801	29	27.62	5–37	2	-	47.1	3.51
CR Miller	5	157.2	37	586	18	32.55	4–41	-	-	52.4	3.72
AA Noffke	3	67.4	16	258	6	43.00	3–66	-	-	67.6	3.81
B Lee	8	186.5	30	752	17	44.23	3–17	-	-	65.9	4.02
ME Waugh	9	24	2	121	2	60.50	1–33	-	-	72.0	5.04
JL Langer	6	2	0	5	0	-	-	-	-	-	2.50
RT Ponting	9	7.3	1	15	0	-	-	-	-	-	2.00
MG Bevan	1	5	0	28	0	-	-	-	-	-	5.60
ML Hayden	10	11	2	44	0	-	-	-	-	-	4.00